D1000893

THE GOLD AND SILVER HOOKS

THE GOLD
AND SILVER
HOOKS

by Ruth Moore

WILLIAM MORROW AND COMPANY, INC.

NEW YORK • 1969

Published simultaneously in Canada
by George J. McLeod Limited, Toronto.

Printed in the United States of America.
Library of Congress Catalog Card Number 69-11244

THE GOLD AND SILVER HOOKS

Astolpho found on his visit to the moon
that bribes were hung on gold and silver
hooks; princes' favors were kept in bellows;
wasted talent was kept in vases, each marked
with the proper name.

Ariosto: ORLANDO FURIOSO

PART ONE

The Randalls

Starball Cove was on the tip of a narrow peninsula which jutted southward from the coast, marking a division between bay waters and open ocean. On the bay side were sloping, gentle shores with pebble and sand beaches, clam-flats and tideholes—a pleasant, dreamy kind of place liked by shore birds—sandpipers and plovers, and occasional blue herons stopping by on their flight northward to the salt marshes behind the town of Granite Hills, five miles away. But a man crossing the peninsula from west to east might think as he stepped out of the trees along the shore that he had come into another country, for this was ocean-side as far as the eye could see, with granite cliffs, black, sea-weed-hung ledges and, nearly always, a wild surf that pounded away all day long. The peninsula itself had no particular name of its own; travelers asking were told it was "down Starball," the way to get to the cove, whose distinction was that a meteor had once fallen into it, affrighting the inhabitants with a great glare and hissing and a horrid smell of brimstone.

The cove was the last sheltered place before the cliffs began; cliffs were its actual protection from the sea. A rampart of tumbled granite made off into the water, curving like an arm bent at the elbow toward the opposite western shore. Behind a tricky, narrow entrance, the small harbor was safe for boats in almost any weather. If a rousing southerly hit at just the right angle and time of tide, it might send rollers racing in through the cove mouth big enough to do the damage to moorings. In that case, boats could be shifted around to the salt pond behind the beach and grounded out there till the weather settled down.

The beach was a high ridge of pebbles joined to the shore only at the southern end. The northern end sloped sharply down to a salt-water brook which could be crossed on stepping-stones at low tide, but which became on the flood a natural waterway into the pond. A small, lazy stream meandering down from deep woodland swamps halfway up the peninsula had created the pond, which had once been fresh water with no opening to the sea; but in some prehistoric storm with flooding rains, a massive pressure of water had burst through the northern end of the beach, or perhaps the sea had helped, eating its way in. The place had been in its day a fine haven for Indians cruising the coast in summer—shelter for canoes in the pond, fresh water from the stream and, at low tide, a splendid expanse of clamflats. They had made good use of these flats and had left their mark. The beach where it joined the shore was a shell mound; shells could be found among tree roots a hundred yards back from the beach. White men, also, had left their mark on the cove. In 1918 it consisted of five old houses, abandoned and falling to ruin across the top of the beach.

The original white settlement in the late 1700's had started out to be quite a community. Spaced around in the sturdy second growth of hardwoods and spruces in back of the pond was what remained of some thirty clearings, each with its fallen-in cellar hole. Hardhack and wild rose bushes had taken over most of the clearings, but the tough grass of the countryside was still battling; it had given up hard. In places it still matted the ground in tufts of old fog a foot thick, through which green shoots struggled in the spring. The cellar holes were what was left after a forest fire backed by a howling northwest gale drove down the length of the peninsula in a long-past dry fall.

The fire started, no one knew how, in a mass of crackling dry slash left by timber cutters from Granite Hills, which had been getting ready to explode throughout a long summer with no rain. When it finally did, it chose midnight in a fifty-mile gale; the fire crowned and spread so fast that the entire width of the peninsula was ablaze before anyone in the town so much as saw it. By that time help could not get through by land and no sailing vessel could weather Starball's western shore. At the cove four families in the four northernmost houses were burned in their beds. The rest of the community made it to the beach or to small boats in the pond.

The five houses on the beach were saved partly by the impractical place on which they were built—for two generations people had said that some day a southerly would wash them off of there—and partly, the legend is, by an old gentleman with an exceptional voice, Uncle Rudolph George Tufton, who owned one of them. He got up on the roof of his house and prayed loud enough for God to hear him. By 1918 no one living was old enough to remember the scene, but some had heard their grandfathers tell what a mighty one it was—the peninsula aflame from shore to shore for five miles to the north and thirty houses burning, and above the roar of wind and fire, the bull-bawling of Uncle Rudolph, standing on the peak of his gable where he could hold onto the chimney and telling God what to do.

"Godalmighty! If you don't know what to do, I'm the man to tell you. Send rain! Send a thunderstorm!"

And over in the west a grumble and flash began that could

hardly be seen at first over the glare of burning, until all at once there came a rip of chain lightning that laid open the sky and thunder like the crack of doom, and God let down a cloudburst that practically washed Uncle Rudolph off the shingles. He came down mopping his eyes, which had taken some damage from flying cinders, and said it was too smoky up there for him to use his voice as well as he might have in a normal situation; but probably that was a good thing, because if he had been able to, no knowing what God would have done. When some skeptic asked him if he thought that carrying-on of his had drummed up rain, he said, Hell, no, anybody knew that that kind of a nor'wester was likely to end up in a thunder shower, but it was good and goddamned time somebody had the forethought to hurry it up a little.

Later on, as he grew older, it seemed that this single success had gone to his head. He kept saying he could fly like like a bird and he went around telling people that in a time of catastrophe he might be a good man to know. He put a curse on sea urchins, which bothered lobster traps, and on eelgrass which was filling up the salt pond, without any practical results anybody could see; but when, in the next century, after he had been dead for fifty years or so, sea urchins vanished from the coast and the eelgrass all died, for no reason, there were some descendants who wondered if, after all, the old man hadn't been able to fly.

After the fire no one had any desire to rebuild at Starball. For one thing, the womenfolk were all too nervous, and with reason. In a dry year, with a northwest gale blowing, the peninsula had turned out to be a fire trap and could again. Not that there was anything left to burn, but in a few years there would be; nobody wanted to go through that again. For another thing, the smell of the burned-out forest was horrible. Dead stumps smoldered all winter, their roots on fire deep underground. Even after snow fell, the air was full of metallic stink—stale ashes and carrion-reek from carcasses of dead deer and rabbits. Most of the game on the peninsula, from small creatures to large, had got as far as the edge of the pond before the flames caught up with them.

The community buried its grim dead; then it packed up what few possessions were left and went away. Some families went to Granite Hills, on the river at the head of the bay; others who found it necessary to blame someone for the fire blamed the Granite Hills lumbermen who hadn't cleaned up their slash, said they wouldn't be caught dead in the place, and moved to distant fishing villages along the coast where they could make a living with their boats. Among those who moved up into the town was Frederick Randall, whose great-grandfather had built one of the houses on the beach.

Fred Randall, together with his father and brother, owned a two-masted coasting schooner, in which Fred made periodic trips to Boston, carrying shiploads of locally bought products and bringing back necessary staples and freight of one kind and another which could be sold for profit in the coast towns. The Randalls had always been prosperous people, competent and able, with a built-in talent for making money. John Constant Randall, the pioneer settler of Granite Hills, had had his pick of lands rich in lumber and marketable stone, along with other products of a wild, untouched country. Being himself a seaman with an itchy foot, he did not stay long in the place; but his large family of sons made the most of his land claims. For years, until the bonanza began to give out, the Randall men were the owners of ships and shipyards, lumber mills, stone quarries, and offshore islands, where a number of them settled when Father's claims on the mainland were exhausted or taken up by brothers, sisters, and cousins. Among them they accomplished a good deal of devastation on the new countrysides, but it could be said of them that with great fortitude they brought to the wilderness the civilization of their time, planted it and made it grow. Fred Randall's father, at the time of the Starball fire, owned, as well as his share in the schooner, the big general store in Granite Hills and a prosperous four-hundred-acre farm which Fred's brother ran. Fred skippered the vessel and did the trading along the coast and in Boston, partly because he had a genius for trading, but mostly because he was, like his ancestor John, a seaman, with a terrible distaste for working either under a roof or too long on land. He lived down Starball because he liked it there. If he had to drop killick anywhere ashore, he told his wife, May, it had got to be somewhere within the sound of water.

"And, after all," he said, "the family owns the place. It's a nice solid house, and it ain't sensible not to use it."

May didn't like Starball. The house was a good one, two-storied and gabled, with ample rooms. If it had been in town, she would have loved it. She was a town girl who loved company and a good time; she found herself at the end of no-where, three-quarters of the time alone with the two little girls, one in arms, the other four years old, and nothing to do but watch for Fred's sails and go half out of her mind listening to the *hussh-hussh* of water along the beach and the *rabble-dabble, rabble-dabble* of the brook running in or out of the salt pond. She was alone on the night the peninsula burned.

Fred, on that night, was headed home, driving up the coast in the roaring gale. He had had to reef down, which he hated. What he liked was to come booming into Starball Cove through the narrow passage to a flying anchorage which raised the hair under the hats of his crew. It was always a pretty piece of navigation which, he prided himself, not many skippers could have done; and May was always watching—that was part of it.

He was not going to be able to make even Granite Hills Harbor tonight, he thought, as the gale worsened and the night wore on, and one by one his sails had to come down. Northwest wind, dead offshore, the best he could do would be to let her drive, under the foresail, or maybe heave to under bare poles; he could tell better when he got there and saw what the weather was then.

It was about that time that one of the crew spotted the fire.

"Godfrey mighty!" he yelled. "That's on Starball!"

The only thing they could do was to let the schooner drive on by, while they watched the horror grow. By that time there was no question of landing or even heaving to. Fred managed to claw in under the lee of an offshore island, where, half crazy with worry, he waited out the gale.

He found his wife and two children safe in Granite Hills on the second day after the fire, when the gale finally blew out; at least the babies were all right, but May was never the same. She had taken such a horror of fire that a hot one in a cookstove could set her off, crying and shaking. She had terrible nightmares and would wake screaming that she was on fire.

"Burning," she would say. "Burning, burning, burning."

Fred found she could not now be left alone for any length of time. His house at Starball was saved, but the community was gone. There'd be no living there any longer. He loaded his household goods aboard the vessel and sailed up the river to Granite Hills.

"That's right," his father told him. "Leave May to Julie. And you work with me in the store for a while. Julie can help her if anyone can."

Julie was Fred's mother, a placid, pleasant person, known for her good heart and skillful hand with sick people. But not even Julie could help May. In a few months May lost her mind completely. For years she sat mumbling in a chair by the window in Julie's kitchen, until she died.

Fred blamed himself bitterly for what had happened to

May. All his life long he never got over thinking that if he hadn't been away, he might have got her and the girls out of Starball before she got so scared; if he had listened to her when she pleaded with him to live up in town—if, if, if. It had been his fault. Well, he had his girls left; he wasn't going to leave them, ever again. In case of trouble he would be on hand to take care. He would go no more to sea. Lance, his brother, would have to take over the schooner. Fred would help in the store, run the farm. Thus he punished himself; and he told himself that the punishment was just— it was what he had coming. He made his decision and he stuck to it—he was a stubborn man; but in doing so, he accomplished his own ruin. As a storekeeper, a farmer, he lost his pride and his love of living and was not again in his lifetime the gusty skipper who could bring the *Julie Randall* past the foaming ledges at the entrance to Starball Cove. He became round-shouldered and touchy, a pecker-away at trifles, who had to know where his daughters were every minute of the day.

His mother, Julie, told him time and again that if he didn't loosen up on the girls, he'd see the day when he'd wish he had.

"Heaven's sake, Fred!" she would say. "What a fussbudget! Abigail is all right, and Grace would be, if you'd let her alone."

But Fred was there to take care, to prevent the something awful which could creep out of some unknown place of darkness at any time and happen. It had once, it could again.

Grace was the elder of the two girls, by four years, a rebel who had fought her father from the time she was big enough to say, "I won't." At eighteen she disappeared. Gossip had it that she had run away with the captain of a lumber schooner which had lain for a week in the harbor waiting for cargo. At least she had been seen with him, and the schooner had left on the night she vanished and was not seen again. Grace sent back no messages. After some years vague word came that she was dead.

Fred mourned her as lost; silently, grimly, he dug into his job. Whatever else he had abandoned in his old, good life, he had kept his business sense. When Lance lost the *Julie Randall* in a wild night off the Isles of Shoals, with himself and all but two of the crew, Fred replaced her with two smaller vessels of shallower draught. Big ships had gone out of Granite Hills like a flight of birds, cargo-carriers to the world, in their time; now the river was beginning to silt up with debris and waste, not only from the town itself, but from the bigger and more flourishing city of Bristol to the north. Looking ahead, Fred saw that cargoes, too, would be more plebeian, now that the proud pines were mostly gone. He and his father could do well enough with what remained, and for some years they did better than well, with shingles and barrel staves, turnips and dried beans, salt fish, and sea birds' feathers for the comforters of Boston. And with smaller ships, if you lost one, you did not lose so much. By the turn of the century, when the old man died, he and Fred were already wealthy men in a growing town, which had become not only a small city but a county seat; and when Fred dropped dead of a stroke in 1909, he left his remaining daughter, Abigail, a considerable fortune.

Abigail was different from Grace. She was a quiet child and steady, with a sense of responsibility which sometimes worried her grandmother Julie.

"Such a sobersides!" Julie would say. "My young ones was always rackety. And that Fred was a devil."

For one thing, you could not lie to Abigail. All the pretty fairy tales, the pleasant little deceptions, like Santa Claus and babies coming from under stumps in the pasture, which Julie's own children had absorbed happily from their mother's knee, were received by Abigail with a quiet, steady gaze from a pair of clear greenish eyes—polite and uncontradicting, but nonetheless skeptical.

"She's too darn bright," Julie would say, throwing up her hands. "She'll have to learn to temper the wind to the shorn lamb someday, but I guess it won't be from me."

At fourteen Abigail had learned, though neither Julie nor anyone else found it out. Abigail was the only one who knew why Grace had run away. Grace had got herself in trouble. She had had to do something; but it had been a mistake to confide in Abigail, to whom, at fourteen, good was good and bad was bad. Grace had fled after an all-night quarrel carried on in fierce whispers in the girls' bedroom; in the morning she was gone.

Abigail said nothing to anyone then, nor ever did; nor did she let anyone know about the tears shed at night in the now lonely bedroom. She went on quietly helping her father at the store on Saturdays and after school—she was smart with figures; Fred took enormous pride in the way she kept the store's books with never a mistake or an erasure. In time she went to the State Normal School in Bristol, was graduated with honors, and taught school for a few years, but when Fred Randall died, she left teaching, came home, and took over the store. In 1910 she married Felix Plummer, who, with his brother Josiah, owned the town creamery and dairy farm. By him she had six children—Charles, Maureen, Nan, Elsie, Julie, and Miles.

Josiah

The five houses abandoned at Starball weathered down into the beach as the years went by, becoming the same soft gray as the pebbles, brown inside as seaweed rotting placidly in salt wind. Generations of swallows used them, flying in and out of glassless window frames; squirrels, mink, and other small creatures made havoc in the empty rooms. In time a kind of race memory of tragedy and bad luck closed in around the place. Some foolish persons claimed Starball was haunted; they declared that Uncle Tufton had certainly been seen and heard shouting around the ruins of his house on stormy nights; they even mentioned the ghost of May Randall. The crew of a dragger, putting into the cove for shelter overnight, started rumors of a queer sound—something going *plop, plop, plop,* like heart's blood dripping in the dark—the story becoming no less true because they made it up.

Abigail Plummer had inherited the old Randall house from her father. She seldom thought of it as anything but a worthless shack set on top of a few rods of beach rocks; she had no inclination to go there and seldom did. She was not superstitious and she had been too young to remember the Starball fire; what she did remember and could not bear to be reminded of was the demented creature in the corner of

13

Grandmother Julie's kitchen, who had cried all day and sometimes all night that she was on fire, that she was burning.

Nothing of note happened at Starball until the years following the passage of Mr. Volstead's Act, when Josiah Plummer, Felix's older brother, realized the possibilities of the place for landing and storing contraband liquor. It was secluded enough, certainly; on a dark night a man who knew his way around there could slip into the cove, run his boat on the high tide up into the creek to the pond, and unload in undisturbed leisure behind the beach. The old Randall house was just the place to store cases of liquor until they could be disposed of safely; and Josiah saw no reason why he shouldn't use the old ruin, nobody else was. Josiah hadn't a strong respect for other people's possessions, anyway, and besides this was in the family—belonged to Felix's wife. Even after Josiah repaired the old building, made it as weather- and thief-proof as he could, he saw no necessity to say anything to Abigail. He had no use for her, for a number of reasons. Among other things, she disgusted him because she had been a schoolteacher. Books and learning weren't in his interest. He himself had managed to finish only the fifth grade, and he was proud of it.

"Godalmighty!" he said to Felix, when Felix announced his marriage intentions. "What for? You might as well marry a razor clam."

Felix usually did what Josiah told him to, even to selling tainted butter. The Plummer boys had inherited the town dairy from their father, who had run a clean, solid business for a fair return; Josiah wished to provide for a prosperous future a little more quickly. He did not propose, he told Felix, to spend his life tending cows and trickling milk into bottles. So take the milk cans to the pump, substitute light cream for heavy, don't be so particular when the component parts of a mouse show up in the butter. Hell, you could sell it down on River Street, them apes down there wouldn't know the difference—they might even like mouse. Josiah had always dominated Felix.

But in the matter of his marriage, Felix declined to be run. He was unsteady in many ways, not a strong-minded man; his father had always tried to stand between him and Josiah's tormenting. Josiah was a great practical joker and a tease. Now the old man was gone, but there stood Abigail, honest and stedfast as a rock. Felix needed her and he married her.

At the wedding a paper bag hidden in the flowery arbor over the bridal couple's heads was overturned by an ingeniously rigged length of string. Josiah was very clever with his hands. The bag showered down not only rice but a bright green garter snake which was too dazed and smothered to move much. It lay on the floor in front of Abigail. She stooped and picked it up.

"I've had schoolboys play snake tricks on me before," she said. "This is yours, I expect, Jos." She stepped out of the arbor holding the snake.

Josiah turned his own shade of green. He was scared to death of a snake; he figured any normal person ought to be. When he had caught this one, he had handled it with a forked stick. And here *she* was, holding the slimy thing in her hand. What was she—some kind of a witch?

"Come on, take it," she said. "Put it back where it came from."

"Git—git away from me with that," he said, backing up nervously, for she was sticking it right in his face.

"What's the matter? The poor thing's half dead, it can't hurt you." And she dropped the snake into his coat pocket.

The company roared, seeing how fast Josiah got out of his coat.

Josiah was known for his practical jokes. What he usually got was laughter and backslapping, people telling what a

card he was. But this time the laugh was on him. He shook
out the snake, stamped on it, and walked away from the
wedding. Right then he declared war.

Damned battle-ax, couldn't take a joke, turned it right
back on a man. Wasn't even a proper female. Any woman
he knew—and he knew any number of nice little pretty
jumpy ones—would have screeched and squealed, hopped up
on a chair and let herself be rescued, whether she was scared
or not. By the God, there was no need to make a man feel
like a fool, and in a nasty way, so that he'd be a long time
hearing the last of it.

Well, this decided him. He was through with the dairy
business. Felix, that gutless wonder, wouldn't be able to keep
her out of it. She'd be into everything, bossing, like as not
nosing into the books and accounts which Josiah did not
care to have anyone but himself see. It would be just like
her to blat around all over town that he'd been cheating the
pants off Felix for years.

It took Josiah some eight months to arrange the financial
affairs of the business to his own best personal advantage;
then he told Felix he was pulling out. He was going to build
a lobster boat and go fishing.

Felix was appalled. He hated the creamery and dairy
farm; he wasn't good at running a business. He couldn't
even keep books; Josiah had always done that, sent out the
bills, collected the money. He had no idea how much money
there was, nor what Josiah's share of it might be. He did
know that the creamery had lost a lot of customers since the
episode of the mouse in the butter.

"Lord, I can't run this place alone, Jos," he said. "You
know I can't. Besides, I don't know what I'll do if you take
your cash out of it now. We need every cent we've got to
keep running."

"You call on your cute little razor clam," Jos said. "She
knows how to handle business. Yank some of that money old

Fred Randall left out of her. God, she must have half a million socked away."

"Oh, hell," Felix said helplessly. "Let's sell the damn place, and I'll go lobstering with you."

"Not on your life. Have you frigging around with my engine outside on a choppy day, likely playing tic-tac-toe on the spark plugs with a hammer?"

Felix nodded. He was a fumble-fingers and knew it; at least, he'd been many times told he was.

"So you trickle the milk, Fee, my lad. All yours from now on." And Jos went his way.

He left the business in such a mess that Felix couldn't make head or tail out of it. Bills and complaints piled up; Jos hadn't left him any cash at all, either in the till or in the bank. He had signed a paper stating that Felix was now sole owner of the property—a fair division, wasn't it?

Felix staggered along alone for a few weeks before he went to his wife. He had to have help from somewhere.

Abigail could keep books and she could certainly run a business. She had taken over the Randall store, had enlarged it, was making money. She was busy, putting in a full day there; but she was already pregnant with her first child and had made arrangements with a competent man, Norman Hardwick, to manage the store for her while she had the baby. She got Norman to come in sooner than she had planned to, and then she waded into the jumble of accounts at the creamery. It took her quite a while to find out what had happened.

"Fee," she said one night at supper, "your brother Jos has cheated you something scandalous. It looks to me as if he's been doing it for years."

"Well, I don't know," Felix said, "as I can think of anything to do about it now."

"You could go to see him, ask him for your fair share. It's outrageous, Fee!"

Felix said nothing. She could see that he was rapidly losing his appetite for supper.

"Don't you want to?" she asked.

"Lord, Abby, I can't handle Jos. They way things are, I'd be a fool to try."

"Well," she said, "I'm sorry. I didn't mean to spoil your supper. But would you mind if I saw him about it? We could win a lawsuit pretty easily, you know."

Felix swallowed. His throat made a clicking sound, and looking at him, she saw he had turned quite pale.

"I can't have you tangle with him, Abby," he said finally. "He's real rough sometimes, Jos is."

Abigail left it at that, seeing how upset he was. But she made up her mind that when she saw Jos she'd tackle him, and she did. He came into the store one day after a suit of oilskins.

Abigail wrapped the bundle for him. "That'll be fourteen ninety-five," she said.

"Hell, write it down on the book," Jos said. "I don't have the cash right now."

"You should have, shouldn't you? I'm not trusting you for anything, Jos, until you pay Felix what you owe him on the dairy."

Jos grinned. "What's it to you?" he asked. "You've got enough socked away to paper the goddamned dairy with hundred-dollar bills."

"That's neither here nor there, and none of your business, really. Felix needs his cash to operate on."

"Let him come and ask me for it."

"No. If he asks at all, it'll be through a court of law. He could win a lawsuit pretty easily."

Jos guffawed. "Fee?" he said. "He does that, I'll kick his pants up over the top of his head, and he knows it. Besides, what's a lawsuit in this town? All you got to do to win one is sweeten up the Judge. I can't see you in all your holiness doing that. I would, like a shot. The Judge's a friend of mine too. We go hunting together."

"How nice for you both," Abigail said. "I expect we need some new legal talent, don't we? We expect you to pay that money, Jos."

"That money," he said, mimicking her precise tones, "has every goddamned cent of it gone into my new lobster boat. You tell Fee to whistle for it. He's a pretty good whistler. About the only thing he is good at, if you ask me."

Abigail said nothing. A customer had come in and she walked out from behind the counter to serve him.

"Well, well, well, well!" Jos said, as she passed in front of him. "From the looks of you, he must be pretty good in bed at that. Jesus, that's really a job he done, damn if it ain't! You look like a lamper eel swallered a rock." One of his bristly black eyebrows crawled slowly upward toward his hatbrim, and he stood grinning, dangling the package of oilskins by its string.

Being tall and fairly big-boned, Abigail had not taken to pregnancy gracefully. She really showed, and she knew it. She flushed.

"You tell old Fee many happy returns," Jos said. "From his only living, loving relation," and he turned to go.

Abigail said, over her shoulder, "If you walk out of here without paying for those oilclothes, I'll call the sheriff and have you arrested for stealing."

"I bet you would at that," Jos said.

He tossed the package into the air, caught it on the toe of his boot with a hefty kick. It sailed over Abigail's head into a shelf stacked with canned salmon, sending cans rolling and scattering on the floor. Jos went out and shut the door behind him. Then he opened it again, stuck in his head. "Know what I'm going to name my new boat?" he asked. "The *Abigail Plummer*. After you, dear."

He did too. The new boat slid down the ways with *Abigail*

Plummer lettered in black and gold on her glossy stern. Jos used her for lobstering and trawling and, after 1920, for two years as a rum runner. He also entertained aboard her. She had a cuddy equipped with a stove and bunks as well as other homelike comforts for ladies from about town, some of whom came to refer to Jos as "the man I go lobstering with." He took out deep-sea fishing parties which generally ended with the doughty sportsmen flat-out drunk on the platform among the fish; and when, following the end of the war, holiday celebrations started up again in the coast towns, he invariably won the Fourth of July Fishermen's races with her, always throwing a fine party aboard to congratulate himself on victory.

"She's lucky, this old hooker," he would say, keeping the joke on Abigail going until he wore it out. "Why wouldn't she be, named after the toughest, honestest, holiest witch in town? Wouldn't believe, with a name like that, she could throw a wingding like this, would you?"

Then, all of a heap, Jos's luck ran out. Federal men caught him red-handed, headed in from outside the three-mile limit with a load. In the wild chase that followed, the *Abigail* was holed by gunfire and sank before she could be towed ashore. Jos paid a heavy fine for his night's work and had to spend the next year or so, as the saying was, "away."

Painstakingly, through the years, Abigail had restored Felix's dairy business. In the beginning she had got back the lost and complaining customers by sending postcards, signed with her own name, and printed in large letters for anyone to read who saw or got postcards in the mail: WE HAVE CHASED THE MICE OUT OF THE BUTTER. Anyone, also, knew that what Abigail Plummer said she had done, she had done; and customers at her store knew from experience that whatever was bought there would be of high quality and sold at an honest price.

The creamery and farm were valuable property now. Somewhat to her relief, Felix had from the first refused to manage it. He couldn't, he said; he would work there, since he had to, but let him do odd jobs, maybe save the wages of a hired hand. Poor Felix, he couldn't do odd jobs either. He really was a fumble-fingers. Given a nail and a hammer, he could not drive the one without bending it or mashing a thumb with the other. If he touched machinery, he disabled either it or himself. What he could do even to a simple construction like a hand lawn mower, no ordinary man could believe. It was uncanny, the way, for Felix, the devil rose up out of the machine.

He was willing to try; and yet, when he did, it almost seemed that having been all his life told that he was no good, he went out of his way to prove it. Abigail found a steady, competent man, Clarence Bickford, who could manage the business and let Felix alone to do what he liked. What Felix did was not much—less and less as time went on, and he became more and more bored with the work and with himself. Whatever one might think about Jos, with him away the place was dead. When he had been around, he might have been tough to get along with, but things happened—he always had something cooking on the fire.

On the fine, sunny day in spring when Jos got back from "away," Felix was sitting behind the desk in the creamery office, feeling useless and glum, wondering what next to do with himself. It had seemed simple enough to him to tighten a loose screw on a cream separator. If the screw broke off in the hole, it must be because it had a flaw in it, not because he had put out too much strength. Clarence Bickford couldn't be blamed for getting mad—he'd been in a rush and needed every machine he had to fill his orders on time. He had cussed for half an hour. Owner or no owner, Felix had got cussed out like a hired hand. He supposed the fellow who came in the door was Clarence and he didn't even look up.

"Well, for godsake, look at you! There you sit like a new-born aig, not a thing in the world to do."

"Jos!" Felix said. He jumped to his feet, holding out his hand. "I'll be darned! When'd you get back?"

"I'm just back," Jos said. He looked about the same. Jail hadn't seemed to faze him any. "Where's your old razor clam? She around here anywhere?"

"Over at the store," Felix said. "Gosh, Jos, it's good to—"

Jos waved his hand. "Ne'mind that," he said. "I'm in a kind of a sort of a hurry. I got a proposition. You always said you'd like to come in with me on a boat. You still want to?"

"I'd give my eyeteeth to! But—"

"But nothing! I'm getting a new business going. I need a man. I need a new boat and I need the dough to buy one. So the thing for us to do is sell this goddamn creamery."

"Gosh, I can't do that, Jos. Not without talking to Abby. She put a lot of money in here to straighten things out after you quit."

"Uh-huh," Jos said. "So she wears the pants? You want to remember that anything she's put in here's a free gift to us. You own half, I own the other half."

Felix jumped. "You signed off to me, Jos. Didn't you?"

"Hell, no. Of course I didn't."

"What's that paper, then?"

"Oh, that. I give you a kind of agreement, you to manage the place whilst I done something else. Nothing legal about it. I never signed off my property to you, not for a few odd cents I didn't. I'd ha' been a fool to. I'm still part owner."

"I don't remember the paper was worded quite that way, Jos—"

Jos grinned. "Dig it out and see. If you can find it." His grin grew wider. "I bet you a dollar you can't find it."

"Well, I—" Felix began. He flushed a little. He hadn't the

faintest idea where the paper might be. "Abby'll know where it is in the file. She takes care of all the paper work."

"Look, you leave her out of this. You know damn well what she'd do. Gaggle and gargle to raise the roof, she hates me like a potful of poison. This is you and me, or me and nobody. How much cash can you lay your hands on? You got some, you must have; this place must be making a mint now."

Felix did have access to some cash. He and Abigail had a joint savings account. There was quite a sum in it.

"Uh-huh," Jos said. "I see you do have."

Felix sat staring at the office desk. It was neat—not the way it had been in the old days when Jos had had it. Abby had been in the night before and had cleared up everything. Papers were where they belonged, letters answered, bills paid. The desk was dusted; even the pencils were sharp and a new nib was in the penholder.

"Shoot, Fee! You could help me pay for the boat and be half-owner of it. You're a young man and you might as well be spending your life in a spud cellar. God, boy, I'm ten years older than you are and I may have lost some time in jail, but I'm out now and I'm about to have some fun. Sweet lilies of love, boy, you wait till you see the plans for that boat!"

What Jos was saying was no more than Felix had always said to himself. Jos had the fun. As a boy, Felix had tried to trail around after him, envying the good time he had.

"Get shed of this damn creamery, and you come along with me. Burn the cussed place down. Or don't you carry much insurance?"

"Oh, we carry a lot of insurance," Felix said. He had turned slightly greenish. "But, God, Jos, I couldn't do that!"

"No, I guess you couldn't. Be a nice way out, though, wouldn't it? Look, how about you and me having a look

through the file there for that paper I signed? I'd kind of
like to know what I did say, wouldn't you?"

The paper was in the file in a folder marked *Plummer,
Josiah*. They hardly had to hunt for it at all.

Jos pulled it out, glanced at it. "Well, I sure did sign off
to you," he said. "We didn't get it witnessed, though. You
mind if I take this along to a lawyer, see if it's legal this way?"
Without waiting for Felix's answer, he thrust the paper in
his pocket. "You think it over about letting me have that
cash, Fee. You and I get that boat, we'll cut a wake in the
water won't close up behind us for fifteen minutes."

He waved a jaunty hand and left, having got what he had
come after and found out what he had wanted to know.

The dairy building itself did not burn down, but the big
cattle barn on the edge of town above the pastures did, and
most of the dairy herd went with it. For all anyone could
tell, the fire had started in the haymow. The town fire chief
suggested spontaneous combustion in the hay. Some of it
must have been stored in there damp.

"Damp nothing!" Clarence Bickford told Abigail. "Now,
look, Mrs. Plummer, you good and well know I wouldn't put
damp hay in a barn. I know better. That hay was sweet and
good, every load of it, and dry as a bone. If that fire started
in the mow, what I think, somebody touched it off."

Clarence was boiling mad. He had a reputation as a man
to be trusted and he valued it.

"Do you have any reason to think someone did?" Abigail
asked.

Clarence gave her a straight look. "I'm out of a job," he
said. "And I don't know where I'll turn next. But I'll tell you
what I overheard and you can make what you want to out
of it. Jos was in the office the other day trying to get money
out of Felix. It wasn't any of my business to listen, but Jos
has got a voice like a moose, carried all over the place. I

heard him say to Felix that a way out would be to burn the dairy building down for the fire insurance. Now, if you want to fire me for snooping, you go right ahead."

"I expect you know I wouldn't do any such thing, Clarence," Abigail said. "About your job, you can start in tomorrow, at the same wages. See what you can find out about a modern dairy barn, get some estimates. Come and see me again when you do."

Clarence let out his breath in a long sigh of relief. "I sure will," he said. "I guess you know what a load that takes off my mind too. There's just one more thing. They took a paper out of the file and Jos went off with it. I guess with what you know about them files, you won't have any trouble finding out which paper it was."

"I expect I won't. And thank you, Clarence."

By golly, she was a tough one. Never turned a hair, he thought. Hadn't, right along. Hadn't the night the barn burned. Just stood there.

He himself knew quite well what paper Jos had taken. Hearing only snatches of a conversation which was turning out to be interesting, Clarence had gone along to the door and had taken a quiet peek through the keyhole.

Now, if anyone knowed that, he told himself, they'd have a good reason to think that I was snooping.

Abigail had no doubts about what paper was missing; she could have told without looking. It would be, of course, the only existing record that Felix possessed of his brother's signing over the property to him. Now that Jos had it—and in any case, it was probably destroyed by now—he could collect half the insurance. In the end, he would probably worm the rest of it out of Felix, whom, she had reason to know, he could wind around his little finger. There was nothing to be done about that. Even if there were, she would not do it. She would not, under any circumstances, touch a penny of money gained in such a way. Whether Jos had cudgeled Felix into setting the barn on fire, or whether he had done it himself, the man was a criminal with no kindness or mercy in him. To burn up a barnful of helpless dumb creatures . . . She had stood outside the flaming building and ever since had not been able to get out of her head the terrible sounds. A selfish, inhuman beast. Someday justice would catch up with him, it had to. Only one thing gave her a kind of grim satisfaction. There was probably not quite so much insurance as Jos thought on that rickety old barn, which for some years she had been planning to modernize.

The old Plummer pasturelands were worn out; a good deal of the dairy equipment had been out of date, though some of it she had bought new and the bills of sale were in her name. Meticulously, she listed what she owned and could prove she owned. The rest—pastureland, hayfields, the remaining building—she abandoned. Any money she had put into the establishment for Felix's sake she gave up as lost—a bad investment. She was having no more to do with any property which, conceivably, Jos could get a finger into. So far as the goodwill of the business was concerned, that was hers and had been for years.

The MacGregor place, three hundred acres on the north side of town, a mile or so out, was for sale. The two Mac-Gregor boys were anxious to sell, and for a price that was more than fair—they were young, wanted to leave and get themselves jobs in the city. The place would make a fine dairy farm. It included plenty of good pastureland which only needed to be cleared a little and taken care of, a dwelling house where Clarence could live with his family, and two old barns which could house the new cattle herd until a new barn could be built. It also included something else that she had had her eye on for some time. To the north of it was an outsized hill, known as Mulligan's Mound, high enough to overlook the town, the river, and the ocean—a magnificent view. At present Mulligan's Mound was a worth-less jungle of timber slash—the MacGregors had mined the property for every available dollar they could get out of it, cut down every full-grown tree, and left a mess. But clean up that mess, let the hill sit for a while and heal, and there would be as handsome a bunch of building sites as anyone could wish for. And the growth of the town was toward the north.

Well, now was the time, if she were going to buy the MacGregor place. She would, and turn Clarence Bickford loose on it at once.

She said nothing about the project to Felix. In the years she had been married to him, she had learned him like a book. A good-hearted, lovable man, with no stuffing. He was pleasant company, fun to be with; he had a dry, crackling wit which could bring down the house, set everyone roaring laughing. Abigail loved him dearly—in fourteen years she had had six children by him—and the children adored him. When he was at home, his kids were a kitetail, racing at his heels.

But he was a cripple, she had had to admit, and at first it had been hard to. Josiah had made him so. Almost worse than cutting off a man's legs was beating the spirit out of him. Fee could not meet problems; he could not make up his mind. Faced with a decision, he became another man alto-gether, limp and stricken with worry, changing this way and that, until he could scarcely remember what the original problem was. His rudder completely gone, he would be sunk in a kind of stupor unless somebody else made the decision, told him what to do. It was not his fault; it was Jos's. She had the same fierce, protective affection for Fee that she might have had for a crippled child. An empty sack, she would remember from the school copybooks, cannot stand upright.

Abigail had lived most of her life by copybook maxims.

They were something to abide by, and not worn out, either, as certain snickering people implied.

"Oh, those old chestnuts," some would say.

But she could not see how words possibly could be worn out which dealt with simple good manners or decency.

Honor thy father and thy mother. Neither a borrower nor a lender be. Honesty is the best policy. Do unto others as you would be done by.

And the one, above all, which Grandmother Julie had worked into a sampler to hang over the bureau in the bedroom:

Wear integrity as a coat of mail.

What the extent of Jos's operation had been Abigail did not know, but she found out on the day she went to the bank to draw money from hers and Felix's joint savings account, which had contained more than enough to buy the Mac-Gregor farm. Felix had drawn all of it, except a hundred dollars.

"Yes, he was in yesterday with Jos," the bank teller said.

"Oh, was he?" Abigail said calmly. "Mercy, we've been so busy getting squared around since the fire that I've hardly seen him. Did he take it in cash or a check?"

"Check. Endorsed it to Jos, I believe." He was leaning forward, eying her curiously. The whole town, of course, knew about her feud with Jos.

"Oh? Well, now I won't have to bother with it. Thank you, Johnny."

"You going to close out the account?"

"Mercy, no. We'll leave it open with that hundred. We'll both want to use it again."

She left him staring after her, looking, she was pleased to note, disappointed. Well, he had another think coming, if he'd expected to see her blow up in public, talk her business around. Jos had the money. Felix had given it to him, under the pressure of who knew what threats or promises. The thing was over and done with. Felix would be miserable, wondering how she was going to take it. She decided she would not add to that misery; she would not mention the affair unless he did. Jos would not have access to money of hers again—she would see to that; and what Felix did with his from now on was his own affair. In the meantime, she had to decide what to do about buying the MacGregor place.

To do it now she would have to get a loan, a mortgage through the bank, or disturb her father's money—a solid legacy, solidly invested as a backlog for her children. Looked at sensibly, she supposed that whoever said, "Neither a borrower nor a lender be," was probably somebody who had had a lot of experience with bad debts. Nevertheless, the idea of borrowing went against the grain. Why do it if you did not need to? Investments, if used, could be replaced in time.

A decision was something you had to make; if you made a wrong one, well, then, so you had. You picked up the pieces and did the best you could. She would go ahead with the MacGregor place on her own.

Felix came home to supper that night, silent, preoccupied, and glum. Usually mealtimes were fun. Nettie Hill, who kept the house and took care of the children while Abigail was at the store, was nearly as witty as Felix was; the two of them would pass a ball of foolishness back and forth across the table until everybody fell out of chairs laughing. But tonight Felix said nothing. He didn't eat either, but got up leaving a plateful and started for the stairs.

"Hey, Pa!" Charles called after him. "How about the movies? You promised to take us to the movies tonight."

Felix went on without answering. His feet sounded heavily on the stair treads.

"Aw, what's the matter with him?" Charles said, aggrieved.

"Let your father alone," Nettie said. "Maybe he don't feel well. I'm going to the pictures. Anybody wants to can come along with me."

"Nuh, everybody'll think I'm hard up for a girl," Charles said.

"Well, you sure will be if you hand out that kind of fresh backchat to the ladies," Nettie said. "Stay home then. Who cares?"

"Nettie, you've had nothing but youngsters all day," Abigail said. "You don't have to spend your evening with them too."

"Well, they've had *me* all day," Nettie said. "I can stand it if they can."

Nettie had kept house for Abigail for nearly fourteen years, ever since Charles had been born. She had come originally from River Street and her early childhood had been, according to her, "nothing to write home about, if you had a home to write to." It was true that, before coming to the Plummers, she had never had a regular home, having been handed around among distant relatives after her parents' deaths, until she was considered old enough to get a job, which she had done at the age of twelve. She had been a big girl, tall for her age, and Abigail, who had given her the job —at first clerking in the store—hadn't realized how very young she had been. But she had never had any cause to regret hiring Nettie.

Nettie was now twenty-eight, a woman of spirit, who ran Abigail's house like silk and produced excellent—and prodigious—meals, always on time. She was big, rawboned, and homely, standing almost six feet tall in her boots, and she took no nonsense from anybody, including children, who adored her. She considered this family her family and this home her home; she now fixed Charles, across the table, with a mean eye.

Charles squirmed. "Thanks, I'd like to go, Nettie," he said hastily. "What's the picture?" he went on, hoping to divert her from whatever disaster she had in mind for him.

"Pearl White," Nettie said. "She's going to get run over by a railroad train. Prob'ly her head'll go bouncing along the tracks, but it ain't nothing to worry about. She'll be back, head'n all, next week. First show's at seven, so if you're going to help me clean up the dishes and get your good pants on in time, you're going to have to hop up off your fat cannery, Buster."

Charles let out a howl. "I wasn't going to change my pants, I don't have to—what's the matter with these? And dishes is girls' work! I won't—what's the matter with Maureen helping?"

"Maureen didn't hand me a mouthful of the fresh and juicy," Nettie said. "You did. I don't take to spriglets with tomato down one leg of their pants telling me I'm not pretty enough to be seen on the street with them."

"Aw, I never did say that," Charles protested.

Abigail smiled quietly to herself. Before she was through, Nettie would have everybody duffing in, doing the dishes and putting them away—everybody, that is, but Miles, the youngest, who was already drooping with sleep in his high chair. Miles was one and a half, too young for movies. Abigail scooped him up as she left the table and took him upstairs to bed. She heard, behind her, the amiable wrangle remove itself to the kitchen, where it continued with some spirit. Charles and Nettie were actually very fond of each other.

She found Felix lying, fully dressed, on the bed with the light on.

"Mercy, Fee," she said. "Take your shoes off, honey."

He didn't seem to hear her. He said, as she came up beside

him, "I may as well tell you. I've used the money from the account to buy in with Jos on his new boat."

Abigail nodded. "I know you've given it to him."

"Are you sore?"

"Well, I wondered why, let's say. Isn't he due to collect insurance from the barn?"

Felix winced. He said, after a moment, "I suppose you think I touched off that barn, don't you?"

"Why would I think that?" Abigail said. "You aren't a man who'd burn down a barn full of live cattle."

"You've heard some talk then? That somebody touched it off?"

"I suppose people always wonder, when a building burns for no reason anyone can see."

"All that gas and quack about the insurance policy getting hot in the bureau drawer, sure. Well, someone's made it to the insurance company. They're on the prod and they're holding up the money."

Abigail couldn't help it. She said, "That makes it very rough on Jos, doesn't it?"

"Probably it was Clarence," Felix said, going on. "Trying to shift the blame onto somebody else for his moldy hay. What? Of course it's rough on Jos. He's got this contract with the Gilmore House in Bristol to supply seafood. He'll lose it if he can't pay for his boat. That was why I—Jos needed— Oh, hell! I own half of that boat now. I'm going fishing with Jos. He needs a man."

"Well, all right. If you want to, Fee, why don't you?"

Felix stared at her. "What do you mean, all right? Don't you care? I thought you'd hit the ceiling."

"I thought I would too. I might have once. But I guess it's your own business, you've made it so. All I hope is you've got your agreement about the boat down in black and white."

"Of course I have. D'you think I'm a fool?" He blustered

a little, smacked his fist into the palm of his hand. But his timing was bad—the smack came too late for proper emphasis. Felix regarded first his fist and then his palm and grinned bleakly. "That fell pretty flat," he said. "No, I haven't got any agreement at all from Jos. How about that? Are you going to say, 'Honesty is the best policy'?"

"No," Abigail said. "Only to the children, sometimes, Fee."

"Be darned, I thought you'd be sitting up there high and holy, ready to come down like a rainstorm."

This was straight from Jos; it sounded too much like him not to be, and Abigail didn't answer. She couldn't think of anything to say, anyway, that wouldn't make him feel worse than he did.

"'A lie well stuck to is better than the truth wavering,'" Felix said. "And blast it, I waver, don't I? Oh, I can match copybook maxims with you, all right, only mine aren't the same as yours. Take that thing over the bureau your grandmother made, I've looked at that every day of my married life till it's stuck in my craw like a fishbone. I had to write that, let me tell you, fifty-one times, one night after school, when I was, oh, say, fourteen. Even that far back, man, oh, man. 'Wear integrity like a coat of mail.'"

"Fifty-one?" Abigail said. "You must mean fifty, don't you? Or was the teacher unreasonable?"

"She was sore," Felix said. "On the forty-ninth time I found I couldn't write it again. So I wrote, 'I myself am but indifferent honest,' and signed it *Hamlet*. She made me do one extra."

"Fee, you'd never have read *Hamlet* at the age of fourteen, you know you hadn't."

Felix grinned. It was the same bleak, unhappy grin. It told her that she couldn't fight Jos for him, that she might as well stop trying.

"Well," he said, "I've read it now."

*   *   *

The *Abigail II* was built out of state, because Jos did not wish anyone to know about her happy secrets. He left off the *Plummer* since the name was too well-known now in certain official circles, and he did not wish to call attention to himself again. He had had time in jail to design in his mind the kind of hull he wanted; his design was very smart. The new boat was no long, low, raked-back speedboat, looking exactly like she was, a rumrunner. She was, obviously, a lobster boat somewhat larger and longer than the usual type, painted gleaming white as a lobster boat should be. She could be spotted a long way off on a moonlit night; but any Federal men investigating Jos now would find him peaceably hauling or setting trawls, with his kidboards partly full of fish and three or four fairly noisome tubs of bait standing around the platform, all of which smelly cargo would have to be dumped out if a thorough examination were to be made. There was nothing unusual about a man setting his trawls in the middle of the night to catch the right time of tide, so that he could haul them on slack water . . . a man who had learned his lesson, now carrying on his honest trade. News got about very soon that Jos had a contract to supply fresh fish to the Gilmore House in Bristol.

While he was waiting for the *Abigail* to be finished, Jos had done a real job of repairing the old Randall house at Starball, putting in all the refinements he had planned before his career had got interrupted. He had replaced the roof with cedar shingles and the rotten sills with new six-by-sixes; he built a couple of bunks and acquired a cookstove. He wanted, he said, a fish house—a place to keep fishing gear and where he could camp out if he felt like it. Anyone peering in would have said that was exactly what it was. Gear was what was in sight—lines and rope, toggles, buoys, and all the paraphernalia for building lobster traps. A good many tubs of one kind and another stood around or were stacked against the walls—tubs for trawl, hogsheads for salted bait, and some stoutly built half-barrels which might contain mussels or clams or haddock filets for the Gilmore House.

Jos had built and coopered his half-barrels himself. Each one was actually two tubs, one shallow and one deep enough to accommodate a case of whiskey. The shallow tub, filled with sea products, could be set on top; with a slight twist, cleats on its bottom could be fitted neatly into a set of notches, so that the two tubs became one, the division line hidden beneath a stout iron hoop. They could not be taken apart by anyone who did not know how the cleats and notches worked. They were of a comfortable size to handle —two men could lift one easily and, in a pinch, one man could do it alone.

Jos had always been clever with tools; he loved fooling people, and he enjoyed the whole construction project immensely, particularly the new floor in the Randall house, built over and higher than the old one to leave storage space between.

Not that, Jos told himself, he was going to keep any stock stored for very long. It wouldn't be smart, and this time he was going to be smart. He wasn't going to get hauled up, not this time. Everything would be open and aboveboard. Gilmore's truck could back up to the town dock, in full daylight, and any snoop who was interested could see that what he and Felix were unloading was what it was expected to be. He'd have to be sure to keep up his supply of fish and stuff—a lot of clams would have to be dug down Starball. Felix would have to do that, or, if he couldn't dig enough, they might hire a clam digger or two . . . No. There was no point in having anybody snooping around Starball, anybody you didn't need. Jos chuckled suddenly to himself. Why not hire Felix's kid, Charley? He was big enough now to be a lot of help, and around the boat too. Take him on some trips, learn the kid a few things he wouldn't get around home.

Make Felix's old razor clam madder than a wet hen. Boy, he'd do it—start up a little fun. Hadn't had any fun with her since he'd burned down the barn.

He brought the *Abigail* home at last, and she was beautiful. She had everything he'd wanted. Faster than a streak, if you called on what she had packed away in that big engine. He'd opened her up, once, coming along the coast and found out for sure what she'd do—better, of course, when the engine was broken in. But he wasn't going to let anyone know, not even what her horsepower was. A nice, new, big, old slow lobster boat jogging around. Let 'em think so.

Felix was impressed with what Jos had done to the old Randall house. In the beginning, when he had supposed that he and Jos were merely going to supply seafood to the Gilmore House, he wondered why Jos had gone to so much trouble and expense.

"Why not?" Jos said. "Nights when we don't go out, we'll sleep down here. It's nice too. Not a soul around to bother you. Most folks think they might see Uncle Tufton's ghost honking out flames of fire, so they stay away, thank God."

Felix said doubtfully that he hadn't planned on staying away from home too long at a time.

"What's the matter with you? Most nights we go out, and when we go, we go."

"Well, I thought likely you'd pick me up at the town dock."

"Yeah? Five miles up there, five miles back? I see myself. We start out from Starball here, we're out where we need to be in a couple of hours. How much time d'you think we're going to have, anyway? We got to have clams too. Somebody's got to dig 'em. Say, how about us hiring young Chuck for the summer? Don't he want a summer job? We could pay him a damn sight more than kids get fooling around with jobs in town."

Seeing Felix had his doubts, he went on, "If your old razor clam don't like it, wait till she sees how much dough you and the kid bring home."

As to that, Felix wasn't so sure. He had known Jos a long time. But one day, to his astonishment, Jos presented him with a bill of sale for the new boat, made out in Felix's name.

"There you are," he said. "All shipshape now, ain't we?" He grinned. "Even named for your wife."

"What the hell, Jos?" Felix said, staring at him bewildered. "You said half of it. This, unless I'm crazy, gives me full title to your boat."

"You been pretty decent about letting me have cash," Jos said. "When I've made enough to pay you back, maybe I'll take title again. After all, us working together, don't make no difference who owns it."

He glanced around at Felix sideways, running his hand with a raspy sound over the growth of whiskers on his chin, and went on in a voice that wasn't Abigail's but was near enough to it so that the caricature was unmistakable. "'Neither a borrower nor a lender be,' huh?"

Well, there was some reason for it. There had to be.

Once or twice a week a big closed truck, refrigerated, would back up to the town dock, load, and return to Bristol, full of Jos's trick tubs, everything open and aboveboard. The truck was well-known in the town, as was its driver, a companionable young chap named Ronnie Gilmore, whose father was owner of the Gilmore House. Depending on the time he was passing through town, he would stop for a meal at Bunny's Seaside Diner; he never seemed to be in a hurry and would linger to talk with anyone who was around, while his truck, parked openly at the curb, dripped ice water into the gutter.

"Oh, heck, no," he would say, when someone suggested that maybe he'd better step on it, his load was melting. "My

old man sticks ice enough in there to cool double that load
of fish. That'd last if I didn't roll in till suppertime. My old
man, he's too smart to skimp on ice."

"You use a hell of a lot of fish for just one hotel, seems
like," Bunny said to him one day.

"Sure do," Ronnie said. "City folks, they sure go for the
fresh, don't they? My old man's got it made with this deal
in seafood. Get rid of the middleman, that's what counts,
boy, in the hotel business. My old man and Jos Plummer,
they got a gold mine." And humming softly, with a nice
word to the waitress about her pink cheeks, Ronnie would
pay his check and be on his way.

"Nobody in the God's world would have thought," Bunny
said afterward, "that there was ever anything in that truck
but fish."

"But there was," the young waitress said. "Wasn't there?"

Abigail had always been busy. During the next months
she was busier than she had ever been in her life. She ran
the store; she had conferences every few days with Clarence
Bickford over the new dairy buildings, the modern equipment for the creamery, the breed of cattle to replenish the
herd; she had long talks with Chris Cartwright, the Bristol
contractor who was doing the construction work. She left
home at six in the morning and often did not get back until
six at night.

She seldom saw Felix. He was gone most nights. He had
to be, he said. He and Jos were trawling, making night sets
while the tide lasted, on other tides lobstering or clamming.
Jos had two hundred traps set and the Gilmore House used
clams and mussels by the ton. He was so tired when he did
get a chance to sleep that he didn't even consider trying to
make it home—he just crawled into the bunk and died there.

"But what bunk? Where are you sleeping, Felix? Is it a
comfortable place?"

"Oh . . . aboard the boat, of course. Jos has got it fixed up something plush. Innerspring mattresses. I'm fine, don't worry."

Jos had cautioned him not to say anything about the old Randall house, so he didn't. He didn't think Abby would care about the old ruin; still, the way she felt about Jos, she might. Felix knew now what Jos's real enterprise was. At first the idea of being a rumrunner had made him shake in his shoes. Every time they made a trip outside the twelve-mile limit, he had had what Jos called the nervous jerks. Jos had laughed him out of that, and things were better now. To date they hadn't even seen a revenue cutter and they were coining money.

But Jos had said, "You keep your trap shut about us using her house down there, see? Be just like her to start nosing around. Throw us out of there. At least throw me out."

Abigail said, "Well, wherever you're sleeping, it's certainly agreeing with you, Fee. You look wonderful."

He did look well—brown and huskier, as if he had put on some weight.

"You like it too?" she went on. The few times she had seen him lately, he had seemed happier in his mind, though right now she could tell something was troubling him. He was getting that overcasual look which meant he was going to propose something he knew she wouldn't agree with.

"Have you looked in our savings account lately?" he asked.

"Why, no, I haven't."

He must know why she hadn't. There was next to nothing in it.

"It wouldn't hurt you to look, see what's there. We're doing pretty well, Jos and me." And then he slipped in his proposal. "By the way, I've been taking Chuck with me, a few times. You don't care, do you?"

"Chuck?" Abigail said, puzzled.

"Oh," Felix said. He grinned uneasily and looked away

from her. "Charles. Jos calls him Chuck, and I guess I've got into the habit of it too. We needed help," he went on, in a hurry, seeing her face. "Shoot, Abby, Chuck—Charles is old enough and big enough, you're always carrying on about teaching the kids to work. Charles is having a swell time, earning his own money too. Jos is—we're paying him regular wages, and he's taking to it like a duck to water. You ought to see him aboard that boat. He can run her a darn sight better than I can already. Well, what's the matter?" he demanded. "You see anything wrong with his having a good time and making some money while he learns a man's trade? It's a lot healthier than sulling away in the store, if that's what you're going to make him do. Or do you want him to go to school till his brains drop out of his eyes? Well, it never did me any good, let me tell you. Turns a man into a big baby . . ."

This was pure Jos. Abigail recognized it with no trouble at all. Felix ran down slowly, as his words dropped into her frozen silence.

"Well, are you going to tell him he can't go, when I've already told him he can? He loves that boat, and he's a darned good little worker, too. He's already made a big difference to us. If you make him stop now, he won't forget it as long as he lives, and I don't know as I'd feel very good about it either."

"I wish you'd told me about it first, Felix. Why didn't you?"

"You know why. You'd have said no like a building falling down. You hate Jos like a potful of poison."

"I don't know as I do." She realized suddenly that she didn't. It wasn't hate. It was more, perhaps, what she would feel if she had to defend her household against an enemy—a burglar or, yes, a poisonous snake. "Jos is none of my business, so long as he doesn't interfere with me. When he does,

I'll fight him. I can't fight him over you, Felix, you know
that."

"Jos is all right. You won't give him a chance—" He turned
on her suddenly, his face white and pinched. "I set that barn
afire, if you want to know."

"No, you didn't Felix. You'll say what Jos wants you to say,
but I know you, you'll stop somewhere. I know who burnt
the barn down. And Jos isn't the kind of man I want to teach
Charles anything."

"I suppose you think I wouldn't have the guts to," Felix
said.

"I expect you're just trying to make me think Jos didn't."

"You don't know he did."

"You can't prove arson unless you catch the man with the
match in his hand, can you?" Abigail said.

"Clarence's damp hay—"

"Look, Felix, we must stop this. The thing's over and done,
no use hashing. Don't you honestly see any harm in letting
Charles be around too much with Jos?"

"Well, Abby, I may not amount to much, but I guess I
can look after my boy aboard the boat."

How could she tell him he couldn't? When he couldn't
even look after himself, with Jos?

"Look," Felix said. He suddenly sounded quite cheerful.
"We're not doing a thing on Sunday. I was going to spend
the day home with you and the kids, but if it's a decent day,
why don't we all pile into the boat and take a picnic off on
one of the islands? You can see how Charles is aboard that
boat—maybe Jos'll let him run it."

"Well, I don't think . . . not if Jos goes."

"That was kind of the idea, Abby. I want you to see how
Jos is with Charles. It's not the way you think, honestly it
isn't. Couldn't you just give things the once-over, before you
drop the building on us?"

* * *

Jos's manners, on the picnic, couldn't have been better. He was pleasant to Abigail; he romped with the children. He had brought candy and little presents for everybody. It was the first time Abigail could recall seeing him clean-shaven and neatly dressed. He took great pride in his new boat; apparently he was also proud of the way he had taught Charles to run her.

"Why, two or three trips with us"—he beamed—"and he's handling her darn near as well as I can."

He did not bully Charles; they were man-to-man together. And Charles, who steered the boat and tended the engine on both trips, out and back, strutted like a peacock. He showed his sisters around the boat as if he owned her. He had always been quite a self-important boy, inclined to tease and lord it over the younger children. Abigail had had to put her foot down hard more than once about that—she had seen enough of it, in her time, to know what it might lead to. Today he was pleasant and interested, and the girls were too.

He loves this boat, Abigail thought, watching him. Oh, my soul, I don't see what I can do about this now. I could say no and start fighting, but how can I when Felix has already said yes?

It was a great success, this day of the picnic. Apparently, a great success. The children had a fine time; Abigail did, too, and Felix seemed happier in his mind than he had been for days. But on the town dock, when the boat had pulled away with Jos and Felix aboard, Abigail was startled to see two of her daughters, Nan and Julie, matter-of-factly toss into the water the presents Jos had brought.

"What'd you do that for?" Charles demanded. "That's a heck of a thing to do with Uncle Jos's present. They cost a lot!"

"We don't like him," Nan said.

"We hate him," said Julie. "He's horrid."

Both girls turned to look at Charles. They were very much alike; the two pairs of eyes, identical in color and expression, stared at him with the same clear, knowing, speculative gaze.

"Darn fools!" Charles said. "You must be crazy. You could have a lot of good stuff if you showed him you liked him."

"Oh, *I* do!" Elsie said. She clutched to her bosom her own present, a small, fancy pink doll. "I *love* Uncle Jos."

"Oh, you love everybody," Julie said.

This was very nearly true. At seven, Elsie was a beguiling child in a blond and dimpled way. Grownups had always gone "Oo" and "Ah" over Elsie. She did love almost everybody, if only temporarily. She would love Jos as long as he had something for her in his pocket. "Darn fools," she said now to her sisters, parroting Charles.

"That'll do," Abigail said. "Nobody loves anybody for what can be got out of them. That isn't love, that's greediness. Charles, Elsie, you apologize to your sisters for that kind of talk."

"Oh, yeah, sure, excuse me," Charles said. He started off up the dock with his hands in his pockets; then, suddenly realizing that he mustn't do anything to jeopardize tomorrow —he was going on the trip with his father and Jos—he came back and took the picnic basket out of his mother's hand.

Troubled, Abigail trailed him and the rest of her brood up the dock. He was so valuable, so dearly loved, so full of promise. Under pressure, she had said he could go, for the summer, with Jos and Felix. The mistake was already beginning to show.

She felt beleaguered, driven into a corner.

Well, she thought, at the end of the summer Charles will have to go to school, and that will be the end of it.

She realized suddenly that one of the children was missing and, glancing around, saw her eldest daughter standing at the edge of the dock.

"Coming, Maureen?" she called.

Maureen glanced around at her; almost reluctantly she opened her hand and let a small object fall into the water.

Abigail waited.

"I expect that came hard, didn't it?" she said, as the youngster came up to her. "You liked that necklace."

"Yes," Maureen said. "I wanted to keep it. It goes with my blue dress. But I don't like him, either."

She walked along soberly at Abigail's side. Maureen was thirteen. She was much the quietest of the four girls, and in many ways the most perceptive, though perhaps not quite so bright as Nan and Julie. "Miles'll be glad to see us, won't he?" she said. "Seems as though we've been away a long day."

"Mm—hm, he will," Abigail said. Miles had stayed at home with Nettie. "Did the day seem long? I thought you had a lovely time. You weren't still a minute."

"Oh, I did. Yes, I did. It's nice out on the island, isn't it? Uncle Jos is an awful tease, though."

"Did he tease you, honey?" Abigail hadn't noticed that.

"Oh, not very much. He did Nan, though. And he pulled Julie's hair quite hard when no one was looking."

"*Did* he?" Abigail said grimly.

"He doesn't like girls much. Oh, he likes Elsie, she's smarmy, but we three didn't smarm, so I guess that's why he plagued us. Charles is who he likes. I'm glad it's not me. I wouldn't be Charles for anything."

"So you all threw your presents away."

"Yes, we agreed to. Nan was awful mad when Julie cried."

Well, we won't be doing that again, Abigail thought. And Charles won't either for very long . . . if I can only think what's best to do about it, without hurting Felix too much.

Abigail's two middle girls, Nan and Julie, were alike in looks and somewhat in temperament. They were not pretty

in the candy-box way Elsie was, but they were handsome
children, dark-haired like Abigail, and with extraordinarily
beautiful eyes. Grandmother Julie's eyes, Abigail would tell
herself, or, remembering with a clutch at her heart, Grace's
eyes, long-lashed, brown with a tinge of hazel, though in
some lights and when either of the girls lost her temper, the
hazel would turn very nearly green. Nan was more stable
than Julie, not quite so high-strung; she was older, eleven
to Julie's eight. She had a formidable temper which she did
not often lose; it took provocation. When she did lose it, her
contained fury was silent and lasting; it smoldered inside
and was a long time cooling. Julie's tempests flashed out into
tantrums and were quickly gone. Abigail dealt firmly with
the tempers. She would not put up with them and she did
not often have to; the girls were, mostly, bright, sunny little
things who got a great deal of fun out of life, particularly
together. They were very close. When problems arose, they
sided with each other—it was Nan and Julie against the
world.

Abigail had no favorites; all the children got the same
affection from her. But she could not help knowing that,
sometimes, the focus of her attention was on these two. The
others had their qualities, of course. Maureen was a good
sturdy plodder and she was reasonable—not like Charles, to
whom no reason was good if he wanted something—and
Elsie would perhaps grow out of being a flitterbug. Abigail
sometimes felt a little sorry for Maureen. It was not her fault
that she could not keep up with Nan, or even Julie, in school.
She wanted to, desperately, Abigail knew; she also wanted,
desperately, to have their talent for music, which she did
not have and never would, no matter how hard she tried.

Music, to Nan and Julie, came as naturally as breathing;
rhythms were spontaneous. They could already play the
piano. The walls of the house fairly rocked in and out when
they sat down to it together. Abigail had started all three

girls early with music lessons. A very good music teacher
lived in town, Mr. Graves, an oldish man, now retired from
teaching in Eastern Conservatory. He was delighted with
Nan and Julie; over poor Maureen he could do nothing but
beat his breast. She, being older, had been at it longer than
they had, but she still could not count, or if she tried to, she
at once lost all connection with the notes she was playing.
It had to be one thing or the other—either you played and
stopped counting, or you counted and stopped playing. Still,
she would not give up.

"She just sits there," Julie would say. "Going *plunk, plunk,
plunk,* till she busts out and cries."

It was the kind of tough stubbornness that Abigail admired, though with reservations. A waste, in a way, she
thought, of good energy misdirected; but Maureen would
have to see that by herself. Abigail was not going to make
her give up.

"You can stop that, Julie," she said. "Maureen may not
play as well as you can, but she's got other things she can
do better than you."

"Well, I'd like to know what they are," Julie said.

In her heart Abigail wondered too. Julie could do a number of flashing and brilliant things. If she wanted to.

"I can't see you sitting down and trying the way Maureen
does, if you didn't have the gift of playing off the top of your
head," Abigail said. "And she didn't go merrily off to school
this morning without making her bed, the way you did."

Poor lamb, she told herself, thinking of Maureen, she
wants to flash and sparkle too. And she's out of it, and knows
she is, with those two smart scamps, cuddled together in
their own world of brains-come-easy. It's lonely for the
plodders.

Since the addition of Miles to the family, Abigail had been
a little less concerned with Maureen being out of things. Up
to then Elsie, of course, had been the youngest, too cute,

too pretty, too admired—too much of a nuisance, making her presence too often felt, to be more than taken for granted and put up with by any of the other children. She was loved, but avoided when possible, and by Maureen as well. But Miles was another matter. He was too little still to own any character—a homely, chunky baby with a wide, pleasant, toothless grin—and Maureen adored him from the beginning.

As the days went by, Abigail became more and more absorbed in her new project at the MacGregor place, with more and more demands on her time. The new dairy buildings were going up fast. Cartwright, the Bristol contractor who had taken the job, she found was more than a skillful builder, he was a perfectionist. He would okay no part of his construction unless it was not only strongly built, and built to last, but right—suited to its purpose. He seemed to know a great deal about modern dairy barns; Clarence Bickford told her that Cartwright had not built one before, but had gone to endless trouble to get information about what would be needed.

"And it's going to be a real model," Clarence said, with deep satisfaction. "A pleasure to work in. That guy is a whizz."

Abigail agreed. She had had conferences with Cartwright and arguments with him about some ideas of her own. More often than not he turned out to be right. He was a lanky, laconic, self-contained sort of fellow, who made his point in as few words as possible. Once he had, he sat back, silent, listened to a different opinion, and did not give an inch. Abigail liked him. After a while she realized that he knew much more about what he was doing than she did, and she made no more suggestions, but let him go ahead. When the work was finished, he went over it from foundations to ridgepoles, inspecting, and then, before he departed for good, nailed to a beam in the new barn a metal plaque, which carried an inscription as laconic as Cartwright was himself:

CARTWRIGHT BROS.
Bristol

"That's his sign that it's his work and as good as he could do it," Clarence said. "George, his brother, told me that. If it could be done any better, by anybody, he wouldn't put the sign up. And he's right, Mrs. Plummer. That's a job, that is." Clarence, a conscientious worker himself, also with considerable pride about it, sighed with admiration. He had been busy supervising the gang of men who had cleared and fenced the new pasturelands. He felt that was a pretty good job too. It was ready for the arrival now of the new dairy herd—Guernseys, with a pedigreed Guernsey bull.

"Kind of wish we'd mixed a few Jerseys in with that bunch of cows coming," he said tentatively, looking at Abigail out of the corner of his eye.

They had had a long argument about the breed of cattle, which he had lost, though he had already, on his own, mixed in the few Jerseys. He didn't know whether Abigail knew this or not, and by bringing the matter up, he had hoped to find out. He did, for she lifted an eyebrow slightly and fixed him with a look.

"You're a hard man, Clarence," she said. "You don't give up easily, do you?"

She knew, all right. Clarence got up to go, trying not to seem in a hurry. Still, if she'd been going to say anything more, she would have. Maybe she was too tired—she looked it. He certainly was. He was tired as a dog. It was Saturday afternoon, and he'd think she'd be dead, the week's work she'd put in, and all summer too. Too bad that husband of hers couldn't be around to help out some. Not that Clarence would ever want to see him again around the place, now that they had new machinery that would cost a pocketful if it got scrambled.

Abigail was tired. The store was always busier with summer trade, and she had Norman Hardwick helping, but she had had to divide her time. She was as glad as Clarence was that Sunday was coming up. And why go back to the store at all today? she thought. Why not go home now? There was nothing going on here at the MacGregor place, and Norman could close up for the weekend without her, for once. She smiled to herself, thinking how he would growl about it on Monday morning, but she was too tired anyway to be of much help. She would climb into the Ford and arrive home early to everyone's surprise—because this was something she seldom did; she was more likely to be late than early. She could see that Nettie didn't grab all the hot water for the kids' baths, so that there'd be some left for Felix and Charles. They were due in tonight—at least Felix had said they'd surely be back by Saturday with the Gilmore House's Sunday supply of fish. It would be nice to have them home for tomorrow too. She saw so little of either of them these days.

When she had seen them, throughout the summer, she had been relieved and pleased with the way they both were looking—and acting, too, both brown and lean as Indians, obviously having a fine time doing something they liked tremendously. Charles had lost most of his adolescent pudginess; he had broadened across the shoulders and grown taller; he was pleasant around the house and nicer than he had ever been to the younger children. Felix, too, seemed contented and happier than he had been for a long time. For the life of her, Abigail couldn't see that Jos's company was hurting Charles. At first she had kept her eyes open for changes, and she was not surprised to hear that Nettie had too.

"I'm all cocked back," Nettie had said, "to climb him the

minute I catch him bringing that Jos's manners into this house."

But Charles hadn't. He did wish now to be called Chuck and insisted on it around home, which nobody minded. Abigail did her best to try to remember; she herself liked the sound of "Charles," but if he wanted a nickname, it was his own affair. After a while, when nothing else happened, Abigail had relaxed. Charles was all right; she couldn't see any real reason for stopping him going with Felix and Jos, and she did not.

Tonight, as she swung the Ford off the main highway into her own street, she almost collided with a motorcycle, traveling on the wrong side of the road and at a high speed. She managed to miss a sideswipe by pulling partially up onto the sidewalk while the machine squeaked by and flashed around the corner out of sight so quickly that she caught only a glimpse of the helmeted person riding it. Jolted and indignant, she determined that the minute she got home she'd call the office of Jerome Green, the county sheriff, and report the incident. What a crazy fool, racing around like that through town, with no thought in the world of anyone else on the street!

Felix and Charles were at home—at least Felix was in the kitchen.

"Oh, good," she said, kissing him. "I hoped you'd be here tonight. Tomorrow, too, please?"

"Uh-huh," Felix said.

He was sitting at the kitchen table, leaning his chin on one hand, still in his work clothes, and looking, she saw, drawn and tired, pale under his tan.

What on earth now? she thought, hanging up her hat and jacket. Nettie seemed to be upset too. She was banging pots and pans, something she never did unless she was good and mad.

"Feeling all right, hon?" she asked, coming back to the table.

"Oh, sure. Pooped out is all."

"Just get home?"

"Uh-huh. Going up to wash and change in a minute."

"A good hot bath'll help, I expect. I told Nettie this morning to be sure and save plenty of hot water."

"I," Nettie said in measured tones, "have saved all the hot water anybody's likely to need."

Abigail raised a questioning eyebrow at Felix, who managed a weary grin.

"Nettie's sore," he said. "I've been trying to promote a flock of chicken sandwiches for a picnic tomorrow."

Nettie, never one to contain feelings, expressed them in a loud snort. She slammed a kettle into the sink with considerable clangor.

"Oh, come on, no need to dent the tinnikins," Felix said. "You've got a chicken. I saw it in the icebox, two of them as a matter of fact." He was trying hard on his usual give-and-take basis with Nettie and not getting anywhere. He himself sounded lugubrious, and Nettie was madder.

"A picnic on the boat, Felix?" Abigail asked doubtfully.

"Yeah, Jos won't be there. He's gone to Bristol to see Gilmore. Won't be back till Monday."

"Why, I think it would be fun, then. Nettie, if you mind doing sandwiches, the girls and I'll be glad to."

"They won't be as good as Nettie's," Felix said in a hollow tone.

"Don't you butter me up, Felix Plummer," Nettie said. "Why didn't you tell me in the first place your blessed brother wouldn't be going? You don't deserve any sandwiches, let alone the good that goes with a picnic. Now, let's see, what else have I got? Pies, I can make two-three apple pies and—" Her good humor completely restored, she went on muttering to herself about supplies for the picnic.

Ordinarily Felix would have bantered back; instead he pulled himself to his feet and started for upstairs, moving stiffly as if he were lame.

"Now, what d'you suppose ails him?" Nettie said. "I guess he must be tired. I'm real sorry I got mad, but he knows I won't have the girls hanging around that feller—he ain't fitten—and then he tried to talk me around, saying how good Charles could run the boat and wanted to show you, and I like to popped my garters—"

"Where *is* Charles?" Abby said. "Didn't he come home with his father?" Nettie coming out of a temper was like someone coming out of a drunk with a talking jag. To get a word in, you had to interrupt.

"What?" she said. "Oh, Felix said he stopped downtown to buy work gloves. Said he might drop over to Jack Russell's, seeing it was early and he had time before supper. Think he might realize some of us would like to see him, where he's been gone so long, but kids that age they don't think of—"

Nettie was going on, but Abigail wasn't listening. Something more than being tired was wrong with Felix, she was sure. After supper, after he was fed and rested, perhaps she could find out what it was.

Charles came thundering in at suppertime, exuberant, dirty, howling for food. He kissed his mother, fetched Nettie a mighty smack on the bottom, avoided the swipe she made at him with her dishcloth, poked and tickled his sisters.

"Food any better in this joint than it was last time?" he said, grinning at Nettie. "What's for supper?"

"You won't get *nothing* out of me for supper till you clean up," Nettie said. "Phew! You smell like an old haddock."

"So would you if you'd been up to your button in 'em the way I have for the last two days. You going to make us chicken sandwiches for the picnic?"

"Button!" Nettie said. "What kind of talk is that?"

"Neck, I mean. Well, you going to?"

"What picnic?" Maureen asked. "On Uncle Jos's boat?"

The girls had been out together all afternoon. They had just come in.

"Sure, on the boat, why not?" Charles said.

Nan said quietly, "I won't go on the boat with Uncle Jos."

"Oh, phooey!" Charles said. "He don't like you, either."

"Doesn't, Charles," Abigail said automatically. "Uncle Jos isn't going, Nan."

"Well, he *doesn't* like her," Charles said. "He hates her guts." Then, seeing his mother's eye on him and the look on her face, he turned brick-red. "I'm sorry, excuse me," he mumbled.

"Well, I should think so," Abigail said. "I don't want to hear that again, Charles."

"Okay, Ma. I said I was sorry, didn't I?" He sat down at the table, picked up his knife and fork, and wiggled his ears at Maureen who sat across from him. One of Charles's accomplishments was that he could wiggle his ears.

"Smart, aren't you?" Maureen said. "That looks *hideous*."

"More than you can do," Charles said. "Aw, come on, Nettie, can't we eat? My stomach thinks my throat's cut. Please," he added hastily, for the benefit of his mother.

"When your father's ready," Nettie said, "we'll eat. Not before." She folded her arms and stared at him.

"You might as well start serving, Nettie," Abigail said. "I'll call Felix."

Troubled as she was about Felix, her mind was no more than half on the children's wrangle, but as she went along the hall she heard Charles say something to Maureen and Maureen's reply.

"Yes, and I know you. You've got something mean up your sleeve. I just hope Mama finds out before you do it too."

Sometimes, she thought, bringing children up not to tattle

on each other has its drawbacks. What could that be about? Well, she'd doubtless find out when the time came.

Felix was dressed and ready, but he was standing by the bedroom window, looking out.

"Supper's ready," Abigail said.

"I'm coming," Felix said. He did not move, however, and she went over to stand beside him.

"What's wrong, Fee? Something is, I know."

"Well," Felix said, "I'm sort of trying to make up my mind, Abby." He grinned slightly and shrugged. "You know what that does to me."

"What about? Can I help?"

"I guess you'll have to. I think the time's come to get Charles away from . . . out of that boat and keep him out. It's going to be a rough deal . . . for everybody."

"Well, I've thought this right along—" Abigail began.

"Don't, for godsake, say I told you so, or I'll drop dead right here on the bedroom floor," Felix said. "I'm damn sick of spending my life having to admit that somebody else is right."

"What's happened? Has something—"

Felix did not reply at once. "Look," he said heavily. "We've got to go on this picnic tomorrow. Chuck—Charles wants to show you how well he can handle the boat. I've promised him, and I can't see slamming him in the face with everything at once. Wouldn't do any harm to let him have one more day, but after that, that's got to be it. So we'll go?"

"Of course. I don't mind. I'll enjoy it, so long as we don't have to put up with Jos. Tomorrow night after we get home, I'll talk with Charles. School will be opening in a couple of weeks, anyway, and he hasn't had any vacation. Perhaps he'd like one."

"You think he'd like anything better than the roaring good time he's had all summer?"

"Perhaps not. But if you want me to, I'll handle it, Fee.

Charles can blame me. And so can Jos. Jos will, anyway.
There's no problem—not to get so torn out over, anyway.
Come and have your supper. You need it and you'll feel better." She slipped her arm around, leaned against him. "You
wouldn't like to quit, too, come back and help Clarence
manage the new creamery?"

"Oh, God, no! I can't drink a glass of milk now, let alone
sell one. Maybe I'd like to quit at that. Guess I'd just as soon
have Jos eat me out—it's all in the family—as have Clarence
curdle the cream every time I bust a diamond-studded, gold-
plated screw."

At supper Felix was at his best, talking about the picnic,
joking with the kids until they screamed with laughter, kidding Nettie about the quality of her supper, which was very
good. But occasionally his voice would shoot upward, almost
with a squeak, into a higher register—which he pretended
happened on purpose, to be funny; and Abigail, watching
him, saw that his cheeks were flushed, as if with the flush
of fever.

What had happened to Felix was the revenue cutter which
had spotted the *Abigail* the night before, offshore, on her
way in from rendezvous with the Canadian supply boat, and
had put chase. This had not happened to Felix before; Jos
either by luck or by know-how had so far managed to avoid
it. He had always told Felix that if they were overhauled, he
would heave to, fast, and start setting trawls. "And, hell,"
he'd said, "having Chuck here aboard's as good as an insurance policy. Nobody's going to believe we'd bring a kid on
a jaunt like this, huh?"

But Jos had bragged a good deal to Charles about what
the *Abigail* would do if he opened her up, and last night he
had raided a case of the stock and had sampled it. He was
sitting in the stern, at ease, with the bottle in his hand, when
suddenly he stood up, pointed his nose into the wind, and

sniffed it like a hound. Felix had seen him do this before, listening in fog or darkness for the rote on ledges which would confirm to him where he was. It was almost as if he listened with his nose. You had to admire Jos, aboard a boat; he seemed to have a sixth sense, particularly for sounds.

"Slow down, Chuck," he said to Charles. "Idle her a minute." And then even Felix could hear, from somewhere out in the blackness to windward, the thrum of heavy engines.

"Well, well, well," Jos said. "B'God, if there they ain't!" He twirled his bottle around his head, let it go with a mighty heave, splashing into the water. "You wanted to see what she'd do, Chuck, old socks-o," he said. "Give that throttle a shove ahead as far as it'll go, and stand aside!"

It was not a long chase or a close one, but while it lasted, it was wild. Jos made the most of it. He was, in part, showing off to Charles—he was not even sure that what he had heard was a Government cutter, but Felix and Charles thought it was, and maybe it could have been. The night was a very dark one, he knew where he was and what the *Abigail* could do, and it was a chance, he roared gleefully to Charles, to step on the old girl's tail, for once.

"Look at the damned old scairt goose go!" he yelled. "But blast that sea fire, likely they'll spot that. Chuck, get below and break out them rifles. Give one to your pop, if he knows which end of it to shoot, and if they git any closer, let 'em have it!"

The sea, since dusk, had been full of luminescence. The *Abigail's* side waves rose up tall; she seemed to be thundering down a chute between two solid walls of cold fire.

Things had happened a little fast for Felix. He had barely saved himself from sprawling flat when the sudden thrust of speed had tumbled him backward; and then his first frantic thought had been that what he was sitting on was the case of whiskey which Jos had opened and left in plain sight on the platform—God, they mustn't find that!—and he had picked it up and dropped it overboard. He was turning back from doing this when Charles thrust the rifle into his hand.

The *Abigail* carried two high-caliber rifles, beautiful and expensive guns—Jos would have nothing less—in an unobtrusive compartment behind the paneling in her cuddy. On most trips, throughout the summer, he had had them out, teaching Charles to shoot. Their marks had been numbers of harmless and defenseless creatures; they had shot seals off the ledges of the islands, porpoises rolling up to surface, sea gulls. Felix had regretted the creatures; he liked seals and, particularly, porpoises—"puffers" always seemed to him to be having such a good time, a humorous kind of sea animal playing games in the water, making a pleasant sound of held breath letting go almost like a human sigh when it came up for air. But shooting was a manly thing to learn; Felix would have tried it himself if he hadn't known beforehand that he would be a duffer at it, and that Jos and Charles, too, would laugh their heads off at him. Charles was no duffer —not now. He could shoot nearly as well as Jos could.

Something about the feel of the icy metal in his hand turned Felix sick with horror. Shooting at animals who could not shoot back was one thing; it was for fun. These men coming up behind, gaining, if they were gaining, had guns, too, and they would use them. This wasn't fun, though both Jos and Charles seemed to think it was. Jos, at the wheel, was yelling. Even over the thunder of the engine Felix could hear his bull-moose bawl. "Look at 'er go, by God! I can't hold the bitch back!" And Charles, with the cold glint of the sea's luminescence on his rifle barrel, was peering intently into the darkness, where the boat's wake disappeared in a boil of icy light. By the same light Felix could make out Charles's face, pale but excited, even eager.

He laid his hand on Charles's arm. "Put the gun down, Chuck."

Charles seemed not to hear. He tried to pull his arm away, but Felix did not let go.

"I said, put the gun down, Charles."

"Oh, for godsake, Pa, let me alone! *Leggo*, will ya?" He jerked his arm backward; his elbow caught Felix, hard, in the pit of the stomach.

Felix staggered, knocked off balance. The boat's motion, a quick pitch-and-rise, kept him from catching himself, and he sat down with a crash on the platform. The gun in his hand went off. The bullet sang past Jos's head, shattering the windscreen in front of his face.

For a brief moment Jos thought the revenue cutter had indeed caught up with him. After all, he had had one boat, the first *Abigail*, shot out from under him and he knew what it sounded like. If they were that close— He yanked the throttle back as far as it would go, slammed the gears into neutral, and stood staring wildly out into the empty blankness astern. There was nothing. The engine idled, the boat lost way, the eerie boil of her wake began to die in the water.

"Well, then, what in hell was it?" Jos began. Then he caught sight of Felix, or some dim form, sprawled on the platform. And nowhere in all the black expanse of water around them was there a sign of a searchlight or even the sound of a heavy engine.

Charles was babbling frantically, "Pa, oh, Pa! Are you okay? I didn't mean—"

"I'm . . . all right," Felix managed. He was still struggling to get his wind back, which seemed completely gone.

Jos picked up his flashlight, kept handy by the steering wheel for emergencies, held it on briefly, long enough to take in the scene. He was speechless. Then he let out such a moan as he might have if Felix's bullet had indeed caught him in a tender place.

"Wouldn't ya know!" he demanded of sea and heaven.

"Wouldn't ya, for the love of old Aunt Nancy's busted petti-coat string, for godsakes, *know?*"

"He might be hurt, Uncle Jos—"

"No," Felix said. He had got some breath back, not enough to get himself on his feet yet, but enough, sitting flat on the platform, to stand up for the first time in his life to Jos.

"What are you . . . trying to do, Jos, make him a car . . . carbon copy of you? What kind of a has . . . hassle is this to put a young boy through? Well, I won't have it! I'm . . . stopping it. Tonight."

"Why, you wrangle-gutted son of a dead cream puff!" Jos said. He had got half the message, but not all of it. "Stopping it, are you? Is that what you tried? By the God, did you take a shot at me?"

He started down the platform, and Felix, breathless again, wearily heard him coming.

"He fell down!" Charles said. His voice scaled up, falsetto, went down as he checked it. "He fell down and his gun went off, is all."

"Haw!" Jos said. He began to chuckle.

Quick change, Felix thought. He's not going to do any-thing to put Charles off him.

Jos burst into a guffaw. "By gum, if we ain't the cookies!" he gasped between gusts. "Me, I was so darn scared there for a minute that *my* legs pretty nigh went out from under *me*. And, you know, Chuck, I don't believe that was any-thing in the God's world but some damned old sardine car-rier, heading somewhere after a load. Give her a spin, will ya? Got to get rolling, or old Gilmore's truck'll be there before we are."

Whether or not Jos thought the craft off in the darkness had been a sardine carrier, he was being mighty cautious, Felix saw, as they neared the coast. He took a roundabout way through some narrow island channels—a nice piece of navigation in the dark—and then, instead of going up to his

mooring in Granite Hills Harbor, as he'd planned, he slid
the boat quietly in through Starball Narrows to the Cove,
up the creek into the pond behind the beach, where they
unloaded cargo and stored it in the space under the floor of
the old Randall house. By the time the job was done, Charles
was too tired to stand up; he staggered into the cuddy and
fell, boots and all, into one of the cuddy bunks. Felix followed him, took the boots off, and tucked him under a
blanket.

Felix himself was worn out; he still felt sick and dizzy
from his fall, and the hard work carrying the cases up the
beach hadn't helped any. He was about to go to bed himself
when Jos called to him to come on deck. It seemed there
was more to come.

Jos was busy backing the boat, getting her headed out
through the creek. Then, instead of dropping anchor in the
cove, as he usually did, he turned out through the narrows.
He seemed to be none the worse for wear, for all his night's
work.

Now where's he going? Felix thought. Damned if I'll ask
him. He can speak first.

But after a while he said, "If you don't want anything,
I'm going to turn in."

"Feel all right?" Jos said, without turning his head.

"Bushed."

"Yeah, that was quite a tumble you took. Lucky you didn't
break something."

"Wasn't it?"

"I'm going up to lay in the harbor tonight. If that was some
of them fellers on the hop, I don't want to be cornered in
Starball Cove. Tomorrow I'm getting glass to fix that windscreen. I'll have to go to Bristol for it."

"Okay," Felix said. "So it wasn't a sardine carrier, after
all."

"Dunno. Could ha' been. Could ha' been somebody we

wouldn't want to meet up with too. If it was, they'll be
nosing around for a while, looking boats over, this one and
that one. Now, I want you to take Abby on a picnic Sunday,
all the kids. Sail all over the bay, show yourself. Go out to
Finney's Island." He chuckled suddenly. "Tell Abby I won't
be going."

"Why?" Felix said. "What's all that for?"

"Well, use your bean. They won't overhaul you with a
woman and a mess of kids on a picnic. Next time they see
the boat, they'll know it."

"Everybody knows it's your boat."

"And we know it ain't, don't we? If they bother you, all
you've got to do is show your papers. Nice family man, out
with his wife and a potful of kids on a Sunday picnic. Hell,
they'll want to go too."

So that was why, Felix thought. If we'd got caught tonight, if we ever do get caught, whose boat is it? Not his.
Mine. Hell, I might have known.

"Chuck done good tonight," Jos went on. "It's about time
I give him his bonus. If he ain't awake before I leave in the
morning, you tell him it's waiting for him over in my wood-
shed. Hey, we all done pretty good this summer, hanh? You
and him both got quite a wad laid away."

"Yes," Felix said. "You've paid me back every cent you
owe me for the boat. So you better have that bill of sale
back, hadn't you?"

"Don't you want to know what Chuck's bonus is?" Jos said.

"Well, hadn't you?"

"Shoot, I ain't paid you back for what I took out of the
creamery money. A motorcycle, by God. A dandy. The best
money can buy."

Nausea choked Felix's throat. My boat, he thought, And
my boy. I'm the kind of a man who'll take his kid into a mess
like that, and nobody'll ever believe different. I'll get the
works and Jos'll be just the hired hand.

What boy could resist Jos's boat, Jos's things? Jos's presents, all the best money could buy? Charles's catcher's mitt, his fancy fishing rod, his new hunting rifle, all stored quietly away in Jos's house, in case Abby made a fuss?

Stuff I always wanted when I was a kid and envied Jos because he had them. If I'd been the kind of a boy Charles is, Jos would've done the same for me.

"What's the matter, don't you want the kid to have any fun? Or are you scairt of Abby?"

"He's not old enough . . . he can't—"

"Can't ride a motorcycle? He sure can. He learnt how on Jack Russell's, that kid he bats around with in school. Jack's sixteen, but, hell, look at Chuck, he's nigh half a head taller than Jack is. Any cop gets rooty about it, he can say he's sixteen and you can back him up, can't you?"

"Abby'll—she'll be afraid he'll kill himself."

Jos guffawed. "Let her pucker," he said. "He won't. He ain't like you with machinery. He can do anything with his hands, the little baster."

The picture flashed into Felix's mind of his son's hands— the young, stubby, grimy fingers taut around the gleaming wood and metal of the rifle; and he leaned over the side and vomited quietly into the water.

When he awoke in the bunk, sunlight was streaming through the cuddy portholes; he saw by his watch that it was four o'clock. He had slept nearly all day. Charles and Jos were both up and gone; tumbled bunks showed that they had been there, but that was all.

Felix lay for a while slowly coming to; he still felt sickish and queasy, his back was lame, and his stern felt as if it had been pounded with a board. Well, in a way, he guessed it had been. The boat was apparently tied up at the town dock. He could hear the rub and squeak of her fenders against the piling.

Feet sounded on the dock and someone jumped soundly up on the boat's bow, setting her to rocking. It was Jos. Heavily gloved, he began ripping out the shattered glass pieces of the windscreen.

Felix sat up, put his feet over the side of the bunk. He wished he had waked up earlier; he didn't want to see Jos or talk to him.

"For godsake," Jos said. "You still down there knocking it off? I better come down there and dump some salt on you, you'll rot."

"Yeah," Felix said. "I already have."

"Jees, I been to Bristol and back and Chuck's been out since noon on his motorcycle. You ought to see him, he's having the time of his life."

Felix said nothing. He was putting his clothes to rights as well as he could. He had slept in them, and he would have to walk up through town to get home. God, he thought, I hope Nettie's got some hot water.

Jos met him on deck. "I'll give you a ride home," he said. "My car's right up here at the head of the dock."

"Don't bother. I'll be all right. I can walk it."

"Hell, I want to talk to ya."

"All right." What could you do?

"No place like a car to talk secrets in, is there?" Jos said, as he climbed in and started the engine. "Look, I see Gilmore in Bristol, told him we wouldn't have no load ready today. Told him why. We decided we wouldn't unload anything but fish here at the dock for the next few trips. For anything else, we'll operate out of Starball. That old road's bumpy, ain't been used much, but I patched up the worst holes when I was hauling lumber down there to fix the camp, so I know Gilmore's truck can get through. He can back up close to the bank of the crick, and I'll lay the boat in there alongside. It's going to be tricky, and it'll have to be fast. We've got to use every minute of the high-water slack, before the waters starts out of that goddamn pond. It'll have to be at night, and we got to wait on the tide. Wednesday night's the soonest we can do it, high-water slack's at ten-fifteen then. You getting this, or are you too thickheaded to listen?"

"I'm getting it," Felix said.

"Okay. Ronnie'll spend the night down there with us in the camp. Then in the morning we'll light out of there early. Ronnie'll make sure nobody sees the truck when he ducks out of the Starball road onto the highway—it's all woods along there anyway—and we'll meet him down at the dock with a load of fish. And I mean fish. There ain't going to be one other goddamn thing aboard that boat till them buggers out there quit nosing around and go elsewhere. They will. They got territory to cover. When they're gone, we'll go back to regular. Innocent as virgin maidens. How you feeling? Any better?"

"No."

"That picnic tomorrow'll put you right. Ought to be a nice jaunt for everybody."

"Godalmighty, Jos! I've got to get some rest. All that work you've laid out, I can't—I feel like hell warmed over."

"Sleep all day in a bunk, if you want to. Chuck'll run the boat."

"What if Abby won't go?"

"She'll go if I don't. Fun for the kids? Sure, she will. Now, look, Fee." He shot a look at Felix, his eyebrows drawn into a scowl. "You're going, see? Damn it, can't even a half-wit like you see what it means?"

In a minute, Felix thought wearily, he'll get red in the face and start in. And I can't take it. Not a screaming row, not now.

"All right," he said. "I'll go."

But, he told himself, for Charles, it's going to be the last time.

This was what had happened to Felix on the night of August 15, 1924, and on the following day when he started to try to undo what he had let happen to his son.

Sunday, the day of the picnic, was beautiful, the weather made to order for a boat trip. The bay was smooth, rippled here and there by a light, warm southwest wind, the sky a soft baby blue with a few woolly clouds. On the horizon, far and middle, the offshore islands were withdrawn and mysterious in a thin, smoky haze, which vanished as the boat neared each one, to replace itself over the mainland as the distance grew behind.

"That isn't fog, is it, Felix?" Abigail asked.

"Just August weather," Felix said. He glanced over at her from the stern, where he had the four girls clustered around him, telling them, as nearly as she could make out above the sound of the engine, stories about the islands, who lived there now and who had gone away. His night's rest had done him good; he was feeling better, she was relieved to see, and looking better too. Except for the dark half-moons of shadow under his eyes, he seemed almost himself again. Today would rest him, she thought. A nice quiet time, with nothing to do but lie in the sun. "Busman's holiday?" she called, smiling at him.

Felix smiled back and kept on with his yarn, which apparently was about the island they were passing, where an ancestor of hers had settled in colonial times and had founded a community.

"Only feller in the world ever had two tombstones," she heard him say.

She had heard the old story before and so had the children, but it never lost anything in the telling.

Charles, at the wheel, was beckoning to her, and she went up to stand beside him.

"Now look, Ma," he said. "Pa don't know anything about

the weather. I've got to keep my eye on it. That *could* be fog. And this wind, it might be calm now, but then again it might blow up into a smoky sou'wester this afternoon, be quite rough."

He glanced at the sky, swept the horizon with narrowed eyes—the expert, being one.

She glanced at him thoughtfully, which he did not notice, being occupied with his job of letting everybody know who was boss here, skipper in charge of the boat. He had been doing this ever since they had left the dock, ordering the girls around, ordering his father to cast off and do other deckhand chores; he had yelled at Nan when she had started to investigate the cuddy, "G'wan, get out of that! Mind your own business!" and had banged to the companionway doors practically on the end of her nose.

Ordinarily Abigail would have put a stop to this with a firm word or two. It was Jos at his best, bossy and tiresome and an overall stuffy great bore, worrying people unnecessarily and in the end spoiling everybody's good time. And downgrading Felix, of course, was pure Jos. Felix had asked her not to say anything to Charles until tomorrow, and she wouldn't.

But it's time somebody did, she thought sadly, and put some teeth into it, poor lamb. What a know-it-all!

She made her way aft and rejoined the group in the stern. This time she sat closer to them and quietly slipped an arm around Nan. Nan's eyes, she observed, were still quite greenish, and so were Julie's, which naturally followed—if one of them got mad, the other did, too, and it took both a while to get over temper. She saw now that Felix was really laying himself out to help, and she sat watching with appreciation. At his best he could be very funny and entertaining; he was engaged in smoothing out ruffled feelings and succeeding. Before long he would have everybody doubled up laughing. She waited, listening, and when the shrieks came, as they did almost at once, she found herself laughing harder than anybody—and couldn't have helped it, she thought, if I'd tried.

"Oh, Felix," she gasped, as soon as she could speak. "That was wonderful!"

The boat was entering a long gut between two islands, a narrow, deep channel, sheltered and glassy calm. The islands looked as if they had never been touched or lived on, perhaps never even been discovered since the beginning of time. Their tall spruces grew down to steep, pink granite ledges, where a small white scarf of foam let itself be seen before it disappeared. The only living thing in sight was a pompous white sea gull who sat with his head pulled down into his neck and did not bother to stir from his ledge as the boat passed by.

"Look at him," Julie said suddenly. "No neck and chest stuck out. Uncle Jos."

"It is *not!*" Elsie said.

But there was a resemblance, if only in manner, which nobody could deny. The three older girls burst into yells of delight, which went up a shrill octave when the sea gull stretched its neck, put up its head with an affronted stare, and flapped away.

"All right," Abigail said, "let's not be unkind. It's too nice a day. You scared the poor thing, and it was having a nice peaceful time too." I wish, she thought, that I was.

She was not, however, to have one. Peace, it seemed, had departed for the rest of the day. Charles said in a sudden loud voice, "Listen, everybody. Now everybody hang on. I'm gonna show you what she'll do." And he pushed the throttle ahead as far as it would go.

He hadn't really given anybody much time to hang on to anything. The boat leaped ahead with a great jerk; Abigail saved herself from going over backward by grabbing with one hand at the cheeserind, and her other arm held Nan.

Felix, thrown off balance himself, managed to snatch at the two children nearest him, Maureen and Julie, but Elsie crashed backward into him, bumped her head on his bony knee. A tub behind Charles fell over. Its cover came off and its contents, a half-bushel or so of spoiled lobster bait, distributed itself along the platform.

Elsie was crying, but Abigail could not hear her above the thunder of the engine and the crash and roar of water along the boat's sides. She could not even hear Felix, who was, apparently, yelling at the top of his lungs at Charles, at the same time gathering Elsie into his lap and trying to extricate himself from the flying arms and legs of the other two. She said into Nan's ear, "Hang on tight, honey," and made her way grimly forward along the platform. She was therefore quite close to Charles when the grizzled black head and bristly whiskers of Jos himself thrust up out of the companionway hatch, and she did not miss the quick grin and wink he gave Charles or Charles's response.

He has been here all the time, she thought. And Charles knew it.

Jos grabbed at the throttle, thrust it back to "Slow." He then proceeded to give Charles a loud and raucous dressing down, which Charles took without looking at him.

"I ought to turn you over my knee and slam some sense into the seat of your pants," he finished. "I thought I'd learnt you how to run a boat, but I see I ain't learnt you enough. You do that kind of a fool stunt again, by gorry, I will. You hear me?"

"Yeah," Charles said. "I won't do it again, Uncle Jos."

Well, Abigail thought. An act. And not a very good one. Neither of them is actor enough to get away with it.

"Well, my gorry, I hope nobody got hurt," Jos said. "My gorry. That engine like to hove me right out through the side of the bunk. I overslep' down there," he went on, unlatching the companionway doors and heaving himself out

PART TWO: Josiah   69

on deck. "I was planning to go to Bristol today, but I was so pooped out last night, I darn nigh slep' the clock round. So here I am."

He was in his work clothes which stank of tobacco and fish, and as he paused beside her, she caught a rich, ripe smell of rum.

She said, "So I see."

Jos grinned. "And ain't you glad to see me, though!"

There was no telling how drunk he was. Sober, he could be mean enough; she was not going to argue with him, not in a boat full of children. She nodded briefly and said nothing.

"Well, I know somebody who is," Jos said. He picked the tear-stained Elsie out of her father's lap, boosted her high. "What's the matter with Uncle Jos's best girl? All puddled up! Get rid of them puddles, I got something for you."

"In your pocket?" Elsie said. She began poking in his jacket pockets and presently stopped, frustrated.

"Tch! Must ha' forgot it, left it ashore," Jos said. "Now ain't that too bad!"

Elsie's face puckered. Two big tears formed slowly and rolled down her cheeks.

"Hey, wait!" Jos said. "Why don't you go down in the cuddy and see if I left it on the bunk?"

Elsie scuttled. She vanished down the companionway, and Jos sat down agreeably on a tub. "Hey, Chuck! Chawles, I mean. You don't have to set dead in the water. Le's go, hah?"

Charles, apparently, felt none the worse for his bawling out. He seemed quite pleased with himself and with Jos— Abigail had seen him hide a quick grin at Jos's "Chawles" and his unmistakable imitation of her own voice. So Uncle Jos was terribly, terribly funny; anything he said was gospel. Felix was already of no account; she was prim and foolish— an old maid, perhaps, who by some accident had become a mother. If they were going to make fun of us, she thought grimly, they had much better have done it behind my back.

Elsie came struggling up out of the cuddy with her present, a huge box of candy decorated with pink ribbon bows. She could barely lift it. The big flat box obscured all of her except her head, ankles, and sneakers. Charles had already set the boat smoothly in motion, which made her progress difficult, but she finally made it across the platform to Uncle Jos, laid the box in his lap, and stood looking up at him with melting brown eyes.

"Now, ain't that some old cute!" Jos said. "Wimmen! All alike, ain't they, Abby? Open her up, Else, see what you got, and you 'n' I'll try how much of it we can put down."

He himself opened the box, when Elsie was too slow at it, ripping off the ribbon, dropping it to the platform under his feet. When the cover came off he dropped that, too, and both he and Elsie stared, entranced, at the sight. Rows of brown chocolates, chocolates in gold foil, chocolates with fat nuts, nougats—they looked wonderful.

Jos scooped out a handful, scattering fluted paper cups to the air as he filled his mouth.

"Good!" he said thickly. "God, ought to be, cost me ten bucks. What's the matter with you kids? Stand-offish, ain't you? Come on over here, ask Else if you can have some. It's her candy."

Disgusted and furious as she was, Abigail kept her voice down. "Not too much, girls. Remember Nettie's chicken sandwiches. You don't want to spoil your lunch."

"Spoil their good time, more like," Jos grunted. "What's chicken sandwiches, anyway? Hell, I got lobster in mine."

Nan had not moved. She sat, taut and silent, looking out over the water. But both Maureen and Julie had, beguiled —as, Abigail thought, who wouldn't be?

"Well, come on," Jos said to Nan. "Have some. Come over here. For all you know, I might have a present for you too."

"No, thank you," Nan said. Polite, remote, she went on staring at the water.

"If she ain't the spitting image of you, Abby," Jos said. "You better come, or I'll give it to little sister here." Suddenly aware of Julie, he did a double take. "Another one, by God! Three Abbys! It ain't possible!"

"Elsie," Abigail said, "that's enough. Not one more piece."

"Aw, eat all you want, Else," Jos said.

"I don't want her to be sick. No, Elsie. That's all."

Elsie, however, was already diverted. Maureen had bent down, rescued the pink ribbon from under Jos's feet, and was brushing it off and folding it.

"That's mine! You can't have it!" Elsie let out a squall.

"You didn't want it before," Maureen said. "It was getting all dirty."

"It's nothing to fight over," Abigail said. "Here, bring it to me." She held out her hand for the ribbon.

Julie suddenly screamed, high, shrill and piercing, a sound only Julie could make. She went plunging across the platform into her mother's lap, still screaming. It was a moment before Abigail could get anything coherent out of her.

"Something awful cold . . . slippery . . . he dropped it down my neck," Julie sobbed. "Get it . . . oh, get it out . . ." Julie shuddered, turned greenish, and was sick.

Abigail got it out. She undid Julie's blouse and found the cold object, which was a raw clam out of its shell, dropped it overside, and wiped the quivering small back with her handkerchief. "Better now?" she asked quietly.

But Julie was not better. She was outraged, revolted; she began screaming again.

"She'd better lie down," Abigail said. "Felix, isn't there a bunk? Will you carry her?"

Below, in the cuddy, she soothed the hysterics as best she could.

"Felix," she said, "I want you to go out there and tell Jos

we are going back. I won't stand this any longer, and I won't subject the children to it."

"Well, I'll tell him," Felix said. "I don't know what he'll . . . he's . . ."

"I know. He's drunk. It's disgusting."

"What'll I tell him?"

Abigail stared at him. He looked, she saw, strained and pale, and he was sweating.

"I swear I didn't know he was aboard, Abby. He told me he was going to Bristol."

"Charles knew it. That was obvious, wasn't it?"

"Yes. It sure was. I'll tell him Julie's sick, we've got to see a doctor."

"Tell him what you like. And send Nan down, will you? Sometimes she can help when Julie's like this."

Julie was often like this. Abigail had dealt with her tantrums before, never quite sure how much was to be taken seriously and how much was Julie's articulate bid for attention. Usually a little firmness was all that would be needed. But not this time. Julie didn't even begin to quiet down until Nan came, sat on the bunk beside her, put both hands on her cheeks, holding hard.

"Listen, Julie. Listen, it's all right. I've got something to tell you." She leaned close and whispered in Julie's ear.

After a while she said, "She's better now, Ma. I'll stay with her if you want. She's going to sleep."

Abigail nodded. Yes, that was probably the best thing to do. If Julie slept awhile, she'd be all right again. She was a child who snapped back quickly. And it was really wonderful the trust those two had in each other.

On deck, Jos himself had taken the wheel. Charles was sitting on the bow in front of the pilot shelter; Felix was talking with the other children aft. The boat had not turned back. She was still headed for Finney's Island, where they usually picnicked.

"By God, I come on a picnic, and on a picnic I'm going to go," Jos said as Abigail came up the companionway steps.

When she did not answer him, he went on, "That kid ain't sick no more'n I am. All she needs to straighten her out's a couple of good whacks acrost the stern. You can do what you want to, but I'm going ashore and eat my lobster sandwiches."

"It's a nice day for it," Abigail said.

She went on by him and joined the others in the stern. Felix was doing his best to get a laugh or two out of the girls, making heavy weather of it. They looked at her apprehensively as she sat down; Felix pulled out his handkerchief and mopped his forehead.

"Julie's all right," she said composedly. "She's asleep. Isn't the island pretty today?"

Faces began to clear almost at once.

"Now, don't anybody forget her bathing suit when we go ashore. I expect you'll have time for a swim before lunch."

There was nothing to be done about Jos. An argument would only make him worse. She would keep the children as far away from him as she could, and the only other thing, she would try as best she might to see that they had a good time.

They went along. After a while Jos slowed down, turned the boat into Finney's Island cove, and yelled to Charles to drop over the anchor.

Nan came on deck to tell her mother that Julie was all right now; she was waking up.

"Good," Abigail said. "Want me to come down?"

"Oh, no," Nan said. "We'll be up in a minute." On the way she skidded a little on the platform and thumped down on all fours, but she wasn't hurt, she said. She gave everybody a sunny grin and vanished into the cuddy to Julie.

At least she's over it, Abigail thought thankfully. If Nan was, Julie soon would be.

Julie was. While Charles was bringing the punt alongside, preparing to load and ferry everybody ashore, shrieks of high glee rose out of the cuddy, and presently Nan and Julie came on deck giggling, as happy as any two kids on a picnic ought to be.

Jos paid no attention to them or to anyone else. He rummaged out his dinner bucket and, surly and taciturn, plunked himself into the stern of the punt with the bucket on his lap. Ashore, he lay down on the beach in the sun and went to sleep with his hat over his eyes.

Thank God, Abigail told herself. Either the rum was wearing off or he had gobbled too much candy.

Peace descended. Felix and the kids swam and dried off in the sun and swam again. There was only one slight disturbance, when Charles started to tease Julie about the clam.

"Ho, a raw clam! Some present he had for you, I'll say!" He started a raucous hoot, which cut off suddenly when Felix leaned over and closed his fingers hard around the back of Charles's sunburned neck.

"You knock that off!" Felix said, in a voice which Abigail had seldom heard him use. "And knock it off right now!"

Well, that's a help, she thought. A surprise too. She wished he'd do something like that a little more often. She didn't miss, however, Charles's sullen stare at Felix as he jerked himself out from under the hand.

Tomorrow. Tomorrow there'd be changes made. And pray God it comes soon.

"If you're ready," she called, "lunch is out and on."

Jos woke up feeling better, at least hungry. He opened his dinner bucket and stared into it with gusto before he began pulling out one fat, thick sandwich after another and gobbling with huge bites.

"Will you have a chicken sandwich, Jos?" Abigail said, offering him the plate.

Jos stared past the plate, ignoring it. His eyes turned slightly red. "Will you kids for the luvva God quit *looking?*"

he demanded. "It's enough to make a man lose his appetite."

Abigail glanced around. Nan and Julie were sitting side by side on a beached log. Their lunches were in front of them, so far untouched. They were simply sitting and staring at Uncle Jos, and each pair of identical eyes was a clear, hard green.

"Ain't your ma ever learnt you no manners?" Jos said. "What's the matter with you, anyway? Can't you take a little joke?"

"Yes," Nan said, "we can. Excuse me, Uncle Jos."

And Julie echoed politely, "Excuse me."

Abigail caught back her smile in time and soberly proffered the plate again.

"Well, it's about time somebody said excuse me for this and that," Jos said. "Here I give you a nice picnic, my boat and my candy, and you— Hell, no, Abby, what I want one of them finicky doodas for? Ain't fit to eat. Female samwiches, phooey! They ain't a woman living can feed a man on a picnic or anywheres else, so's he don't git up from his dinner hungry. Don't git a piece of meat big enough to feel in your mouth, and nine times out of ten some kind of a slipp'ry pudding ain't no more flavor nor body to than a potful of Bay o' Fundy fog. I'm some old glad I never got married. I can fix my own stuff, feel it when I chew it too. Now, these, it took five big lobsters, tomalley and all, and darn nigh a pint of mayonnaise before they was fit to eat." He shoved the fat sandwich he had just picked out of his bucket under Abigail's nose. "You smell that, by gorry? Ain't that good? Smell that across the street and around the corner, hanh?"

Abigail recoiled. The thing was horrible. It smelled like nothing she had ever run across before, a combination which, if it did go around corners, probably walked on feet.

She gasped, "Jos! What is it? You can't be eating that," and put out a hand to stop him, but she was too late.

Jos had already taken a ponderous bite and was going on. "Now, there's something a man can—awrrk!"

His eyes bulged, his mouth dropped open. A look of complete horror spread across his face as he stared at the sandwich in his hand. Suddenly he dropped it, lunged to his feet, and fled down the beach, where he rinsed, gargled, spat in the salt water, and presently threw up with noises which might have been heard anywhere in the land.

Maureen suddenly clapped both hands over her mouth, but the half-choked squeal got away from her. She sat rocking back and forth, a series of explosive snorts bursting from between her fingers as she tried to stop laughing and could not. The other children weren't laughing. Charles stood frozen, horrified; Elsie, as usual, was puckering up to cry. Nan and Julie sat soberly, almost, it seemed, with wonder, watching the antics on the beach.

"Felix, what on earth?" Abigail said. "It smelled dreadful. You couldn't think anybody would—"

"No, not knowing it," Felix said. He had picked up the discarded sandwich and was sniffing it. "Wow!" he said under his breath.

"Pa, we got to help him. He's awful sick," Charles said. "We gotta do something!"

"Yes, sure," Felix said. His lips suddenly twitched into a grin he could not control and he fled down the beach to Jos, his shoulders shaking. Abigail saw him at the water's edge pull back his arm and loft the sandwich as far as he could into the cove.

"I don't see what's so darn funny," Charles said. He himself had not gone near Jos. Abigail knew why—the sight of anyone as sick as that had always made Charles throw up too. It was the noises they made, he had once told his mother.

They watched while Felix loaded Jos into the punt, rowed him off to the boat, helped him aboard. Apparently he had also helped him below into a bunk, for Jos disappeared down the companionway and didn't reappear.

Felix did, however. He started the engine, left it idling, and went up on the bow to pull in the anchor.

Charles at once began to dither. "He can't *do* that," he began. "He don't know how, not without me. Oh, my Lord, he's running inshore here! He'll get her aground sure as hell! Pa! Pa! Keep her off, will ya? Oh, the darn old—"

Abigail reached over and took him firmly by the ear. "Stop that right now!" she said. "You father's as well able to run the boat as you are, if I can judge by the act you put on on the way out here. Whether Jos put you up to it or not, and I know very well he did, it was a foolish and dangerous thing to do and could have hurt somebody. You both behaved like slobs, and you know it. If I hear one more word out of you about what your father can't do, I'll turn you over my knee. Your father's running the boat inshore so he can pick us up more quickly, that's all."

Felix, she hoped and prayed, would not run the boat aground. She was relieved when he didn't. He stopped well off the shore in deep water, at least deep enough, idled the engine, and gave the punt a good stout shove toward the beach. Then he turned the boat around, jogged off a little way, watched while the light wind blew the punt toward shore.

I hope Charles noticed that he knows which way the wind is, she thought. She was still almost angry enough to call attention to it, but she had said enough. Let him alone now.

Behind her she could hear the picnic gear being gathered up quietly. The girls were doing it without being told; they were as ready to leave as she was.

Then she heard Nan's clear, cool voice say, "Well, he can't take a little joke either, can he?"

Abigail spun around. "Charles," she said quickly, "will you take care of the punt, please, when she drifts in? I'd better make sure we don't leave anything."

Charles's face was crimson with rage and his fists were

doubled up, but he went without a word, caught the punt by the bow, and grounded her on the pebbles.

I had much better not have heard that, Abigail told herself. And I'm not going to let on I did. Justice is what it is, and there can't be anything much worse than a raw clam down the back of the neck.

On the way home Charles, very lofty and stand-offish in his manner, went up on the bow, where he stayed with his back to everyone. The girls, even Elsie, stayed aft, as far away from the cuddy as possible, though there was not a sound from Jos except an occasional snore. Abigail went to stand by Felix at the wheel.

"Is he awfully sick, Felix?"

"Sleeping it off," Felix said. "He said he was dying, get him to a doctor quick, he'd been poisoned. But he got rid of most of his, uh, trouble, and a couple of hefty slugs fixed him up. He's all right."

"Felix, what was in that sandwich?"

"A witch's brew." He glanced at her, his eyes crinkling with laughter. "Lobster bait, cylinder oil, maybe a touch of engine grease to hold things together. God knows what else. We have got witches in our family, two green-eyed ones, know it?"

"My soul, yes, I know it," Abigail said. "No wonder he thought someone had poisoned him." She almost added "at last," but didn't.

"A comeuppance, by gum," Felix said. He began to laugh, but quietly, holding it in till the tears streamed down his cheeks. "Serve the old baster right. I'm not going to say anything about this, Abby. Are you?"

"No," Abigail said. "I don't believe so."

On a Saturday morning, shortly after school had begun its fall term, Nan, Julie, and Elsie ran away. Nettie had supposed they were out berrying—she had promised pies if they would pick the berries. She could see the pasture from her kitchen window, and for a while the girls were in sight, their heads bobbing among the hardhack and juniper. But when she looked out at ten, they had vanished and they did not come in for their lunch at noon.

Maureen came in at twelve—she had not gone with the others because Saturday morning was when she had her music lesson. She was looking very glum, not at all pleased with herself. She sat down to her lunch with a doleful sigh.

"Oh, dear," she said, "I was just no good again, Nettie. And Mr. Graves got mad and hollered at me, and when he hollers, I can't even read the notes."

"That's too bad, honey," Nettie said. "Maybe somebody hollered at him when he was learning, so he thinks that's what *he* ought to do."

"Naw," Charles said. "Old Graves is ugly anyway. He's sore at the world because he's got that stinking-looking club-foot. What do you keep on for, 'Reen? You got fingers like a handful of carrots."

Maureen, already convinced of that, burst into tears and fled upstairs.

"That was pretty, I must say," Nettie said. "What'd you want to go and do that for?"

Charles made no answer. He was gulping down the last of his lunch, in a hurry as he always was on Saturdays. This weekend he was going to spend with a school friend, and he was all packed up, ready to go.

"I see you can't be bothered to answer me," Nettie said. "Before you light out, you go out and find the girls and send them in. They ought to've been back an hour ago."

"Go yourself," Charles said. "You know I got my own plans, for godsake."

Arms akimbo, Nettie stared at him. "Look here," she said. "I'm about done listening to sarse from you, young feller."

"So what are you gonna do about it?"

"My soul, you ain't been fit to live with ever since your mother stopped you going on Jos's boat and made you give him back that motorcycle, and I don't blame her—all you was learning was a mouthful of cusswords and how to knock people off the road into the bandstand. Believe you me, if it hadn't slipped her mind to call up Jerome Green that night, your mother's monkey'd have had his tail in a crack and a good deep one. The idea, a twit like you with a motorcycle!"

Nettie, mad, had very little stopping power and no judgment. She went on, "You go find them girls, do as I tell you, or your mother'll hear about it."

"Telltale tit!" Charles said. He began to sing:

> "Your tongue shall be split,
> And all the dogs in our town
> Shall have a little bit."

"I'll telltale tit you! Are you going or ain't you?"

"Hanh! You used a dirty word yourself. Tit, tit, tit!"

He scraped back his chair, grabbed his overnight kit, and made for the door.

Nettie's hard fingers suddenly had him by the collar.

"You leggo! You old bitch—"

Without a word she spun him around and slapped him solidly on the cheek.

"I'll take that talk from nobody!" she said. "The next time you let go Jos Plummer's filth at me, you'll get the same and your mouth washed out with soap. You go find them kids!"

He went, but he did not come back, and as the door closed behind him, Nettie sat down and cried. He had always been the apple of her eye.

After a while she mopped her tears with the corner of her apron and called Maureen.

"Honey, those girls can't be far off, but I'm worried. I'll

keep your lunch hot—" She stopped, interrupted by a loud hiccup.

"I'll go look, Nettie."

"Maybe Nan and Julie's plaguing me because I made 'em take Elsie along. Oh, dear, dear, dear, Maureen! I just don't feel fit to lug enteruls to a bear today!" She began crying again, and the patient child comforted her, as best she knew.

"Don't mind him, Nettie. He's dreadful, I know. He just hates Ma is all."

Maureen could not find the girls in the pasture. She walked across it to the town highway on its far side without seeing a sign of them; but at the entrance to the road down Starball she found their berry pails carefully hidden behind a bush and saw a line of barefooted tracks heading along the muddy gravel out of sight.

For goodness' sake, they knew they weren't allowed to go off into the woods alone, and not *barefooted!* Among all those sticks and prickles too!

The berry pails were full, and Maureen gathered them up and thriftily took them back to the house.

"The Starball road!" Nettie said. "My heavenly day, and I've just set bread!"

"What?" Maureen said, not quite following.

"I'll have to traipse down there, gone the Lord only knows how long, and it'll have to be batted down in the pan. If it ain't, it's ruint."

"Why, I'll go, Nettie. I only came back to bring the berries and tell you where I was going."

"You will *not* go anywheres near down Starball! That place ain't fitten for man nor beast, let alone young girls. No knowing what kind of a nasty twitchamacallit you might run into. You stay here and keep care of Miles and bat that bread down when it hits the top of the pan. I put in two yeast cakes for quick rising."

She tied a scarf around her head, put on a raincoat and a

pair of Felix's rubber boots in case of mud and hornets, and departed, muttering that when she caught up with them kids she was going to grab them baldheaded.

She was gone a long time. It was late afternoon before she got back and she hadn't found the children. She hadn't, as a matter of fact, found the Starball road either; she had gone into an old woods road near it which led her to an abandoned pulpwood clearing and a swale where she said she would have sunk out of sight if she hadn't grabbed a tree. The heavy boots had rubbed a blister on her heel; she was wet and worn out and frantic with worry, and had Maureen batted the bread down?

Maureen had. She had tended the bread, baked it off, and it was now cooling on the bread rack.

"Well, thank God, at least they's something," Nettie said. "That place down there is bad luck and the creeping horrors. I've got to call your mother—she'll have to get the policeman."

"I'll call her," Maureen said. "You get dried off and rested."

The telephone in the dairy office didn't answer. While she was ringing the store, Abigail drove into the yard.

Abigail's everyday transportation was an old Model-T touring car, of which not much could be said except that it would go anywhere and that it ran.

"But you can't drive down there," Nettie told her. "You'll sink, car and all, just like I did, and then we'll have to hunt for *you*. You get hold of Jerome Green and them."

"I will if I need to," Abigail said. "Now, you calm down, Nettie. They can't have gone far, not with Elsie tagging."

Nettie surely must have got sidetracked, she thought, as she rattled along the bumpy gravel road. She had planned on walking from the edge of the wood. The road, abandoned for years, would of course be overgrown and impassable for cars. But someone with a truck had been using it, it seemed, and not very long ago. Whoever that was had done some repair work. Alders and brush had been cut back, the worst mud sloughs patched with gravel. Surprised, she kept on going.

There was no sign of the runaways, except occasional prints of bare feet where the road was muddy. Now and then she stopped the car, leaned out, and called. Nothing answered except, once, a white-throated sparrow, whose pipe was hoarse and rusty from all summer's use. Then she realized that for quite a while she hadn't seen any footprints —only the deep-cut tracks of the truck tire treads.

Oh, Lord, the little idiots, had they got into somebody's truck and gone for a ride? They could have—they were crazy about any kind of an automobile. But what on earth had got into them? Into Nan? Usually she could count on Nan, who certainly knew better than to go off in a car with strangers. Well, there'd be a reckoning when she did find them.

The worry grew. It was five miles to the end of the peninsula; she traveled the whole way without seeing any further sign. By the time she came out on the bank of the inlet that opened into the pond, she was too concerned to drive as carefully as she usually did.

After all, whose truck? And three little girls . . .

Going faster than the road allowed for, she almost rammed head-on into the hood of a big closed truck that was parked in a small graveled turnaround somebody had built at the edge of the creek bank. She managed in time, set the brake, and got out, breathing hard. That had been close.

GILMORE HOUSE, *Fish and Shellfish a Specialty* was painted on the side of the truck. That was—yes, it was—the hotel in Bristol that Felix and Jos supplied. What on earth was their truck doing down here on a Saturday afternoon? At least it had some connection with Felix. She hadn't seen him for three days and hadn't expected him home for the weekend, but maybe he and Jos had got back sooner than they'd planned and had put in here after clams. There certainly were fine clamflats, laid bare far out now in what looked to be a low-dreen tide. She hadn't heard him mention Starball, but perhaps the kids had. They might have come down here hoping to find him—it could be the truck driver had given them a lift. Still, there was no boat in the cove. The tide had turned, though; quite a strong little stream was purling up the brook, along its channel at the edge of the flats. Felix and Jos could have come and gone; if Felix had found the girls there, he would have loaded them aboard the boat to take them home that way.

At the edge of the bank she solved at least a part of the mystery. All three children had crossed the brook; so had the truck driver. There were all four sets of footprints in the blue clay leading down toward the water and up the bank on the other side. Thank goodness, the children hadn't been barefooted; they'd had the sense to bring their sneakers with them. At least she wouldn't have to spend the evening pulling sea-urchin spines out of everybody's feet. That brook was loaded with sea urchins.

She eyed the stream flowing up past the end of the beach. It was not deep yet, but whoever waded it now would get almighty wet legs. The kids had obviously got down here when the tide was low enough to cross—no, they couldn't have, not if Nettie had seen them in the pasture at ten. High tide would have been around twelve. . . .

She shook her head, bewildered. They had certainly gone over there at some time or other; she could see where they had clambered up the bank on the other side. She would have to check, make sure they were not still there—wade the brook, shoes and all, unless she could yell loud enough to raise them, wherever they were.

She opened her mouth to let out a good loud shout. It stayed open, slowly opening wider with astonishment.

That old ramshackle house of her father's—the last time

she had seen it, years ago, it had been a ruin. Somebody had fixed it up. New shingles, new underpinning, windows . . .

Why, that's my house, she thought. I suppose it doesn't matter too much, but what's been done to it's been done without a word to me. Somebody's gall's enough to be divided into three parts.

She had to go over there anyway. While she was there, it wouldn't hurt to take a look, see what was going on on her property.

Just then, around the end of the beach, a young man appeared leading Elsie by the hand, Julie and Nan bringing up the rear. All three were laughing. At the sight of her the girls stopped, but the young man was still grinning when Elsie said, in a voice squeaky with fright, "Oo, look! There's Mama!"

I wonder who he is, Abigail thought. Perhaps somebody who's been in the store. He had a very familiar look to him, she couldn't think why. He was nobody she remembered ever having seen before.

"Hi," he said. "These yours? I guess I've made them a little late getting home."

"They are and you have," Abigail said.

"Well, don't blame them. It's my fault, I guess."

"Not all of it," Abigail said, eying her offspring. "They knew better than to run away into the woods or ride around in strange men's trucks. Who might you be?"

"Me? Uh, Gilmore. Ronnie Gilmore. Gee, I did pick them up in the truck. They seemed kind of young to be all that ways into the woods, and I found out they were Felix's, so I—I know Felix, he's a friend of mine. They—I thought he might be down here."

"Oh? What made you think he might be here?" The slight stress she put on "here" and the glance she gave around the deserted place implied that this was somewhere nobody

could have a desire or a purpose to be, and Ronnie agreed
with her.

It wasn't any idea of his to be kept hanging around the
Godforsaken hole for hours on end. He hated the place, he
couldn't say why. He wasn't superstitious, didn't believe anybody's old worn-out ghost stories, but when he was down
Starball alone, he felt jumpy. He had been here since yesterday afternoon, expecting Jos Plummer to show up with the
usual load at eleven last night. When high tide came and
the ebb set in and Jos still hadn't appeared, Ronnie had fer-
ried himself around to the pond side of the beach in the punt
Jos kept for his use and had gone to bed in the camp. He
had orders both from Jos and his father not to drive the
truck out of Starball at night. Everything open and aboveboard, that was the idea, but it wasted a lot of Ronnie's time.

Since he had gone to bed late, he slept late. When, at
noon, Jos still hadn't shown up or sent him any word, Ronnie
got the jitters. Something must have happened—maybe Jos
had run into trouble. The thing to do was go up to town and
telephone his father. Either that, or hustle straight back to
Bristol with an empty truck. If he did, though, and there
wasn't anything the matter, his old man would be sore as a
boil. He hadn't made up his mind what to do, when halfway
up Starball, he had met Felix's kids, who said they were going down there to meet their father. It seemed kind of an
irresponsible way to send word—by a pack of kids—but then,
that was Jos, you never knew what kind of weasel work he'd
think up. The idea of using kids in a deal like this shocked
Ronnie, but it was Felix's business, not his, and Felix apparently didn't hesitate to—he'd taken his fourteen-year-old
boy with him all summer. Anyway, here was the information
Ronnie'd needed. Jos would be coming. If he had a load, he
wouldn't of course bring it in until the next high tide, around
midnight tonight, or if he did he'd be a fool to. And that
would mean another long wait for Ronnie. Disgusted, he

thought, well, he'd have to drive up nearly to the town highway before he could turn the truck around.

He offered the kids a ride back; but on the way he got to thinking about the long time he'd have to kill, hanging around that hole alone. He liked kids, and these would be company. After all, they'd wanted to go down there anyway. He could ferry them across the brook in the punt, let them fool around the beach for the afternoon, if they thought they were waiting for Felix, and then, along toward suppertime, bring them back up here in the truck. He mentioned this plan and struck gold. The little one, Elsie her name was, said she loved him and would like to stay with him forever and always, which touched him to the heart.

They had had a darned good time all afternoon, and so had he. They had eaten all the canned beans and bread in the camp—that was all Jos had left in the way of food for Ronnie, but Ronnie was used to that by now. He always brought his own dinner bucket. When Jos provisioned the boat for a trip, he generally took what there was; cleaned out the canned goods. The kids and he had rousted around the beach, dug two arrowheads out of the Indian shell heap —they had tried hard to find three, so that each of the girls could have one; but nothing else showed up, and all of a sudden Ronnie realized that time had gone by, and he'd better get those kids back across the brook before the tide started to run in there. And now he guessed he'd got them into bad trouble, because here was Felix's wife, looking as if she could bite nails. He grinned at her, putting out the charm which nearly always worked with women, and answered her question.

"I was due to meet Felix and Jos here with the truck," he said. "After a load of clams and stuff for the hotel. The Gilmore House—I guess you know about that. I most always pick up at the town dock, but it looked like a nice day to go fishing, so I told them I'd run on down here, be here on the high tide. I dunno how we got crossed up. They didn't show."

Faced with telling a mess of lies in a hurry, Ronnie felt he hadn't done so badly. But she wasn't saying anything; she was just standing there looking at him. Well, maybe he could do better.

"I'm quite a fisherman," he went on confidently. "Sometimes I come down here for a whole weekend. Jos rents me his camp, over there on the beach."

"I see," she said. She glanced away from him, thoughtfully at the building. "That's Jos's camp, is it?"

"Well, it's his fish house," Ronnie said, still trying. "Nice place to stay. He keeps his gear in it, but it's got bunks and a cookstove. Real comfortable in there. Ask your girls if it isn't."

"And you pay Jos rent for it?" she said.

Jos, she thought. Jos again. Grabbing something that doesn't belong to him. Evidently he'd put quite a lot of money and work into it. Why? A fish house? And what was there about it that was making this young fellow lie his head off? He was, she was sure of it. Too many schoolboys had faced up to her with that same dishonest, bright eye.

"I wonder how you go fishing without a boat," she said casually.

Thank God, he could answer that one without making up anything.

"Oh, I got a punt," he said. "She's around on the pond side. Tide went out and left her—she's high and dry now. Reason we're so late, I was waiting for her to float so I could set the kids across without getting their feet wet."

"If you've fished much around here, you must know that by the time there's water enough in the pond to float a punt, the current running in here'll be so strong you'll have to land a ways up the shore and the children will have to plow back through the mud. I expect you'd better carry them across here, and do it soon before the water gets too deep, hadn't you?"

"Oh, gosh!" Ronnie said. He looked distastefully at the purling water. It was already beginning to ripple strongly and it looked cold. He had on a good pair of shoes and a fairly decent pair of pants. He was going to have to drive in them tomorrow. "I dunno as—"

"Well, then, girls, you'll have to wade," Abigail said briskly. "Come on, now, come over here."

"Oh, hell, no!" Ronnie said, horrified. "Oh, great Lord, that's too deep now. And that current running—"

"Then what would you suggest?" she said.

The tallest girl, Nan, shut her mouth tight, stepped into the brook, turned and held her hand out to Julie. The two, hand in hand, splashed into the brook, made it across without staggering too much. It looked, he saw, deeper than it was. But the little one, his friend Elsie, stood where she was. She began to howl, not loud, but gargly, a noise that sounded to Ronnie a good deal like an owl.

He said loudly, "For Christ's sake!" and picked her up. Gingerly he put foot himself into the brook, lugged her across, set her down on the opposite bank. "Are you crazy?" he demanded. "That little kid would have washed to hellangone up into the pond!"

It didn't help any to see that she was looking at him with amusement.

"And fall down and get her hands and knees full of whore's eggs," he spluttered. "Don't you know that crick's plugged full with whore's eggs?"

"Some people say sea urchins," she said. "Especially in front of children. I'm sorry you got wet, but you did get them into this, didn't you? Thank you for your help."

She turned to follow the children, who had legged it for the Ford. They had climbed into the back seat and were lying low, not making a sound.

Ronnie was too mad to hold back. "Goddammit!" he yelled. "And I suppose you'll beat hell out of them when you get the poor little buggers home!"

"Why, no," she said, glancing back. "They're going home to a hot supper and be put to bed. I don't beat children, certainly not for something that isn't entirely their fault. I'm sorry you got so wet. If Jos keeps his rum in that, um, fish house of his, I suggest you heat up a dram on his cookstove and drink it to keep from getting a cold."

Ronnie almost fell down. Did she know something? Had Felix let drop something at home? Had word got around somehow?

For a moment he considered getting into the truck and out of there fast. Felix had told the kids something, must've, to get them to bring word. Maybe she'd overheard, put two and two together. She'd known where to come to find them. Maybe she was in on it. No, not that upright old girl. That battle-ax. What, then? If he went back without a load and everything turned out to be okay, the old man would break him up. Anyway, he'd get double new-mown-hay if he drove back to Bristol soaked like this. He'd have to dry off first.

Sorely tried, and as mad as he had ever been in his life, Ronnie splashed across the brook. He got wetter and colder, because the tide was running faster, the current spurted water against his legs and over his knees. At the camp he dumped his shoes, wrung out his pants and shorts. He built a good hot fire in the stove.

The sun was going down, the sky graying over. Getting dark too fast. Glancing out the window, Ronnie could see why. Out by the mouth of the cove, heading in, was a long, silvery nose of fog. Even as he watched it began to spread both ways, pouring into the cove like milk into a pan.

Ronnie stared at it and swore. No knowing now when Jos would get in, clawing that boat around the ledges and kelp banks out there to find the channel. At the thought of it Ronnie began to shiver. His teeth chattered. He *was* getting a cold! He could feel the back of his nose burning. That old girl, Felix's wife, had been right. A dram, she'd said. Nuts to that—he could use a whole bottle. He lifted a tray of clams off the top third of one of Jos's tubs, hauled out a case of whatever it was—Jos had an assortment here—and pried off the top. He opened a bottle, took a long, grateful swig.

At home, Abigail let her three miscreants undress and get warm in front of the kitchen fire before she fed them, and she quelled Nettie, who was ruffled up like a hen and ready to scold.

"Not tonight, Nettie," she said. "They're too tired."

They were—too tired almost to eat. After a little, when Abigail was sure they were warmed through, she let Nettie take the two younger ones upstairs to bed.

"Don't you want to go, too, Nan?" Abigail asked.

Nan's plate was untouched. She sat over it at the table without a sound, her thin little body, tough as a slat, stiff and upright, as if braced for trouble to come. She shook her head slightly.

"All right," Abigail said. "You want me to talk to you now?"

Knowing Nan, she realized that Nan did. If there was punishment to come, she wanted it over.

"I'm not going to switch anybody for this," Abigail went on. "I think that young man was partly to blame. But I *am* surprised at you, Nan. You're usually pretty dependable. What on earth got into you to start out on a jaunt like that?"

"Charles said Papa was down there. He said it was just a little ways. We wanted to see Pa. Mr. Gilmore said so too."

"I see," Abigail said. "And Nettie wouldn't have let you go if you'd told her."

Nan nodded.

"You do see that this caused a lot of trouble, don't you?

Nettie got terribly scared and upset, and so did I. I think tomorrow, before you and the girls do anything else, there'll have to be a washing done. Your own clothes and Nettie's. She got her dress muddy and torn, looking for you in Star-ball swamp. I'm not going to ask her to clean up after any such mess of foolishness, Nan, and I think you'd better ask her if you can mend her dress. I think that's fair medicine for what you did. Do you? If you do, that will be the end of it."

Nan's eyes suddenly brimmed, but she did not cry.

"Is there something else?" Abigail said.

"You told us to wade across that brook. You knew it was too deep for Julie . . . and Elsie."

"I didn't intend for you to wade the brook. I thought, of course, Mr. Gilmore would help us. But you were too quick, Nan. Or he was too slow. When you came across with Julie, I was getting ready to come after you myself. Are we straight now? If we are, I think you'd better run up to bed."

"All right."

"You still don't want your supper?"

"No." Nan got up. She went straight to the hall door, closed it quietly behind her, and Abigail could hear her feet going slowly up the stairs.

There must be something more, not yet told. Well, that was a tired youngster. Perhaps whatever it was would come out tomorrow.

Heavy-hearted, Abigail thought, Charles again.

There was something more. Nan thought about it as she lay in bed. She had been thinking about it, shaken, ever since the picnic.

Ma had let Uncle Jos do all those horrid things without standing up to him. She hadn't said a word to him for putting the clam down Julie's neck. She hadn't bawled out Charles for speeding up the boat and almost making everybody fall overboard. She had only just sat there taking it when Uncle Jos made Pa look like a fool. You didn't ever expect Pa to talk back to anybody; he never did. Ma always did. She didn't take good care of us. She's scareder of Uncle Jos than she loves us. She sat around and waited. Julie and me, we did it, we were the only ones, we had to. Julie and me, we're together, anyway.

For the first time in her life Nan had seen her mother scared, or thought she had, and it was as if her underpinnings were trembling, about to fall down.

Downstairs, Abigail sat in the kitchen alone. Nettie had not come down after putting the younger girls to bed. She was put out and worn-out, and Abigail didn't blame her. Nettie was one who felt that punishment should follow at once upon the tracks of sin; she had wanted to see the girls scolded and spanked, so that the grownups would feel better. So she had gone to bed, leaving the dishes. Abigail cleaned them up herself. Everybody would feel better tomorrow.

But I won't, she told herself, unless things straighten out some. Charles . . . he was impossible, and he had been so ever since she had forbidden the boat and made him return the motorcycle. He would not listen to simple fact—that for a boy of fourteeen to own a motorcycle was against the law— if he had one, he would only be arrested. Jos's conditioning had gone deep, driven deeper because it had been what Charles had wanted to hear. And what on earth, she asked herself, are we going to do with him? Is it going to turn out that Jos is too much for us all? Jos. Roughshod over everybody.

She had seen him only once since the picnic. He had come of his own accord into the dairy office. With a sinking heart she had thought, He's got around to making a row over that sandwich. But no, Jos was grinning. Perhaps he didn't realize what had happened to his sandwich—Felix had certainly got rid of it fast.

"You seen my tombstone?" Jos demanded.

"It certainly isn't here. What do you want, Jos?"

"Cost five thousand dollars. Could you afford that much for yours?"

"I've no idea what you're talking about. Please get out."

"Haw, right in the middle of the Plummer lot. You'll have to be buried right next to it. Won't like that, will you?"

Great joke. He went away, roaring laughing.

Some more of his childish foolishness. She had thought no more about it until one day, not long ago, a customer in the store had said to her, "Jos must've hit a gold mine."

"Has he? What makes you think so?"

"Haven't you heard about his marble monument? Biggest thing in the cemetery. Cost a mint, they say. Jos is bragging around town that there ain't a gravestone in the county to touch it."

"Goodness," Abigail said. To herself she said, Well, there'll be at least one thing to remember him by.

One thing he bought and paid for, she thought now. And didn't steal from someone. My house down Starball isn't worth a thing to me, but he has stolen one thing too many from me. My husband, my boy, thousands of dollars in money . . . my peace of mind. This is the end of it.

She got up and went to the telephone.

"I wish you'd find out what's going on in my father's old house down Starball," she told Jerome Green, the county sheriff. "Someone has moved in there without ah, yes, or no."

At early daylight, when the tide was low at Starball, Jerome Green and his young deputy, Willy Meader, drove into the turnaround and parked the police car behind Ronnie Gilmore's truck. The fog hung motionless and heavy; fat fog drops lay on the trucks' flat surfaces, speckling the metal, running down in small rivulets to splat on the ground. The sheriff laid his hand on the hood, finding it cold.

"Been here all night, looks like," he said. "Gilmore House, yeah. Young Gilmore's got to be around here somewhere."

"He's not in the truck," Willy said. "What's he doing to hellangone down in this godforsaken hole?"

"That's for you to wonder and me to find out," Green said. "And godforsaken's right. I didn't know a soul ever come here, or even that the road was passable. But somebody seems to have lit down here. Fixed the road, anyway."

"Used it, too," Willy said. "Quite a lot."

"Makes you think, don't it? Well, we better check out Abigail Plummer's place over on the beach, so's I'll have something to tell her. Got to take care of the citizens' complaints."

He paused at the edge of the bank, looking distastefully down.

"I don't like this place. Got a funny stink to it. Always did have," he remarked.

He was a stocky man in his middle sixties, short-legged and stout. He slipped and skidded down the bank, landed sturdily in the blue clay bed at the bottom, where he sank over the tops of his shoes.

Willy, younger by some thirty-five years, jumped across the clay bed and turned around to see the sheriff glumly pulling out one foot after the other, a sucking sound following each pull.

"You can count on it," Green said, joining Willy on top of the flat ledge where he was standing. "Come down here and something happens to you, and it ain't ever good." With considerable care he moved down to the brook and stepped into the water, bending over to scrub the clay lumps off his shoes and the cuffs of his dark-blue uniform trousers. "I was brought up in Granite Hills. I ought to've recalled that clay bed. It ain't unusual, though, that I didn't. I ain't been here for numberless years."

He stumped across the brook, paying no attention to stepping-stones, not needing to now, and squelched up the opposite bank. "Us boys used to come down here hoping to git a glimpse of Uncle Tufton's ghost," he said. "Never did. But the least little bit of noise in the woods would scare the living daylights out of us." He took a long sniff of the dank, smothery air. "Kind of a pretty place, use to be, when it ain't foggy's a fool. Old folks used to say that odd stink was the smell of bad luck. Wouldn't none of them ever come down here. I dunno's I would if I— Godalmighty, don't I hate to git my feet wet!"

In the fog the ruined houses loomed up dark and shadowy, the color and shape of rain-ravaged rectangles of gray cardboard. From under the fallen doorstep of one of them a mink ran, slithering in noiseless panic past Green's feet.

"Jesus!" he said, recoiling. "Git, you monster!" He took a futile kick at the fast-moving thing, his foot rising in the air almost level with his chin. Then he caught up a rock and flung it. The mink vanished in the fog and so did the rock, which landed with a smack in some part of the clamflats below the beach.

"What's the trouble, Jerome?" Willy said, grinning. "You scared of a mink?"

"I hate a rodent," Jerome said. "Of any kind. Now, that busted window frame, right there, is the one I broke out, le'me see, must've been around eighteen seventy-three. I was around, well, a young kid. Well, well. Look at the old Randall place. Somebody's moved in, wouldn't you say?"

There it stood, new shingles, tight windows, clapboards. Jerome put a foot on the doorstep, testing, rocked up and down before he risked his weight, took a kick at one of the risers.

"Solid's a rock," he commented. "Kicked me back, if you want to know. Two-by-twelves, put together with spikes." He knocked on the door once, then again, harder. "Where's Gilmore? Must be around somewhere, unless he come down here to commit suicide, which is what I'd do if I had to spend the night."

"Here, look," Willy said. He stepped back from a window, where he had been peering in between his hands. "He's there, or someone is. Asleep in the bunk."

"Well, dammit, what is he, dead?" Jerome pushed open the door. "Phew! Smothered himself! Burnt up an old billy goat, like. Hey, you!" He stopped in his tracks. "Well, well," he said. "Well, well, well, well, well."

Ronnie lay peacefully in the bunk. The knocking, the loud voice had not wakened him. He only sighed, softly, and settled more deeply into his dream of a long-legged lady with yellow hair. But beside a tray of clams and a ravaged case of whiskey his second bottle lay naked on the floor.

"Shan't you die," Jerome said. "Willy, do you see what I see?" He went over, picked up the bottle. "Imported," he went on. "And solid full, not a brack in it. Ain't that beautiful! Willy, what in hell did I bring you for? If I was alone here, what I could do for m' cold, wet feet."

"Go ahead," Willy said. "Wouldn't be any business of mine, Jerome."

"You," Jerome said, "are sworn to uphold and defend your country's laws. Anything I hate, it's a crooked cop. I wouldn't of believed that of you, Willy. Just you look at that tub, now. That is one pretty job of carpentering. Anybody could see it'd hold a hell of a lot of clams."

"Yes," Willy said. "That'd make an awful big chowder, Jerome."

"Beautiful. Would you know how many bottles supposed to be in one of them cartoons?"

"Nope."

"I ain't going to do it. You'll never see me do it. What's that? Did you hear something?"

"Fellow snoring, that's all."

"Why don't you step outside and listen? I thought I heard a boat engine out there somewhere."

"Okay."

Outside the weather still hung thick and wet. A light southerly wind blew drops heavy as rain, but the fog had shifted a little, because now Willy could make out the dim outline of a punt anchored off in the cove. No, it was tied up to a big lobster car moored out there.

Wonder what's in that besides lobsters, if any, Willy thought.

It wouldn't be the first time a lobster car had been used to stow away bootleg. Some of them were built with false bottoms. He had seen one in a place down the coast, where those fellows had got caught up with too. But so far as he knew, nobody had suspected the Gilmore House's fish supply. That rig, inside, was pretty darned smart.

Behind him, in the camp, he heard a cautious rending of wood and a slight *skreek* of nails pulling out. He grinned, a little wryly, to himself.

The old devil, he thought.

Well, it wasn't his business if a bottle or so more turned up missing out of that open case of whiskey, likely out of the back row where it wouldn't be noticed at first. What Jerome did was up to him—he, Willy, hadn't seen anything.

Everybody, seemed as though, had a finger and the need of a pie to stick it into.

Light, oily ripples broke at the foot of the clamflats, washing up, receding. The tide was turning. They had better get moving, if they wanted to cross that creek before the water started running in there. Might take some time, too, to get young Gilmore awake and started—he looked to be plastered to the eyes. Too bad he got mixed up in this. Willy knew Ronnie Gilmore slightly; he'd always seemed like a pretty nice kid.

From somewhere off in the fog Willy's ear caught a faint vibration; at least he thought so, but listening, he couldn't hear a thing. Then he heard it again, briefly, as briefly lost it. An engine, throttled down? He couldn't tell. Noises over water in a fog mull were tricky—might have been anything, from any direction. Then it came again, muffled but unmistakable. An engine, barely ticking over. A boat, coming up out of the fog, dead slow.

If it turned out to be the rumrunner, he had better not spot Willy standing here gawking in his policeman's cap and uniform. A big log lay stranded halfway up the beach; Willy ducked down, flattened himself behind it. Watching, he made out the long, dim shape on the edge of the fog, creeping up to the moored punt by the lobster car. He could see the man in oilskins standing with a gaff in his hand on the bow, who all at once let out a muffled yell and began making his way, fast, back along the washboard to the pilot shelter.

And then, suddenly, the boat's engine broke into a deep-throated roar. Before Willy's astounded eyes she lunged ahead, came tearing, full-speed, toward the beach. He heard a sound of rending wood as she drove over the punt and climbed the end of the lobster car, and a muffled thud as she struck a rock, or some obstruction, in the shallows. She slammed into the clamflats, burying her bow a foot deep in mud, came to a grinding stop, with her engine still roaring.

For a second Willy was too appalled to move. The big boat had seemed to be blasting in right at him, with intent. The sight had fairly curdled his blood.

Jerome ran down the beach past him, yelling, "That feller on the bow went overboard! I ain't seen him come up, he ain't *come* up, and us with no boat and no way to git out there." He said, more quietly, as Willy came up beside him, "I can't even swim. Can you?"

"Yes," Willy said. He began stripping off his clothes.

"There's somebody," Jerome said. "It's a kid." He started heavily out through the flats mud, sinking over his ankles at every step.

A young boy, his face covered with blood, had plunged

over the side of the boat. On all fours, he was clawing blindly toward the edge of the flats. Racing past him, Willy thought, Jerome'll have to look after him. I can't stop now.

He splattered into the icy water and swam out.

Jos had had his own reasons for not appearing at Starball on Friday night. One was that he'd raked up another customer for Friday night's load. A fellow from down the coast whom he knew well enough to trust had taken the lot off his hands at better than Gilmore's prices. The transfer of the cargo had been made in a cove at one of the offshore islands, from the *Abigail* to the other man's power boat—not so much work and a good deal less risky than the tricky tide-watch at Starball. Jos figured that if he kept the Gilmores waiting awhile the old man might see the light and go up on his prices too.

That was one reason. The other was that Jos had waited quite a time for the tide at Starball to serve on a Saturday night, so that he could outsmart Abigail and take Charles on at least one more trip with him. For one thing, he had promised Charles, and for another, he always had a lot of fun when he could figure out a way to plague Abigail. On this Saturday, Charles was not staying with a school friend and had never intended to. He had gone to a beach a quarter of a mile or so down Starball's western shore, where Jos hove to and picked him up in the early afternoon.

When Felix objected, Jos hollered him into silence.

"You keep on," he said, "and I'll set you ashore and Chuck and me'll go. You ain't a goddam mite of good to me, anyway. Flap around like a scairt hen with a case of the garps. So shut up."

This was true, and Felix knew it. His nerve was going. On every night trip now he was afraid, desperately wanting to get the thing over with, get back on land, out of danger. It took very little to throw him into a panic, and then, shaking and helpless, he could hardly think what he was doing. There was nothing he could do about this; he went aft and sat down.

At early dusk they ran into the fog bank. Jos rammed the boat into it. While daylight lasted it was no problem to him; even when darkness closed in, black and thick, and he couldn't see beyond the pilot shelter, all he did was slow down a little. He knew where he was and what time it was, which was all he needed. The Canadian supply boat didn't, at least not quite. She was late. It was nearly one o'clock before Jos got his cargo and headed back for land. He was very, very put out. Them herring-chokers had made him lose the Starball tide.

"Hell, no use to run in there tonight in this thick mess," he said. "We'll anchor on Tucker's Shoal and get some sleep. If this fog holds, we can unload on the noon tide tomorrow. Nobody'll see us."

Felix felt the familiar shaking start, deep inside him, as if something, his backbone perhaps, were turning quivery and weak. Tucker's Shoal would be quiet enough tonight and there was an anchorage there, but it was exposed. Almost anything could come out of this blackness. Felix longed for land—not tomorrow morning, but now, as soon as the boat could get there. Arms of land, encircling, concealing, secret, an island cove somewhere. The thought of six, eight hours more of open ocean made him feel sick and faint.

"Why don't we run in to Finney's Island cove?" he asked nervously. "You could make that all right, couldn't you?"

"Why? Oh, my God, go on down and make me some coffee."

"There isn't any. We didn't plan to stay out overnight. The coffee's back in the camp."

Jos let out a moan of rage and disgust. "One of these days, so help me God, I'm going to drown you. Drop you overboard and sail off and leave you there. Go on to bed then, so I won't have to see you flapping around."

Charles had already turned in. He had thrown off his blankets and lay sleeping in a hump, his legs pulled up as if he might be cold. Felix pulled up the covers, tucked him warmly in.

In his own bunk he could not sleep. He stared at the dim outlines of paneling which made the roof of the cuddy above him, aware of the quivering, the feathery brush of fear against his heart.

If we get caught, it'll be me, not Jos. The boat belongs to me. Abigail, the kids—they think a lot of me. What'll they think, how will they feel, if I have to go to prison? I'm like a rabbit in a trap, poking here, poking there, for a way out of it. No, a rabbit'd have more guts than I do. Charles . . . Charles is . . .

He heard the engine slow down and stop. The anchor splashed over. Jos came down, knocked around noisily getting out of his boots and oilskins, turned in. Felix buried himself in the blankets, pretended sleep.

In the mornng Jos was up at first light. He wanted coffee. There wasn't any. He wanted bacon and eggs. He was cold, starving to death. He went on, and on, and on.

Charles slept through it. Felix had not slept at all.

"Hell, I leave it to you to lay in the grub. Thought that was one thing you could do right. Horse up there and haul up the anchor, if you can do it without falling overboard, only if you do, that's all right with me. We'll run in and have some hot grub at the camp. It's foggy. So who's to see us? If anybody does, we'll be unloading fish."

It was foggy. The unmoving gray wall circled the boat, seemed not more than ten or twenty feet away. The *Abigail* came cautiously out of it, nosed up to the punt tied to Jos's lobster car. Charles, below, had just finished getting dressed. Jos was up on the bow, ready to gaff the punt, pull her alongside. Felix was at the wheel. When Jos had told him to climb up and hook the punt, he had been unable to make it—he felt too sick and dizzy.

Jos's eye caught the movement on the beach—some fellow ducking down behind a log so as not to be seen. Another man in a policeman's cap stood in the open camp door. Jos started down off the bow in a hurry.

"Back off!" he yelled at Felix. "Green's in there. Speed it up, you lunkhead!"

Felix didn't hesitate. This was what he had always been afraid of—the law there to meet the boat when she came in. His hand flew to the throttle. He yanked it up as far as it would go. He forgot that first he should have thrown the gears into reverse.

The *Abigail* roared ahead with a great jerk, which tossed Jos headfirst off the washboard into the water. He had braced himself for full speed in reverse and the sudden forward leap threw him like a stone. In his oilskins and heavy rubber boots, he sank like one, and the spinning propeller caught him. Felix, seeing him go, made a futile grab, then jumped back to stop the engine. He tumbled over Charles, who had been coming up the companionway steps and now lay flat on the deck. The boat slammed into the punt and the lobster car; the impact sent Felix headfirst into the wooden combing of the hatchway. He fell into the cuddy and lay still.

Willy Meader tried hard, but the water was too cold to stay in for very long. He made several long dives from the lobster car; it was like diving into soup. He could see nothing but the roiled-up debris from the muddy cove bottom. At last he swam wearily ashore, blue with chill.

"Warn't no use, was it?" Green said.

Willy shook his head, clenching his teeth to keep them

from chattering, but it was no use—they seemed to be trying to knock the top of his head off.

"Well, git up into the camp," Jerome said. "I took your clothes up there and they's a fire going."

Jerome had been busy. He had bandaged Charles's face with his handkerchief, got him into one of the camp bunks. He had climbed aboard the boat and stopped the engine; he had found Felix. He had handcuffed Ronnie to a table leg. Ronnie sat there looking dazed and scattered. He seemed still only half awake.

"Here," Jerome said. He handed Willy a nearly empty bottle. "This was in that feller's bunk, cuddled up to him like a baby. There's one good slug left. It better go where it'll do some good."

He waited while Willy got dressed, fidgeting a little. Once he got up, went over to the bunk, and peered in at Charles.

"This kid's all right," he said. "His nose is splattered all over his face and I doubt if it'll ever be the same again, but he's gone to sleep. You ready?" He jerked his head toward the door.

The cold, wet air struck Willy like an icy breath, but the whiskey had helped. He followed Jerome down the beach and out across the flats, caught up with him as he climbed aboard the boat.

"My God!" Jerome said. He stared down at Felix. "Them fellers was either drunk or crazy, which, I d'no. I thought this one was dead, but he's breathing now. Forehead seems to be drove in, don't it? Haul me down a flock of them blankets, Willy. I don't dast to move him. I figured on the hearse, but I guess what we need is a ambulance, so you git going, okay?"

PART THREE

Chris

The Depression was late hitting the coast towns. Rumors, like the sound of minute guns at sea, blew through them, were mulled over and forgotten. As early as 1929 headlines in the local papers had proclaimed that Wall Street had shot itself, but Wall Street was too far away to amount to anything. The coast towns were not rich, anyway, and never had been. Even in the prosperous days of sailing ships the majority of men had been no more than comfortable, living off the land and out of the sea, with the little cash they had going a long way. Since then a continuous slow depression had lazed along, once in a while rearing up enough to produce the condition known as "hard times." Fish would be scarce; lobsters for some unknown reason—the word was they did it on purpose—would vanish from the sea; a foggy summer would rot potatoes, mildew gardens. But the year 1934 was something that even tightened belts couldn't handle. All at once nobody could sell anything; nobody had any money to buy. Nobody had a job; nobody had one to offer.

Hard words were spoken about Mr. Roosevelt, his PWA, his WPA, his handouts of surplus food, projects designed to clutter the freedom of men. Even when, in his memorable voice, he said to Congress, "I want you gentlemen to legalize beer," he got no approval from the coast towns. The disgrace had gone too deep. Husbands could pick blackberries when there wasn't anything else; they could grow beans to feed families and their wives could can some. But where were coffee, flour, sugar? A man with a sweet tooth liked a doughnut with coffee in the morning, and so had the crusty, independent generations behind him—who had fought the Revolution and the Civil War and the war with Spain, and had established the incontrovertible law that groceries, bought and paid for with money earned, were the outward and visible sign of a decent man's freedom. For years after the Depression the coast towns stayed invincibly Republican, while those lived who didn't forget easily that, once, they had had to take handouts from the government.

By 1934 all but one of the five houses on Starball beach had fallen in. The bright, new wood on the Randall house was weathered and grayed, but Jos Plummer's repair job was still sound. The house was livable; and any shelter was shelter when a man had no rent money or the prospect of getting any.

Chris Cartwright, the master carpenter, with his brother, George, had owned a shop in Bristol. They built new houses and repaired old ones; their mark was on fine buildings all over the county. The metal plaque which read:

CARTWRIGHT BROS.
Bristol

had been nailed up ten years ago on Abigail Plummer's dairy barn and was there still.

Up until the Depression hit the coast, Cartwright Brothers had been in demand, with more jobs than they could undertake, because they were known to be dependable and any work they did to be well and solidly done. Chris, especially, was famous in the trade as an inside-finish man. In his hands wood seemed almost to mold itself. When, at last, nobody dared to build or repair anything, only to hold on tooth and claw to what he had, the Cartwrights found themselves with canceled contracts, a raft of bills, and a carload of unpaid-for materials. They set their teeth and paid what they owed. It took their savings.

Both had families of children. George, the younger, had three; Chris had five. His eldest son, Laurance, was in law school in Boston, partly on a scholarship and partly on his own earnings; he was no expense to his father. But the remaining four were still in grade and high school. And there was no longer any money, even for rent. They had lived in rented houses, counting on the time, surely coming, when they could slack off working for other people and build places of their own. Chris had the plans for both, carefully drawn; he did not now even look at the blueprints tucked away in the bureau drawer. He blamed himself; he had over-extended, he had not looked ahead; and more than anything, he could not accept what had happened to him. A man learned his trade; he did a good job at it; he worked hard. There could never come a time when he did not have money enough to feed his children. Unless he took handouts, which, he swore before God, he would never do.

They were men who did not go under without a fight and they fought. They still owned a truck in which they roamed the towns looking for work. There was none. On the way home on an afternoon in spring Chris was more and more depressed—"twitchy," George called it. George was almighty worried about Chris, and today had been the most hopeless jaunt of all.

"Look, there's that old Starball road," he said, as the truck passed it. "Hey, remember how everybody went down there to watch the cops dragging the cove for what was left of Jos Plummer?"

"Un-hunh," Chris grunted. He drove on without turning his head.

George had hoped to interest him in something at least, start him out of the kind of stupor he seemed to be sinking into. George himself remembered that day well. The case had been a sensation, spread all over the newspapers. More people had gone down Starball then than ever had before—or since, he thought, if you went by the overgrown entrance to the road. The Cartwrights, living in Bristol, had known the Gilmores well. They had often gone over to the hotel to eat. George's mother had tried to comfort old Mrs. Gilmore the day the Federal officers had taken Ronnie and his father off to jail. Chris and George had been part of the crowd who had driven down to Starball Cove. They had been on the beach when the sheriff's men had brought Jos Plummer's body ashore. George had taken one look and had promptly lost his lunch. He grinned now, recalling how Jerome Green had turned on him.

"Well, if ya don't like it, git away from my boots," he had yelled. He had looked the color of his name himself.

Old Mr. Gilmore had not survived the disgrace, but Ronnie had. He had come back to Bristol, had tried for a while to put together pieces of the hotel. Then he had sold it and bought a roadhouse on the edge of town. With his mother, Ronnie lived there now and ran it. It had got itself quite a juicy reputation.

George had been thinking about all this when Chris suddenly brought the truck to a jolting stop.

"Hey, what?" George said.

"Those houses down there. Let's go and have a look."

"Great Lord, what for? They were falling down ten years ago."

"One wasn't. I want a look, that's all."

The road down Starball was shaggy with undergrowth, but the truck was sturdy and Chris seemed to be in a mood

to slam through anything. George didn't say a word. If anything could stir Chris up these days, it was all right with
him.

They came out into the turnaround at the edge of the
bank. Some bushes had taken root in it, but it was still usable.

"Built on a pebble base and topped with good surfacing
gravel," Chris said, scuffing a foot into it. "Hanh!"

George grinned. Chris must be getting his wind back.
When he felt like himself, he couldn't help checking the
foundations of anything.

"That was kind of a rough ride, know it?" George said.

Chris was looking at the ruins on the beach. He walked
to the edge of the bank, peered down into the brook.

The tide was on the ebb, but the brook still held water
and a considerable current. Chris climbed down the bank,
and with some slipping and sliding, started across.

"Hey, you'll get your feet wet," George called after him.
He watched Chris go, dripping, along the top of the beach,
and after a moment sighed and followed him. That water
was sure cold.

"By the God!" Chris said, as George caught up with him.
"All a man needs is a hammer and a nail." He jerked his
thumb at the old Randall house.

George shoved a brotherly arm around his shoulders. "And
if you had to cut up a six-by-eight without a saw, you'd bite
it in two," he said. "If I know you. I'm with you in anything
you want to do, Chris, but what's on your mind?"

"Look. We have got all that chriseless lumber on our
hands, and a truck to haul it with. Out there"—he grabbed
George's wrist, spun him around—"out there's the Atlantic
Ocean. It's got fish. That clamflat's got clams." He spun
George again, pointed at a clearing on the far side of the
pond. "That's good land over there. Look at the grass, up
to your belt buckle. It was cleared once and can be again."

"Chris . . . Somebody owns this. Not us."

"Jos Plummer owned it. He's dead. It's abandoned. I'm going to use it. I won't leave it none the worse, either."

"Jos Plummer had a brother—the one that got hurt, remember? I don't know if he's still living, but his son sure is. The guy with the crooked nose, runs the store up here in Granite Hills. We don't want to tangle with him. I've heard tell he's an s.o.b., cheat the eyeteeth out of you if you don't watch him."

Chris turned to face him. "Between us, we have got seven kids to home. We can't feed them or pay the rent. We could take old Roosevelt's black-eyed peas like some do. I ain't going to. Damn things. Full of hookworms."

"What?" George said.

"Sure, hookworms. Grow down South, don't they? Don't come from around here. I'll get that land over there plowed and planted if I have to do it with my goddamned nose, and before the summer's out I'll pick my own peas, out of my own garden. Now, the first thing we do, we haul stock down here and build a walkway over that brook. We chuck the mess out of this house, and then we'll get the womenfolk down to clean. That roof looks tight. If it ain't, it soon will be."

"All right. If something's going to make you come to life, I'll be glad to go to jail for trespassing. But, Chris, what about getting the kids to school? This is a long ways down."

"We'll try. If we can't claw up enough gas to haul them in the truck, Mary'll have to teach them. She could—she reads everything she can get her hands on. School'll be out for the summer, anyway, pretty soon. She could carry it that that far." Mary was his wife.

"You ever eat fiddlehead greens?" George asked thoughtfully.

"No, I ain't. But if there's greens in them woods, we'll get 'em. Berries, too, when they get ripe. Or anything that sticks up. If kids don't eat, they can't learn, that's for sure. So I'm,

by the God, moving where I can scrape up meals for them,
even if it's fish and clams seven times a week."

"Ought to have a boat," George said. "Can't go fishing
here without one."

"Then I'll build one."

"You're a hard man to keep up with."

"I wouldn't be, not for long, if I didn't find something to
do with my hands. Come on, let's get back. Tomorrow we
start hauling lumber. Be a good idea to haul it all down here.
I noticed yesterday the snatch-and-grab boys had already
started to pick out what they seem to feel they're entitled to."

They splashed across the brook. Early dusk was falling;
the dead houses on the beach huddled together, black with
shadows.

George glanced back. "You ever hear this place was
haunted?" he asked, as they climbed into the truck.

"Hell," Chris said. "That ghost I happened to meet up with
under a tight roof'd scare me a damn sight less than the one
I'd sure-God see with my wife and kids out in the rain under
no roof at all."

By mid-April the old Randall house was weathertight
again and clean, and both Cartwright families moved into
it. The walls bulged with four adults and seven children;
but it was a place to be. The grownups were too relieved to
worry about discomfort. The children were fascinated. The
beach was tremendous for them; they had never known the
like of it, being town kids, except on an occasional Fourth
of July picnic. They groaned and griped about having to go
to school until it would be out in June. Chris, if left to himself, might have let them skip the last month and a half—he
needed every pint of gasoline for the truck that he could manage to buy—but he ran head-on into Mary and George's wife,
Sue. The kids were going to finish school, they said, and that
was that.

Chris had a little cash left; he'd planned to parcel it out as best he could on garden tools which he hoped to find somewhere secondhand. He was gong to need a plow and a harrow, and some kind of a heavy bush scythe to clean out grass and undergrowth. For power, he'd meant to use the truck. That meant gas. But instead, George had to start up the truck every weekday morning, drive the kids to school. It wouldn't do, Chris realized, to stir up the womenfolk too much. They had done a miracle of scrubbing and hoeing out at the house; it wasn't the comfortable home they were used to, but neither one of them had complained, except school for the kids was the one thing they had set their minds on and would not be moved.

He didn't know how he could possibly manage everything. In time he realized he couldn't have managed if it hadn't been for Waldemar Larsen.

Waldemar had once worked for Chris, in the days when Chris had had a business. He was a big, easygoing fellow, part Swedish and part Penobscot Indian; at least he said he was, though who Waldemar said he was and where he came from depended largely on the people he was talking to and how he happened to feel at the time. From his looks, he might have been either, or both. His hair was so blond it was almost white and his eyes were bright blue; to go with these he had a dark-tanned, reddish skin and a sharp-chiseled, high-nosed face which looked Indian, if you choose to believe that all Indian faces looked like this. His accent certainly had Swedish overtones, though it was not like any Chris had ever heard. Once, when Chris asked him about it, he said he had taken his talk from his mother. His father, he said, had never spoken a word in his life.

Waldemar hadn't stayed long on the job. When he went, Chris was sorry to lose him. Working, Waldemar seemed hardly to move—George once remarked that you had to put up a mark to see him move—but his work got done, well and on time, and any job he was on went smoothly. Where he was, you could count on good tempers among the touchier men, a lot of kidding and laughing going on. After a while, seeing how things were, Chris offered him a job as foreman.

Waldemar picked up his hammer, stared at it without comment, stared at Chris. He began to drive nails very fast, and the next morning he didn't show up on the job. Some time later Chris heard that he had gone down to the coast, bought himself a boat, and was going fishing for a living.

"Wonder what bugged him?" Chris said to George. "That hammer'd been a tomahawk, I'd have run like a rabbit. Gosh, wouldn't want to tangle with him."

Not many men would. Waldemar stood nearly seven feet in his socks; he was big-muscled and lean and could move fast if he had to.

He came chugging into the cove one morning in his boat and dropped anchor off the beach. For a while Chris wondered who that could be. The fellow had a dory in tow, loaded to the gunnels with something. He pulled it alongside, got into the stern, and sculled ashore. As he came closer, Chris saw that it was Waldemar, and he walked down the beach to meet him.

"Hi," he said. "You're a sight for sore eyes, Waldo."

Waldemar gave a final shove with his oar to send the dory as near to the beach as he could. She was so deep in the water that she grounded some ways out.

"Heave the painter," Chris said. "I'll haul you in."

"Bust aigs," Waldemar said. He gestured to show that he couldn't, or didn't want to, climb over his load to the bow where the painter was. Instead, he stood up, picked up a big burlap-wrapped bundle off the thwart in front of him, and gave it a towering, one-handed heave toward shore. It sailed over Chris's head, landed behind him with a thumping rattle of beach rocks.

"Ham," Waldemar said.

He then stepped overboard and waded ashore. The dory, freed of his weight, floated higher by the stern. He hauled her with him, stern-first, as he came.

"How been?" He gripped Chris's hand, pumping up and down.

"Good," Chris said. "How about you, Waldo? You still sore at me?"

"Sore? Me? Oh, no. I yust don't like bossing yob. Drive me nuts. So I go off islands, camp around, here, there, my boat. Got lonesome. Sugar come lump, lump. When lump too big for coffee cup, I come ashore. I see George up in town, he say you down here now. So I don't go back. Your vife make good flapjacks?" He gestured at the dory with his thumb. "Ham, aigs, bags flour, all that stuff. Maybe she use it, ain't no good to me."

"Great Lord, Waldo!" Chris stared at the doryload of groceries. At the thought of ham and eggs, which he hadn't seen for some time, his mouth watered. "I can't take— There's half a ton of stuff there!"

"That pay my board. I vork, too, you let me stay." He went on to say that he was damn-far sick of his own cooking. If some nice voman made him meals fit to eat, he would bring fish, fish, fish, meat, meat, meat, and pay board.

"Board?" Chris said. "Your money's no good here, Waldo. Lord, I can't tell you! Just the use of those boats of yours— even the kids can catch flounders in the cove. We've lived mostly on clams. I can't pay you now for those groceries, but I guess you know I will, sometime."

"Un-hunh. I like here. Like kids."

Waldo's eyes were on George's youngest, who was making her way cautiously down the beach. She was three and answered formally to the name of Cordelia Ann; but her hair, white as Waldo's, puffed out in a mass of chiffon-like curls, and her brother Martin, a collector of old bottles, had nicknamed her Blob-top. Any stranger fascinated her, and besides, she was nosy.

"Yust you look," Waldo said with admiration. "Oh, I stay. I vork. You fix up old houses, I see here. Maybe ve fix one for me, hanh?"

Chris and George had already started rebuilding the ruin next to the Randall house. Chris had begun looking ahead. There was no work anywhere, nor prospects of any that he could see; they might have to stay where they were through the winter. George's family would need a place to stay. The Randall house was too small for everybody. Things were getting tight; the womenfolks, though they tried hard, were edgy with each other. Seven kids made pandemonium.

Most of the old ruin was rotten, but the foundations were good, made of solid blocks of granite fitted together. About the only thing to do, Chris thought at first, was to set the old wood afire and burn it where it lay. He found it was too wet from the spring rains and too rotten; he and George had torn it apart and stacked the remains temporarily to one side out of the way, for disposal later. So far, they had sills set on the foundation and the subfloor partially nailed.

Chris gestured toward his pile of lumber. "Why not?" he told Waldo. "We've got lumber to patch hell a mile, and right now we've sure-God got the time."

Waldo stayed. He slept aboard his boat, came ashore daytimes. His first job, undertaken on his own, was to swamp a road in to the grass clearing on the far side of the pond. Then, early one morning before anyone else was up, he commandeered Rob, Chris's fifteen-year-old, and made a trip to one of the offshore slands, where there was an abandoned barn. Waldo had stayed on the island, had slept in the barn, and knew what was there. The fact that the day was a school day for Rob bothered neither him nor Rob, though Rob remarked, as the boat chugged out of the cove, that his mother was going to be madder than a hornet.

"Vell," Waldo said, "vhat heart don't know, head don't add up to. Go school tomorrow."

"Yah, fooey," Rob said. "School till June, darn it."

The people who had lived on the island apparently had moved away to a place where they had no use for their farm tools, or perhaps had been too sick at heart anyway, when the house burned down, to bother loading plows, harrows, hoes and rakes, scythes and grindstones into a boat to haul them six miles to the mainland. There had once been quite a village—acres of field, bounded by sturdily built stone walls, all now grown back to a wilderness of trees and puckerbush. Waldo and Rob had to climb three or four of these walls as they pushed through the undergrowth toward the barn.

"Look them valls," Waldo said. "Stand up like kunk-crete. Only tree grow through, push over. Been here long, long ago. And look, there's graveyard. Trees all up around through burying places."

Black boles of spruces a foot thick had pushed over tombstones, grown up through the middle of graves. Some of the graves were sunken and had to be walked carefully around; most of these had only granite boulders for markers. But one tall dark stone stood out above the others, as straight and solid as if it had been set on yesterday.

"This was boss of this place, I guess," Waldo said. "This old one. Got writing on. Lots of writing."

"Gee!" Rob said. "Seventeen-fifty. It's really old, Waldo."

JOHN CONSTANT RANDALL

1750–1810

A Soldier of the Revolution, Sea Captain and Pioneer.
Born in Gloucester, Massachusetts, he first settled
this town and was lost at sea, washed overboard from
the bark ALICIA in a gale off Mozambique. His soul
to God and his body to the sea. Rest in peace.
A GOOD MAN IS THE HONOR OF HIS COUNTRY
AN HONEST MAN IS A BLESSING TO HIS PEOPLE

"He isn't here at all," Rob said. "Got drowned somewhere."

"I guess," Waldo said. "Come on, Rob. Ve go."

The light under the trees was solemn and dim—as it ought to be in such a place, Waldo thought, but this graveyard always made him feel creepy. He pushed along, Rob trotting at his heels.

"They thought a lot of him, didn't they?" Rob said.

"I guess!" Waldo said. "Only man in vorld got two gravestones."

"Oh, come on, Waldo, how could he?"

"Oh, he got drownded, okay. Only not first time. He come back, live here a vhile, move ashore. Lots other people live here, long time. Then he go off on vessel, somewhere, fall into Amazon River. Other gravestone, just like, only say Amazon River, not first place. Over on Randall Hill, nearby town."

"I'll be darned. Honest?"

"You go see. You find it. There's barn. Now, ve vork, Rob."

The barn stood in a clearing of heavy grass and hardhack not far from the burned-out foundations of what must have been a largish farmhouse. The barn did not seem too old— certainly not so old that John Constant Randall could have built it. Shingles had blown off and the roll-back door was gone, but the floor was solid underfoot and some glass was left in the window frames. The abandoned farm tools were still usable. They were rusty; dampness had rotted some wooden handles on hoes and rakes, but Waldo seemed pleased with what there was. He hummed to himself, carrying heavy loads out of the barn. He found a plow complete with whiffletree and set it down outside as if it had been made of glass.

"Plow handles no good," he said. "Got to make new." He put both hands on the plow handles and pushed, drove the share a little way into the ground before they broke off.

"That iron good, though. Ve use a little, she shine like silver dime. You look, Rob, this vood black like teak, smooth like polish. Man's sveat done it. Too bad ain't solid no more."

"Yeah, gee," Rod said. Somehow he couldn't get worked up much over old plow handles. For some time he had been watching with misgivings the size of the pile growing beside the barn. It was a lot of horsing, and was going to be more than that, getting it all down to the boat.

"Look, Waldo, doesn't somebody own all this? Maybe we hadn't ought to take so much. Maybe we ought to ask somebody."

"Joe Crawford," Waldo said. "Dead. His boys go Vest, California. Ve take. They come ask us, ve give back. Come on, little lugging ain't going hurt you."

They got home with their load a little before dark. They had not only enough tools to work a garden, but also a tubful of lobsters which Waldo had extracted from various traps on the way in from the island. Rob, being a town boy, had never seen lobster traps hauled; he had been fascinated, and the fact that the buoys had all been of different colors didn't mean a thing to him.

Mary and Sue fell upon the lobsters with shrieks of joy.

"Waldo, you blessed woolly lamb!" Sue said. "Oh, I'm dying, I can't wait!" She flew to put kettles on.

Mary, who had been worried about Rob all day and was set to hand Waldo a good piece of her mind for taking him off without telling her, forgot about that as she piled kindling into the wood stove. But Chris eyed the catch with doubt.

"I didn't know you had traps down, Waldo," he said.

"You don't?" Waldo said. "H'm, need more split vood, I guess." And he went off out.

Chris followed him. "Waldo, those look like short lobsters to me."

"Little is best kind," Waldo said. "I don't keep big vons, they tough."

"Jesus, you could get shoved as far as the law could send you for that. Short lobsters, they fine you five bucks apiece—"

"I ain't got caught, do I? You vant throw them lobsters avay? Take avay from ladies? *Now?* Vhat's trouble you, annyvay? Nobody miss. I never took no counters."

Waldo sharpened a scythe, went to work on the clearing. He mowed grass, grubbed out bushes. He brought gas for the truck, got Rob to drive it all day on a Saturday, while he himself held the plow. They had a terrible time with the heavy turf. Rob told his father he didn't believe the plow alone had done it all. Waldo broke both new plow handles, but he managed somehow with the stumps—every time Rob looked around, he said, there was Waldo, bent double and looking as though he was doing part of the job with his nose.

When the place was finally harrowed and fitted, Waldo got right down to it and smelled.

"Nice dirt. Black as hat. Need cow dung now, maybe some lime."

He took the truck and went off. Chris saw him come back, looking very down in the mouth.

"What's wrong?" Chris asked absently. He was figuring on the west wall of George's house, and he had barely glanced up.

"Ball-up," Waldo said. "Oh, damn me!" He sat down on a pile of two-by-fours, put a hand on each cheek, rocked his head back and forth.

" 'S trouble, Waldo?" George asked. "Couldn't find any cow manure?"

"Oh, godalmighty, find sixteen-nineteen ton, haul off for free. Big cow-barn-farm up by town, milk, butter, so on. Everythang. Big nosy voman, like schoolmarm, say she own this place, vhat ve do here?"

"Plummer's Dairy," George said. He blew out his breath. "Chris, we built that barn ten years ago. Abigail Plummer, remember her? Jos Plummer's relative, sure's shooting. I told you—"

"Goddmmit, don't you say I told you so to me," Chris said. His dark-tanned face had flushed red. He stood up, his hand clenched on his hammer.

"Hold on," George said. "Everybody hold on. What'd she say, Waldo? Was she sore?"

"Sore, I guess. Nosy. Ask this, ask that. I don't talk. Make out I a Velshman, don't know English good. She say you a squatter. You come see her right avay, or she send sheriff down."

"She sends Green down here, he'll be met with a shotgun," Chris said.

"Oh, gosh, no," George said. "You wouldn't want to shoot Jerome. He's so damn old now all you'd have to do is point your finger at him." He stopped, seeing Chris's face. This was no time to be funny. "Let me go, Chris. I'll tell her how things are. She wasn't a bad old gal, as I recall. Maybe she'll—"

Chris hurled his hammer against the wall. "I'll go," he said.

Abigail was sitting in the dairy office in town when Chris came in. She had been closing out the month's accounts and had not quite finished. From the figures so far she could see that profits were down below what she'd counted on. That was to be expected, of course, in hard times; she wasn't overly worried. The business ws holding its own, but to keep it that way she would have to cut back somewhere. She could, she supposed, reduce the dairy herd, though she was reluctant to. It was a fine one, built up through the years, for one thing; for another, she was supplying surplus milk and butter for the relief program. She was absorbed, jotting down figures, thinking, when Chris walked through the door.

"Cartwright," he said briefly. "You wanted to see me."

She couldn't think who he could be. She said, "Wait just a minute, will you, please?"

"If you want to see me, see me," Chris said. "I ain't got time to wait around."

Startled, Abigail glanced up. She saw a tall, extraordinarily thin man who looked somehow familiar, though she couldn't place hm. He seemed to be all knots and angles. Two hard lumps stood out on his cheeks where his jaw muscles clenched. He was in work clothes and he had not taken off his hat. She put down her pencil.

"You seem to be put out about something," she said. "What can I do for you?"

"I ain't hurt your house down Starball," Chris said. "I've fixed it up, if you want to know. It was abandoned and I'm living in it."

"Oh," Abigail said. So that's who this was, the squatter from down Starball, and a tough character he looked to be. He had said his name, but she hadn't caught it. The man who had come by looking for cow dressing for a garden had seemed very stupid; she had not been able to get much out of him, only that somebody was living in the Starball house. Starball, where Jos had drowned and Charles had been disfigured for life and Felix had taken the terrible hurt from which he had never got well. Starball, which she had hoped never to hear of again.

Not that she had wasted time grieving for Jos. Justice had caught up with him as she had always known it would. For lying, cheating, stealing, for burning up a barnful of helpless beasts, for destroying both Charles and Felix, Jos was now exactly where he should be—under his splendid monument in the town cemetery.

She had sent Clarence Bickford down with padlocks for the Randall house doors and for ten years had put the place out of her mind. And here was this fellow, probably no more responsible than Jos was, who had moved in, up to heaven knew what down there. From the way he was acting, it might be anything.

"You've no right to take over property that doesn't belong to you," she said.

"I ain't arguing. I'm there and I'm staying."

"Please take off your hat. You'll be more comfortable. And so will I."

Chris glared at her. The snotty old battle-ax wasn't even doing him the favor of recognizing him. It was only ten years ago that he'd built that barn for her. His metal plaque must still be on the beam inside the door where he'd nailed it. He did not realize how much he himself had changed, his body twenty pounds lighter, his face seamed and furrowed with worry and, just now, twisted with his fury. Well, to hell with her!

"I don't need to take my hat off. Goddammit, I've said all I've got to say."

"Don't you swear at me, I won't have it. That house is not for sale or for rent, nor do I want squatters in it. You'll move out at once, please."

"You try and make me," Chris said. "I'll be waiting for anything you send down."

He turned and slammed out through the door.

That was an unreasonable man with an ugly temper. Where on earth had she seen him before? He could be one of the drifters who came by the dairy, quite often now, looking for work, and who got it if she had any jobs to give. She turned back to her figuring, and for an hour or so worked without interruption. Then the telephone rang. It was young Arthur Bickford, Clarence's son, out at the farm.

"Mrs. Plummer, I wish you'd make up your mind about that wild heifer. She ain't ever going to be one mite of good to us, and all I need is your go-ahead to beef her."

Abigail sighed. Since Clarence's death of a heart attack two years ago, she had been trying to train Arthur to take over his father's job. Arthur was a theorist who had read a good many books on dairy farming. He had an excellent memory which retained, almost verbatim, everything he read; but since sometimes the theories in the books contradicted each other, Arthur would get muddled when it came to practical application. He was not the man with animals his father had been; he was nervous around cattle and they were afraid of him. He tried hard, however, with the best of intentions, and so did Abigail. She not only felt a deep sense of obligation to Clarence Bickford, but Arthur had been courting Maureen since school days, and they were now engaged to be married in June.

"I think we'll wait awhile longer, Arthur," she told him. "You know, I told you—"

"Sure, I know you told me. Take her away from the herd, you said, and we've done it. Had one god-awful time doing it too. She's ripped around and tackled a couple of the other cattle, and I've sprained my wrist getting her penned up down here. None of the boys dares to go near her, and I sure don't."

"She's got to be milked, that's half what ails her."

"I wish you'd come out here and see what you're asking us to milk."

"All right, I will," Abigail said.

The heifer in question was one of the pedigreed Guernseys whose bull calf had been sorted out with others of the spring crop and later sold. She had always been a nervy creature, temperamental and hard to handle, because she seemed to find life on a dairy farm a great bore. At times, for no reason, she would leap fences and take off down the highway, or she would brace horns with one of her gentler sisters and hustle her backward around the pasture. The best thing that had ever happened to her had been her calf; she had settled down at once to placid motherhood. When he had been taken away she could not bear it. No fence would hold her then. As long as he had been in the smaller pasture, she had joined him, leaping two fences and crossing the highway to do it. Once there, assured that he was all right, she would take out after the other calves, who, when chased, could jump fences, too, so that there were always calves out and free, having to be rounded up and got back into the pasture before they got hurt on the highway. Staked out, she would pull up the stake; penned, she bawled all day long, raucous as a rusty fish horn, wishing she were dead and making all who had to listen wish she, or they, were too.

She was unpopular with the farm hands because of the extra work she made; Arthur hated her, partly because she cordially returned his sentiments and took out after him whenever he came near her, and partly because she was not his idea of what a good cow should be. As a child, he had been read to out of books, poems like:

> The gentle cow all red and white
> I love with all my heart,
> She gives milk with all her might
> To eat with apple tart.

And he was a young man whose convictions, formed early, seldom if ever changed. Most real cows, anyway, failed to match up to his ideals. Whenever he went around among them, he carried a hoe handle.

Abigail suspected that Arthur's hoe handle had been from the beginning what ailed the heifer. It was the first thing she looked for today when she walked into the barn. Sure enough, there it was, leaning against the gate to the pen. Arthur was standing there glumly nursing his wrist. A couple of the farmhands who had been with him eased quietly out of the side door as she came in.

"What's that doing there?" she asked. "Have you been using it?"

"Holy smoke, I had to have some kind of a club or she'd

have killed me," Arthur said. "Look at my wrist. The bone feels all gritty inside. I think she's broken it."

"Don't be silly. If it were broken, you couldn't move it. And if you've been beating her with that hoe handle, I wouldn't blame her if she'd broken your neck."

"Oh, heck, no. I wouldn't do that, you know I wouldn't."

"She looks like a pretty worn-out animal to me."

"If you think she's worn-out, you try going in there."

The heifer stood, legs braced wide apart, head hanging down, in the middle of the pen. Great tears ran from her eyes and rolled down; regularly she bawled, a sound mournful and hoarse, breathless as if she had no wind left. Her bag was so swollen that the teats, swollen, too, stood out at stiff angles from each other. From them drops of milk kept forming, dripping to the floor of the pen.

"Poor thing," Abigail said. "Arthur, get me a milk pail, please."

"Oh, my Lord, you aren't going in there! She'll kill you."

"She's got to be relieved. Do as you're told."

Arthur got a pail from the dairy room. He also brought his rifle, cuddled hopefully under one arm. "Let me shoot her. Let me get rid of the cussed thing. Lord knows, I'd be glad to."

"I don't doubt you would," Abigail said. "This is one of our good Guernseys. She'll give at least twenty quarts of milk a day when she settles down." She unlatched the gate, walked into the pen, closed the gate behind her. "I'm certainly not going to have her killed unless—"

"Look out!" Arthur yelled.

Abigail dropped the pail, dove sideways out of the way, and fell flat, as the cow walled her eyes and charged.

She did not hit Abigail. She had not tried to. What she had been waiting for was the pen gate opening on freedom. Her whole weight landed on the gate. The latch snapped and she kept going. Arthur, whose one idea was that she was after him, personally, whipped the rifle to his shoulder and snapped a shot after her as she went through the door. Since he had been too jolted to aim, the shot went high. It took the hat off the head of Waldemar Larsen, who had been just about to come in the door.

Today was a half-holiday, and Waldo had driven to town in the truck to bring the kids home from school. He had been on the way home when the notion occurred to him that it wouldn't do any harm if he stopped by and talked with the lady who had sent Chris away breathing fire and brimstone. Couldn't make things worse—might even help. Chris had fought her a battle; when Waldo had left Starball, he, Chris, had still been red-eyed mad. In Waldo's experience, you didn't fight battles with ladies, you talked nice to them. So here he was, coming peaceably through the barn door, when some crazy man took a shot and then threw a cow at him.

He ducked back, just in time, as the cow rocketed past him, stared, surprised, as she fishtailed down the highway. He picked up his hat, still staring. It occurred to him that the truck full of kids had been parked just behind him. Somebody could be shot dead and cold, this very minute. Waldo's blood curdled. He strode back to the truck, saw that the kids were all right, all hollering at once, and that the shot had gone somewhere else. Then he got mad. It took a great provocation to get Waldo mad.

"Who you think you shoot, you damfool crazy damn jackass?" he bawled, and stalked into the barn. "Vhat kind people you, annyvay?"

Arthur had already had one fright; it was nothing to this second threat. The look in the eyes of the preposterous big man coming at him was deadly. It raised the hair on his head.

"Hey, I didn't—" he began. He backed away, dropped the gun, and bolted. Inside the dairy room, he slammed the door, shot the bolt.

"You *better*," Waldo said. "I make hash, blood for jooce."
He picked up the rifle. "Thirty-thirty, too, by God." Rumbling to himself, he snapped the cartridges out of the gun,
sending them flying into the air in a stream. Then he broke
it in two pieces across his knee and hurled stock and barrel
at the dairy-room door.

"My goodness!" Abigail said. "How on earth did you do
that?"

"Crazy damn loon!" Waldo said. "He's lucky ain't him I
do to." He did a double take, seeing who was in the cow pen.
"Vhy, poor lady! Vhat you do there? Cow valk all over you,
mercy!"

He stepped through the gate, put both hands on Abigail's
waist, lifted her out to the barn floor, where he took off his
perforated hat and proceeded to bat muck off the front of
her dress.

"Stop that!" Abigail said. "I thought you said you couldn't
speak English."

"You hurt annyvhere?" Waldo put his hat back on. "Little
vatter somewhere? Ah. Yes."

The trough inside the pen contained water put there for
the cow. Waldo reached a long arm, wet his handkerchief,
offered it. When she did not take it, he delicately dabbed
the side of her face. "Little bit of cow on there. Don't look
nice," he said.

"That's enough, I said. Didn't you tell me—"

"Yes." Waldo sighed. "I don't talk good for lady like you
to hear. I shut up, most times, vith ladies. You all right now?"

"I told you I was."

She had been shaken up and her dress was certainly a
mess, but mostly she was annoyed at herself for having done
something foolish. Anyone should have known better than
to go into that pen with the poor animal in the state she'd
been. It was also a part of that same foolishness to take out
her annoyance on this fellow, who, now that he was saying

something more than a grunt, had turned out to be quite a nice man.

"Thank you for your trouble," she said. "But I'm really not hurt. Did you want something? If it's the cow manure for your garden, I told the boys to let you haul away all you wanted."

"Thanks, I do that. I vant ask you for your house, but I come back some other time."

"My house?"

"Down Starball. Chris ask you, but he got mad. Poor Chris, he's vorried crazy, seven kids, him and George, no money, no place to go. Two vifes. Me."

Chris? she thought. George? And hadn't the man said "Cartwright"? Certainly he had.

"Oh, my heavens!" she said. "Chris Cartwright? The Cartwright brothers? What on earth has happened to them?" She indicated the plaque nailed to the beam overhead. "They built this barn for me."

"That's them."

"He's changed out of all reason. I hope you'll tell him I'm sorry I didn't remember him."

She recalled a husky, youngish, well-turned-out man—pleasant, too, though not always easy to deal with, even then. Now he looked years older, stringy and thin, his clothes hanging on him, and that black temper . . .

"Hard times," Waldo said. "Chris, George, they lose business, houses, everythang. Seven kids," he said again.

"Seven children? In that ramshackle old ruin? That's no place for children."

"Vhere else?" Waldo considered wiping away a tear, but his handkerchief was wet and this lady was smart. He decided against it. Too much, maybe. "You come see that house," he said. "Ve fix nice. Other one, too, for George. Soon one for me. Soon as ve get jobs, ve pay you rent. Ve ain't bum people. Please?" Waldo smiled, showing large white teeth, very pleasant. "You ain't using."

No, she thought, I'm not using it. And what I should have done this morning was to tell the man, whoever he was, to stay there if he needed to. These hard times have knocked out too many people for anyone to refuse a shelter, if there is one.

"I'm sorry," she said. "If he had only told me his trouble and not come banging in and out like a thunderstorm. I hadn't seen him for ten years, you know, and he has changed. Please tell him to use anything down there he needs. And tell him, for me, that he has a very nasty and foolish temper. He was really *awful*. Come now, you've used that smile before, haven't you?"

Waldo blushed. "Yah?" he said, flustered. He took two steps backward, recovered himself, and bowed. "You very nice lady. You need help, anny time, annything, you call me, Valdemar Larsen, down Starball. Now, I go."

With considerable dignity he walked out of the barn.

Go, go, quick. Before she changes mind. Might get thinking again about kids in the ruins.

Driving down the highway, very pleased with himself, Waldo entertained the children with an account of the whole triumphant affair. He told how the cow had gone by, like out of cannonball; he took off his hat and showed the bullet hole. He had growled like grizzle bear at crazy man with gun till feller ran like vebbit. Above all, he had talked lady, there, into letting them stay in her house. It made a fine story. The kids were so tickled with it that he told it again, elaborating. He even told how the lady had fallen down in the cow pen. "Plant that lady right now, she grow potato something vunderful."

"Gee, that bullet went right over the truck," Rob said.

"You all lucky. That cussed fool, I see him again I pull nose out of face."

"It made a funny whizzling noise," Liz said. Liz was George's oldest, aged fourteen. "Look, Waldo, there's that scared-to-death cow right now."

"Vhere?" Waldo stopped the truck in the middle of the highway, sat looking intently at the bushes lining the ditch.

"Aw, Waldo, come on, step on it," Rob said. "Who cares about an old cow?"

"Ain't old," Waldo said. "That's it." He got out and started for the underbrush. "I be right back. You pull truck over, Rob. Some car come along knock us topsideupdown."

The heifer was standing a little way off the road in a pile of dry brush, much as she had stood in the pen, legs apart, head hanging down. She wasn't bawling now, she was too tired. She didn't move, even when Waldo came up, ran his hand along the side of her sweaty neck, scratched the wiry tuft between her horns.

"Vhy, poor lady," he said, "vhat you do here?"

What she did here was what she had to do—stand still. Her front feet were tangled in the brush pile. Her sleek hide showed cuts and scraped places where she had crashed through undergrowth.

"Now, ain't you some mess," Waldo said. He patted and stroked, crooning under his breath. "You rest, shod up now. I fix." After a while he moved quietly back, still stroking, his hand avoiding sore places, squatted, and began to milk her. She flinched at his touch on the swollen bag, aimed a half-hearted kick which he had no difficulty in avoiding, setting the trembling hind foot gently back on the ground. "Don't you be voman, fly in air. You let me fix, you'll feel better."

Behind him, the kids lined up, staring wide-eyed.

"Don't come close," he warned. "She awful scared. She hurts too."

They had no intention of coming close. They wanted no part of a live cow, but it had been a long time since they had seen even the milk that used to come in bottles. They were looking at the rich white streams sinking out of sight into the brush pile.

Rob said, "Geest, Waldo, don't waste it. Let me get my dinner bucket, put it in that."

"Nope. Today, milk no good. Cow all shook up. Bad, make you sick. Tomorrow, milk, butter, cheese, all good. We take her home, you see."

"That's not our cow, is it, Waldo?" Liz said. "Doesn't she belong to that woman up there? We'll have to take her back."

"Take back? Let crazy man shoot? Nossir!" Waldo, finishing, got up. "They been awful mean this cow. Ve keep. Pat, talk to, she be nice, she be yost lovely. You kids go truck, pile up on front seat. Rob, you pull brush off of cow feet."

"She don't look as if she liked me much," Rob said. "If she gets loose, what'll she do?"

"I hold." Waldo put an arm around the heifer's neck, stroking and patting again. "Easy, Rob. Don't move quick. One piece, two piece to time."

Gingerly, with one eye on the cow, Rob picked away brush.

"Good. She come," Waldo said. "Now, you scoot back, let down truck dump."

The cow was too tired to care what happened. Except for Waldo's hold on her, she would have lain down where she was. He had to tug and coax before she came, limping indifferently along beside him. She balked, with a half-hearted snort, at the sight of the truck, but Waldo gave her no time to consider action. He put both arms under her and heaved. There was no place to go but ahead, and she went, helped on by another powerful heave on her stern. She couldn't even kick out behind—she needed all four feet to keep her balance.

"Roll up dumper, now, now, Rob." Waldo stood, bracing her, until the truck body was level. Then he fastened the tailgate, climbed quickly in over a back wheel, eased along to the cow's head. He needn't have worried. She had had enough of everything. Here was a wooden floor, no sharp sticks, no prickles. She collapsed on it with a moan.

"Drive easy, Rob." Waldo settled himself beside her. "Now, we go home. You good girl."

At the turnaround the younger children piled out, tore across the walkway over the brook.

"Can't vait to tell," Waldo said cheerfully. "Rob, roll back dumper. Vhen I say 'Go,' you pull ahead. Slow, easy. Don't jerkle." He went around and unfastened the tailgate.

The cow, as the truck body tilted, found herself sliding backward down the slant, helped on by a firm grip on her tail.

"'N there!" Waldo said. "You here, you not hurt. You get up when you feel like."

Rob stopped the truck and came back. He looked admiringly at the cow and at Waldo. "Gee!" he said. "Milk! I forgot what it tastes like. Where we going to keep her? She can't stay here, can she?"

"I take tarp off of lumber pile, make tent for tonight. Tomorrow we make cow place, pasture, over in green grass by garden."

Chris, attended by the excited voices of the children, came striding toward them along the beach. "What in hell, Waldo?"

"Cow," Waldo said.

"I can damn well see it's a cow. Now, you look here, I'm not taking any handouts from that old battle-ax. You can cart that critter back where—"

"You go fry a kite," Waldo said. "I know who you don't take from. F.D. and R., that's who. This not F.D. and R. handout. This *my* cow." He grinned at Chris. "Name Abigail."

❀　　　❀　　　❀

Maureen and Arthur Bickford were planning a quiet wedding at Abigail's house. If Abigail had reservations about the marriage, she did not make them known. Her daughter Elsie had reservations, too, but not the same kind. Elsie had quit school to marry Delbert Smiley, the young teller at the bank. She had one child, Delbert, the second, and was pregnant with another, which circumstance took up a great deal of her time. She had made all her sisters dance in a kettle, she had fulfilled the destiny of a proper woman; of all four, she was now the outstanding one whose words should certainly be listened to, and she could not understand why Maureen wouldn't let her run the wedding or why on earth Maureen wouldn't be married in the church.

"I have *beggared* Delbert Smiley buying a new dress," she told Maureen. "My, you ought to have heard him, he kicked something fierce. He said it was hard times, didn't I for godsake know it, and of course his pay's been cut at the bank, and there I went taking forty-two dollars and ninety-nine cents out of the savings to buy a matron-of-honor dress that I couldn't very well get along without, my own wedding dress I've never worn but once, but in my condition now it would show everything, and I said to him, Delbert Smiley! I am not going to stand up with my older sister at her wedding in a secondhand dress, and here you have got your feet dug in to be married in Mama's house and not in the church at all and just the family. I call it a shame."

Maureen had not invited Elsie to be her bridesmaid; she had already asked Nan, if Nan could get home in time for the wedding—she was studying music at the conservatory in Boston, and she had written that she'd make it if she possibly could. But Maureen wasn't oversurprised that Elsie had invited herself.

"Well, it *is* hard times," Maureen said. "And Ma's not making too much money these days." Maureen, since her graduation from high school, had been helping in the dairy, keeping accounts for Abigail, and was in a position to know. "I don't want to put her to any more expense than I have to."

"Oh, fooey on hard times! Look what Mama's got salted

away, she could give you forty weddings in forty churches. She's got all our grandfather left and all Uncle Jos left, and I'll bet you every last twenty-five-cent piece has got the eagle's neck broke on it where she's hung on. She's give you already a nice apartment fixed up modren, which is more than Charles and Clarice and Delbert and I got, and she worth what she is, she could more than afford to pay Delbert and I's taxes, if she had a mind to. But then, of course you've always been her favorite, Maureen."

"Oh, Lord, Elsie!" Maureen said. Years ago she had given up being bothered very much about anything Elsie said. She could be counted on to say anything that passed through her mind at any time regardless of whose feelings might be hurt. When people did get put out at her, she was always amazed, because she never in the world meant anything mean, she had said whatever it had been only because she'd happened to think of it and it had been interesting. If anyone had told her that sometimes her talking caused damage, she would have been convinced that that person was lying with malice aforethought. Herself, Elsie believed to be an extremely good and moral person, with few faults if any.

It was no use reminding her now that both Charles and Delbert had been offered the same wedding present by Abigail—an apartment in her house, equipped for housekeeping, and that both had turned it down. Charles had had reasons of his own, Maureen knew, for not wanting to live in Ma's pocket where she could see him every day and inquire about the store; he was determined to manage it in his own way, not Mama's, and he and Clarice had set up housekeeping in the rooms above it. And Delbert had a home of his own, inherited from his father. In some ways Maureen wished that Arthur had one too. It might be simpler, when you got married, to live apart from the place where you'd grown up. But Arthur had snapped up the offer to live in Ma's house; he'd been delighted with the idea. And Maureen didn't really see how she could walk away to somewhere else and leave her father. He lived upstairs now, most of the time, in a kind of dream world of his own; but for years she had taken most of the care of him, and when he did have a lucid time, she was always the one he asked for.

Elsie was going on about the wedding. ". . . and I and Delbert was married in the church in a bower just buried in lilacs and the altar was, too, and I had a bouquet of lilies-of-the-valley from them lovely ones that grow over around Carter's manure pile and little sweetheart roses from the greenhouse. Cultivated flowers," Elsie said dreamily.

"Yes. I was there, remember?"

"Well, what ails Ma, she won't let you? Anyone of her stachure in the town, her children ought to have a church wedding, and you her oldest daughter! Everybody'll think she's lost all her money—"

"I told you. It isn't Ma. It's me. I don't want a lot of fuss."

"—or that you and Art Bickford had got to get married. A wedding at somebody's house and nobody invited most always is hole-and-corner, only—"

"It's partly on account of Pa, you know that. He can't stand a lot of noise and confusion."

"—only Delbert told me once that he and Arthur and some other fellows was talking at a card game down at Byron's about menfolks' cussed actions, and Art came right out and said he wouldn't have connections out of wedlock, it was against his morals. Them men like to laughed their head off." She burst into a storm of giggles. "He called it that," she gasped. "That's what he *called* it."

"So now you know," Maureen said. "Look, Elsie. I didn't know you were planning to stand up with me, and I'm sorry, but I guess I'd better tell you that I've already asked Nan, and if she can't get home on time, then Julie."

Elsie stared, astounded. "Why! Of all the— What on earth

was you thinking about? I'm the one. I'm the only one *mar-ried*. And you stood up with me, didn't you?"

"Because you asked me."

"Because you was the oldest, that's why! There's certainly a rituool to follow out of respect for the marriage, or ain't you ever heard of it? I just took it for granit you'd return the compliment, that's all. I suppose Nan in her city clothes and the whatchamacallits she's learnt out of a music college down in Boston will be a little more to look at than me in my forty-two-ninety-nine dress from Bristol, simple little thing, and my homey, country ways. As for Julie, I shouldn't think she'd want to show her face in public, let alone at a religious rite like a wedding. Failing in every last eternal subjeck she's got and probably not even going to graduate. I'd certainly keep myself out of sight, if I was her."

"It *was* you, once, if I recall. Seems to me I remember some D-minuses and E's on the last report card you brought home. And that was only your sophomore year. You had to struggle to get that far, and you certainly didn't graduate."

It was not often that Maureen spoke her mind to anyone. But Elsie's meanderings were getting harder to answer casually and Maureen wished to heaven she'd get mad and go home.

"Maureen Plummer! That was different and you know it! I quit to get *married!* It was not the same thing at all. Now, with Julie, she just won't study and she's smart—sometimes I think she's even smarter than I was in school. But you know perfectly well that I was so in love with Delbert Smiley that spring that I couldn't open a book, much less look at it when it was open. In love makes it different, Maureen." Elsie paused, looking back, and gave an indulgent smile to the helpless lovesick girl she had been in that far-off time. "Oh, I had my reasons, Maureen."

"For all you know, Julie has hers, too," Maureen said, and bit her tongue.

Elsie stared at her, pointing like a bird dog. "Oh-ho!" she

said. "Maybe I'm not so wrong about quiet weddings. What about Julie? What do you *know?*"

"Elsie, times I'd like to shake you. Shake some sense into you. Julie's missing Nan. She hasn't been the same since Nan left. And now they can't be together next year because Julie's grades are low, and she probably can't get into the conservatory. When I mentioned her reasons, that was what I meant and that was all I meant, will you get it through your silly head?"

"Maybe she better *not* be seen, standing up with you in church. Well, I must say, I wouldn't be in her shoes with Ma, if *that's* it. And I'll bet you do know something too!"

A piercing wail from the screen porch interrupted. Delbert, the second, was tired of waiting in his perambulator.

"Oh, the bessy lamb!" Elsie said, but she made no move to go.

"The sun's come around right in his face," Maureen said. "You better tend him, or you'll have a blind baby. And didn't you say you had shopping to do?"

"Oh, my Lord, yes! I clean forgot. For Delbert's supper, and he'll be home now before I am. Why didn't you remind me before?" Gathering up oddments of hat, pocketbook, shopping bag, and jacket, Elsie fled through the door. On the porch, she crooned to Delbert, the second, "Bessy tweetums, dirty old sun right in hims itsy bitsy peepers," and called back gaily, "Bet you two cents I find out what you know," as she eased the baby carriage down the steps.

If she does, Maureen thought, God help all.

Julie had been in trouble at school ever since Nan had left. This year her grades had plummeted; in spite of warnings from the school and from her mother, she had let them drop. In the spring Mr. Graves, her music teacher, came to see Abigail. He felt, he said, that most of her difficulty was with him. He was, Abigail could see, very much put out.

"I'm a busy man," he said. "What Julie's doing for me now

isn't worth my time. She's got the same aptitude Nan has, even better in some ways. But if she won't listen to me or do my assignments, I'm afraid I can't be bothered with her. Too bad. It's a wicked waste of talent." He shrugged and went away.

"What on earth ails Mr. Graves?" Abigail asked Julie. "He says he won't teach you any more."

"Oh, he's just sore," Julie said.

"But why?"

"I don't know." Julie shrugged. "I can play the piano better than he can, I guess."

She was not going to tell her mother about the fight with Mr. Graves. She was certainly not going to mention her real reason for not bothering with the pieces he assigned.

Mr. Graves knew a great deal about music; he had taught it for years and had retired from the city conservatory where he had made his reputation, and from the city orchestra in which he had played piano only because of the growing weakness and disability of his deformed foot, which now gave him almost continual pain. He had got along very well with Nan, who had studied with him for a year and a half after she had been graduated from high school, in preparation for the conservatory; he had taken great pains with Maureen. But with Julie he had no patience at all. He was a classicist and a conservative with a great deal to offer which Julie did not wish to learn. What she wanted to play was jazz. He mourned the, to him, misuse of a talent which might have been molded, in his hands, into something remarkable. For four years he had tried his best while tension and dislike had grown. The girl was a brat. When occasion arose, he did not hesitate to tell her so, and Julie returned his sentiments with interest. The time came when she returned his comments.

No one was going to holler "Idiot!" and "Fool!" and "Staccato, staccato, staccato!" at Julie Plummer, and slam a baton into the corner with "Go away! Get out! I cannot bear the horrible sounds you make!" He used the baton to beat time with, whacking the top of the piano, which was silly when he was beating out the composer's time and she was playing a rhythm of her own—and a better one, she told herself. It was distracting, and she couldn't stand the horrible sounds *he* made, either.

"Bach!" he stormed. "You do this to Bach!"

"Oh, Bach!" Julie said. "J. S., Yo-ho Sebastian Bach! Deedle-deedle, needle-needle, till you go nuts! A lot of jiggly little old has-been tunes anybody could improve on. And Mozart, tinkle-tinkle, he's all right, he did stuff people wanted to hear at parties and balls. But that was *then*. What people want to hear now's Cole Porter. Raymond Scott. And you wait and see what the classics are in the twenty-first century."

In icy silence Mr. Graves retrieved his baton. "You will play what I tell you and how I tell you to play it. Now! Begin. One, two . . ."

"Okay," Julie said. "Listen. This'll break your heart."

He had started beating time on the piano. His whacks grew louder, more frenzied, fell further and further behind. Julie was playing his assignment with a fast, heavy downbeat in the low bass and some treble antics of her own making. "So see?" she said. "That's what you can do with old J. S., if you know enough. If you don't belong back in the eighteenth century playing, oh, madrigals."

Mr. Graves spoke with deadly, quiet sarcasm. "You do not understand, you cannot read *poco rit.?*" He suddenly stamped his aching foot, leaned over and whacked her with his baton on the knuckles. "So what does it mean?" he shouted. "Tell me! *Poco rit.*, what does it mean?"

Julie ended it for good, there and then. If he thought she was a fresh brat, she'd let him know she was. She told him it meant to stop and pick your nose.

"Ignorant! Vulgar! Go and don't come back! I have better things to do with my time."

"Well, let me tell you, so have I," Julie said.

She did have, she told herself. She was supposed to go nights after school to help Charles in the store. It was her mother's idea—some notion she had that all her kids ought to learn how to work, earn some of their own money. Julie was not doing that. Every afternoon when she could, she was sneaking out of the high-school basement door into the alley, and going by devious streets to Jamie Stetson's place to play piano with his dance band. She was also climbing out her bedroom window nights when she was supposed to be in bed, traveling with the band to dance halls in the area, playing when Jamie needed a fill-in. She was not his regular piano player because she wasn't always able to make it, but he had said she could be any time he could depend on her to show up regularly. If she was listless, not bright any longer in school, if her grades were failing, it was because she was tired out. The band sometimes got home very late.

She had been expecting an interview with her mother. She hoped, desperately, that it was only about the fight with Mr. Graves—the old fool had probably blatted out the whole story to Ma, and she would have to go and apologize, which she'd gladly do for the sake of peace. She'd been careful about ducking out nights; since she slept in a ground-floor bedroom, that part had been easy. Abigail went to bed early and slept well. Julie was pretty sure that she hadn't suspected anything. But Jamie Stetson's place was an abandoned railway car down by the station. She'd always looked both ways along the street and then gone in fast, just in case, but somebody could just possibly have seen her and reported it to Abigail. Or maybe Charles had told about her not being in the store. Julie didn't think so. Of course you couldn't depend on Charles for anything, no matter what he promised;

the thing was, he didn't want her in the store any more than she wanted to be there.

She drove him crazy, he said. He'd rather have the devil's own imp around, balling things up and flashing herself in front of half the louts in town who'd hang out there without buying anything, just chewing over fluff with Julie. Of course when Nan had been at home and they'd both worked in the store, it had been better. They'd plagued the life out of Charles and the two of them had been more than a match for him. Julie, alone, wasn't. He always managed to get back at her in some kind of a nasty, mean way. If she'd stay out of there for keeps, he said, he wouldn't tell Ma. That was a bargain and one that certainly suited Julie. His real reason was, she knew, that he'd rather do the work himself than pay anyone wages—he was tighter than a tick with money, so she didn't really think he'd told on her. As far as money went, she'd been careful to let Abigail know she'd earned some. Jamie paid her a lot more than Charles ever had parted with.

She faced her mother with considerable apprehension, nonetheless. You never knew what Abigail might know.

When Ma started in on Mr. Graves, Julie let her held breath go in a sigh of relief. If there had been anything up about Jamie's band, Ma would have landed on that first, like a ton of bricks.

"Of course you can't play better than Mr. Graves can," Abigail said. "I want you to go ask him to change his mind about you."

"Sure, Ma, I will," Julie said airily. She was at the piano, practicing a piece for the dance coming up Saturday night, playing softly because of Pa upstairs, and drawing out the chords so that Ma would think it was one of Mr. Graves's assignments. It was kind of interesting to see what you could do with it that way. She tried a couple of tentative chords and wrinkled her nose at the result.

"Julie, I want you to listen," Abigail said.

"Sure, Ma, I am."

"You ought to be ashamed, putting poor Mr. Graves out this way," Abigail said. "You know how his foot pains him all the time."

"Mm-hm, I am."

"How can he recommend you to the conservatory if you don't do what he tells you? I know you're counting on going down to study with Nan, and I'm more than willing to pay for it. But if you don't pass your grades, you can't go, can you? The school's already notified me that you're going to have a hard time pulling up your grades in the next two months, if you're going to graduate."

"Oh, they're crazy down there! I can pull those grades up any time, on any test they want to hand out."

"Then let me see you do it."

"All right."

"Julie, I can't think what ails you. You act as if you had only one ear and that one not listening."

"I'm listening, Ma."

"Then you'd better hear this. If you can't spend the summer studying with Mr. Graves, you'll have to help Charles in the store."

Julie sat for a moment stone-still on the piano bench. Then she dropped her hands to the keys and sent a series of savage chords thundering through the house.

"Julie! Not so loud! You'll drive your father out of his mind." Abigail got up and closed the piano.

"Well, I *hate* Charles! He's awful to me and oily-greasy all over customers, the ones he thinks have got any money. And all the time he's cheating them blind. I won't work there and I won't work in that rotten old dairy either."

"The store and that rotten old dairy have kept you in clothes and food for a healthy long time," Abigail said quietly. "Everybody has to learn to work, Julie."

"I do work. I work hard on this piano. So you close it right in my face. Okay, leave it closed. You won't even have to lock it."

"When you use it is up to you," Abigail said. "But I can't have you disturbing your father with it. You know that. For goodness' sake, think a little and stop being so self-centered. I expect you'd better go up and see if that racket waked him. He's had a bad day today."

"Okay." Julie got up with an air of relief at getting away that Abigail did not miss.

I wish, she thought, I knew what to do about her.

Julie had always been difficult, at times unmanageable when her temper flew, but this phase of remoteness and unconcern was something new. It dated, Abigail supposed, from last fall when Nan had left and Julie had found out for sure that she couldn't go too. She had been determined to go; she didn't see any reason why she couldn't. She argued that she and Nan had always planned on going away to study together—"Haven't we, Nan?"—and she'd been given to think that her mother had planned to let her go when Nan went; and so why was she backing out now, breaking her promise? She wouldn't believe that there had never been any such ridiculous promise, and when Nan, in obvious misery, had said, "But, honestly, Julie, you know Ma never did say that. Because you can't, honey, you've got to finish high school first," Julie had got furious with everybody.

"Okay, so you don't want me," she'd told Nan, and at that Nan's patience had given out. "Oh, Julie," she said. "For heaven's sake, grow up."

The girls had always had fights, but this had been the first one which hadn't been made up on the spot. Nan's attention was on going; she was excited, looking forward. This was her great thing, and it might be, Abigail had thought, that she really didn't want Julie just now. After all, she was three years older, beginning to be absorbed elsewhere, and Julie, wherever she might be, would demand time and attention. Nan went off in a kind of bemused happiness. Julie sulked.

She had made a terrible fuss over helping Charles in the store on nights after school and on Saturday mornings. So far as Abigail knew, she was doing all right at it—at least Charles hadn't complained, which he surely would have done at any lapses. It might be a little drastic to threaten her with the store for summer vacation; but of course she wouldn't have to do it if she made things up with Mr. Graves.

Julie came downstairs, paused in the hall to put on her coat. She said, through the open door, "He's awake, Ma," and went off out, headed, Abigail supposed, for the store. She sighed a little and climbed the stairs herself to make sure all was well with Felix.

Ten years ago, when local doctors had not been able to help him, she had taken him, with Charles, to a Boston clinic. Whatever hard object Charles had struck when he had made his headlong dive out of the boat's cuddy had smashed his nose flat and ripped two deep cuts across his cheeks. The surgeons had rebuilt his nose—it would be serviceable, they told Abigail, but not pretty; he was lucky he had any nose at all. They did their best with the cuts—the scars, they thought, would fade in time. There was not much to be done for Felix. The terrible blow on his head had left him partly paralyzed and with no memory. He did not know what had happened to him; he did not remember Jos, or that Jos was dead. He had come home a sick man, vague and rambling; through the years he had partially recovered—he could walk now, carefully, with a cane, and on some days was his old, pleasant, quiet self, though never knowing when blinding headache and vertigo would strike him. When they did, he would fall, wherever he was, so that he had to be constantly watched and cared for.

Abigail thanked God that he had never recovered his

memory. Through Charles she had found out what had happened. Knowing Felix, she was sure that he had done the best he could with his unsure hands in a moment of nerveshaking panic. She was appalled when she found out that Charles bitterly blamed his father. She did not know for a long time that he blamed her even more bitterly.

Talk, stemming mostly from Jerome Green, who was a famous gossip about the fascinating business of the sheriff's office, spread quickly through town. Everyone knew that Abigail herself had started Jerome Green on Jos Plummer's trail. Reactions, depending on the state of individual ethics, were varied. Some people blamed Abigail; most were shocked; a few understood well enough to defend and be sorry for her. And Charles, as soon as his bandages came off, could not bear the way he looked or that his world of a fascinating, handsome, young daredevil, soon to be rich, was gone forever.

Through the furor that followed the accident, Abigail steadied herself as best she could. She justified her action in telephoning to Jerome to no one, nor did anyone ever know whether or not she blamed herself. If she had grim facts to face, she faced them alone; if she spent sleepless nights staring into the dark, seeing Charles's young, flawless face, remembering Felix's affection, his gaiety, his wit, it was her own affair, her own trouble which she stiffened herself to meet. She had a great deal to do—decisions to make, problems to meet, ends to tie up. She would make the decisions, meet the problems, tie up the ends, follow the sensible course of doing what she could, what had to be, done.

The stiffening took its toll. It was a hardening process as well. If integrity were a coat of mail, then she would wear one.

There was no question of a jail sentence for so sick a man as Felix, and Charles, of course, was too young. She paid the heavy fine out of Felix's savings account. He had also, in his

name, a safety deposit box, though the money in it turned
out to belong not to him but to Jos and Charles. It contained,
as well, a letter from Jos, addressed to her, and Jos's will.
The letter read:

Abby, old dear, this dough don't belong to Felix, it's mine and
Chucks, and Ive lef every goddam cent of it to you. I don't
plan to die before you do, but if my luck turns aginst me, I'm
goin to set up strait under my pretty gravestone and watch
what you do with my money. Its dirty money, dear, don't you
fergit it and its gut my dirty fingerprints all over it. If a damd
old skinflint like you can pass it up Ile miss my guess and Ile
bet by god you don't. Ill bet the whole pile of it you keep it
and stash it away and if you was to go out to the cemmatarry
any time you can hear me laffin my fool head off.

Your lovin brother
JOSIAH PLUMMER

Abigail had sat for a long time thinking. The amount in
the box appalled her; so did the sum in the manila envelope
on which was written in her son's round, schoolboy hand,
Charles Plummer. So much, for so young a boy! No wonder
Jos had had his way with Charles. If this money were the
price of Felix's destruction only, it would be very dirty
money indeed, but it was more than that.

You could not hate the dead. You could only be glad that
this dead man was where he no longer could do damage or
harm anyone. The man had had not even the excuse of insanity. He had been a cheap bully, a criminal without conscience. A destroyer, a corrupter of children. That he should
leave something to the world besides a five-thousand-dollar
marble monument was only simple justice.

In this, his final jibe at her, his guess had been right. She
would take the money; she would invest it. So far, so good.
He had had the last word in the long battle between them.
But Jos, if there were any thinking atom of him left in the

place where he was, would not be amused, knowing how his dirty money would be used.

During the next ten years Abigail had found the place for the income from Jos's money. Anonymously, quietly, she supplied the need. By 1934 two bright youngsters from poor families had college educations because Jos Plummer had been a rumrunner, and in all that time no one had heard laughter coming from under his tombstone.

Maureen had known for quite a while about Julie's night wanderings, having gone casually into her room one night last spring to find her gone and the pillows neatly arranged in the bed to look as if she were sleeping there. Where she had gone, Maureen did not at first know. She had found out on a night when Arthur had taken her to Ronnie Gilmore's Place, outside Bristol. She had been a little surprised at Arthur's wanting to go there—it had always been a rough sort of place—but he at times seemed to be quite an innocent about such matters. He wanted, he'd said, to take her everywhere, show her everything. She'd been kept under her mother's thumb all her life, didn't know what fun people could have going places.

This was absurd, of course. Abigail had always trusted her children unless she found reason not to. When she did, the offender got set right, and fast; Maureen could remember times when she'd wished she'd never been born—one of those times was when, a junior in high school, she'd been taken by a current boyfriend to Gilmore's Place—though the punishment hadn't been out of proportion to the crime and when it was over it was over for good. Arthur seemed to think, for some reason, that she and her brothers and sisters had led a hard, unhappy life at home. He didn't like to be told he was wrong about something, though, and after a few attempts to put him right, she'd given up trying.

About Gilmore's Place, he'd said that, as his wife and the mother of his children, she'd ought to know what places like that were. Not that he was going to clamp down on *his* kids —that was half the trouble with kids nowadays, their folks riding them—only, as parents, he and she should know there were certain dance halls where kids should never be allowed to go.

Maureen had spotted his lack of logic and had begun to laugh.

"What's so funny?" He was peevish. "Haven't I made plain what I mean?"

"Of course, darling. I was just thinking how far away the time seems when we'll have children big enough to go to dances."

"All right, then. Come on, then. I want to show those toughs what a man feels like when he's going to marry the prettiest girl in town."

Maureen had sense enough about herself to know that that wasn't true. She looked too much like Abigail to be pretty. Abigail had never been, but she had a chiseled kind of composed face which Maureen admired; she supposed that was what Arthur had meant. He was certainly a handsome boy himself, with his clear pink-and-white skin and brown eyes, and that wave in his taffy-colored hair that felt crisp, like good silk, when she touched it.

At Gilmore's he stopped at the cloakroom to check his hat. Two men were wrangling at the door leading in to the dance floor; one of them had his fist pulled back, as Maureen, not noticing, stepped between them. She had intended to wait inside for Arthur. The fellow grinned, dropped his fist, and chunked her on the shoulder.

"Here's a poor girl all alone," he said.

"Stop that!" Maureen said. "Your breath smells."

It did, too, of some kind of liquor. The fellow turned red. She pulled away and stepped inside the door. And the first thing she had seen was Julie, on the platform playing piano with Jamie Stetson's band.

She spun around, met Arthur coming in, just outside the door.

"Arthur, let's get out in the air. I feel sort of sick."

"What's up?"

A gust of music followed them out of the place and Maureen got at once into Arthur's car, parked at the curb.

"Don't get in the car. If you're sick, walk around, walk it off. What is it, something you ate?"

"I guess so. I'm sorry, Arthur, I've spoilt your evening, but I guess you'll have to take me home."

"Aw, gee, Maureen!" Seeing she didn't move, he said, "Oh, shoot, well, okay. I'll get my hat."

He was disappointed. On the way home it turned out that he hadn't been to Gilmore's before, wanted to see what the joint was like.

"And you didn't even give me a chance to look in on the dance floor."

Well, that was good. He hadn't seen Julie then. But others surely must have; there she was, in plain sight of everyone. People from home who knew the Plummers must go there— at least the men did; they didn't often take their own women-folk. It would be only a matter of time before word got back to Ma, especially if Elsie got to nosing around. Elsie would love to tell Ma in the nicest way possible and without a bit of spite something she really felt Ma ought to know.

Of course Ma should know. Julie's too young, and in that dive, and everybody knows Jamie Stetson's reputation.

But Maureen had always felt an awful sense of shame at the idea of telling on anyone, no matter what. It seemed so mean, and did now. People had enough to contend with anyway, the things that happened to them. You had better realize what those things were, and how it was, and why they'd done what they had. If you did, you might think twice before you went around talking, making a good story out of somebody's bad luck for people to drool over and tell again.

I always sort of went for Ma's copybook tiddlebits, anyway. *Honesty is the best policy,* and all those. Most people think they're funny and simple-minded and sentimental, and maybe I do, too, in a way; I don't seem to live up to them very well. Times, everybody has to lie, and I love Arthur too much to be honest with him and rock him back on his heels when he gets on one of those strings of his.

But they'd always seemed kindly things to live your life by, easy to understand until, of course, you got older. Then some of them puzzled you a good deal.

The one over the bureau in Ma's room had seemed simple enough to her as a child, after she'd looked up *integrity* in the dictionary, and then had looked up all the big words in the dictionary definition:

> Soundness of and adherence to moral principles and character; uprightness; honesty. The state of being whole, entire, or undiminished.

Wouldn't it be nice to be always whole, entire, undiminished?

She had got the meaning, at last, perfectly into her head. Once she had, she'd been proud to think that it said Ma to her. Abigail Plummer, you could count on it, wore integrity as a coat of mail.

But now . . . coat of mail?

A coat of mail was a strong thing, stiff, metal. Nothing could get through it. How could you ever wear anything that the people you loved could not get through?

I can't tell Ma about Julie.

Ma might understand that her way with Julie wasn't right, wasn't working and never would. But stark black in front of her would be Julie's lying, Julie's deceit.

Oh, dear, what on earth ails the little idiot? I wish I knew whether she's really got something to be unhappy about or if it's only one of those stubborn black tantrums.

Nan would have known. When it came down to grass roots, Nan had always been the only one in the world who could handle Julie.

I'll write to Nan. She'll be home soon, anyway, to the wedding, and maybe she'll know what to do.

Pushing Delbert, the second's perambulator, Elsie stepped merrily along to the store. She parked the baby in the shade, pulled his mosquito net up over him, and went inside. Two customers were ahead of her. Charles, busy, glanced up, went back to tying up bundles.

"Oh, dear!" she said. "Charles, I'm late and in a terrible hurry. Can't you wait on me next?"

"First come, first served," Charles said, without looking up. "Now, is that all, Ory?"

The stout lady in front of the counter glared down at the parcels, gathering them up. "It better be all," she said. "It's all I got the money to pay for. I hope I can feed my family on that midgeling little chunk of corned beef for the price of all outdoors. I don't know why you won't charge it. Your mother always did."

"Well, now, Ory, this Depression has hit me just the way it's hit you. We're just barely squeaking by, wholesalers' bills to meet, and Ma says we've got to cut down on tick to customers. I know it's tough, old customers like you and Doug, but she doesn't want to—"

"It's the first time in her life she don't want to. I and Doug had a bill here for fifteen years, settled on the dot every month."

"Doug lost his job, I heard," Charles said meditatively.

"Yes, and I'm working as a scrubwoman in the courthouse, if you want to know. That don't mean we won't pay Abigail Plummer's bill, the minute we got the money to. There's

been hard times before and she's carried us right on through
and got every cent just as soon as Doug went back on wages.
You can squawk about your Depression all you want to, but
she never used one as an excuse for hiking prices up to the
sky. Look at that holler toothful of corned beef, for the Lord
sake!"

"Going to have a boiled dinner," Charles said. "With all
the vegetables, I always feel too much corned beef makes it
too salt."

"You," the woman said, "are a cheat and a liar." She swept
up the parcels and lumbered toward the door. The other
customer hesitated, glanced toward Charles, shrugged and
followed her. He had wanted credit, too, it seemed. A third,
whom Elsie had not noticed at first, came out from behind
the grocery stacks. He was a very tall, rough-looking man,
dressed in overalls and a ragged gray flannel shirt. He
wanted a hundred-pound bag of cow feed.

Charles made no move to wait on him. He stood there,
picking his teeth with the little white quill he always carried
in his vest pocket. "No tick, Larsen," he said finally. "You
heard what I told Ory Carter, didn't you?"

"I pay," the man said. "Say how much." He pulled out a
beat-up wallet, counted out the sum Charles named on the
counter.

Charles put away his toothpick and led the way through
the side door to the annex, where the cattle feed and farm
tools were kept.

As they vanished, Elsie, alerted, began going busily from
shelf to shelf, choosing the items she had come to buy. She
could hear beyond the door the murmur of Charles's voice—
still being a snoot to that poor Swede, or whatever he was,
and Elsie giggled, because she knew why. Charles was always grouchy over the cow feed, because there wasn't much
profit in it for the store. Abigail stocked it and used most of
it at the dairy farm, and she wasn't about to pay Charles

retail prices for it. It meant work for him for nothing, except
from people who had a cow, like this Swede. It about killed
Charles to think of all that cow feed going out to the dairy
and him not getting a cent.

He came back, dusting his hands and saying over his
shoulder, "You haven't got enough for that roll of hen wire.
You'll have to wait till you can pay for it."

The fellow said, "Okay. I pay. You write down."

There came a bumping noise and a rattle. A truck started
up and pulled away.

Charles, in the act of putting the man's money into his
cash register, slammed the drawer shut and made for the
door. He yelled something and swore, and then apparently
got busy moving heavy stuff around, because Elsie could
hear bumps and thumps.

Tch! Now you listen to him, she thought. Being mean to
that poor man who wouldn't be half bad-looking if he was
dressed up. And Delbert says Charles is coining the money,
just coining it.

Delbert, being in the bank, of course knew what Charles's
deposits were. He cautioned Elsie against mentioning to a
soul anything he told her about the bank's business, so of
course she didn't, except to a few dearest friends whom she
knew she could trust.

And I and Delbert just barely able to stivver along on his
pay, let alone his pay cut. We deserve just as much out of
Ma as Charles does. There she sets on top of all that money
stashed away, stocks in the electrict-power company, I'll bet,
and I'll bet *they* pay her, the price them people charge for
electricity. Anybody'd think she'd let loose of some of it once
in a while, pay our electrict bill for us anyway. I don't care
if she does think I spend it as fast as I get my hands on it, I
and Delbert have got just as much right to have a few things
as other people, and more than some, where Ma's rich.

It was a poor day for Elsie when she couldn't go home

with something new—at least one parcel to open. She was
the business world's dream, the ideal customer, drowned
and consumed with desire for things. She bought on impulse
and charged where she had any credit left; she drove Delbert out of his mind bringing home gadgets—anything bright
and shiny or cute. No matter if these objects never seemed
quite so desirable when she got them home and out of the
wrappers. They would lie around the house until she got sick
of them and tossed them in the garbage can. A little plant
in a painted pot was pretty—let Delbert storm his head off
and call her a magpie, she'd seen just that same little plant
in a pot in so-and-so's kitchen set on a frilly mat, and she
knew where she could buy the mat too.

Delbert said one day that her altar was a store counter and
her Bible a mail-order catalog. Why didn't she go to church?
—it would be cheaper.

She'd been shocked to death.

"Delbert Smiley, don't you talk that way to me. I do go to
church and I'm just as religious as anybody in this town,
and what you've said is wicked blasphemy. You ought to be
ashamed taking the name of the Lord in vain."

Now, coursing Charles's neat shelves, picking out groceries
and items she needed, she saw two or three little things she
couldn't resist. Charles carried a general line—jackets and
boots and women's wear, as well as meat and canned goods
and farm supplies; some of his things were real up-to-date
and handsome. Elsie chose two pairs of stockings with those
lovely new clocks embroidered up the ankles and a pretty
head scarf. These she thrust down her front, arranging them
just under the bulge of her brassiere where they wouldn't
show.

Humming, she was about to pick up her other things,
when she heard a slight clinking sound. This set of shelves
ran head-high down the middle aisle of the store; they were
wide enough to take dry goods on one side, on the other,

stacked cans. Through a small recess between the peas and the beans Elsie saw two round staring brown eyes. She jumped and shrieked.

The eyes withdrew, their place taken by a can of beans clinked quickly into the recess where they had been.

"What do you think you're doing?" Elsie said. "Sneaking around spying on people?" Mercy, it was a wonder she hadn't dropped her baby right there in the middle of the store floor!

The eyes belonged to her young brother, Miles, whose possible presence in the store she had forgotten about. He did help Charles sometimes, and he must've just come in while she'd been walking around. She got no answer except a shuffling sound. Then the annex door clicked open and Miles disappeared through it, carrying an empty carton.

Putting stuff on shelves, hmf, you'd think he'd say hello to his sister, not scare her like that, peeking. And me pregnant! I suppose he saw me. So what if he did, he'd been brought up not to tattletale, like we all was. That was certainly a course of sprouts Ma gave us when we told on each other. And if he does, I can certainly say I haven't got one idea in the world what he can be talking about.

She went back to the counter. "Charles, for the love of Pete! Have you gone to roost out there?"

Charles came in. He was still mad, she could see that. He said over his shoulder, "All right, you count the rest of those rolls of hen wire, so what if they are heavy? What's all the screeching about?" he went on to Elsie. "You see a mouse?"

"I told you before I was in a hurry."

Charles stared with disapproval at her collection of groceries. "Now, look, this is not a Piggly Wiggly store. I've asked you not to go around fooling with the shelves."

"Well, every time I come in, you keep me waiting."

"I had to count my rolls of hen wire. I think that clunk Larsen made off with one. If he did, he'll get it where the chicken got the ax, when Jerome Green catches up with him.

You want anything else besides expensive olives and the rest of that truck Del Smiley can't afford?"

"Yes, I do! I want two pounds of that sirloin steak you've got laid away for Judge Clawson and them."

"That'll cost you."

"And cut off that wad of suet before you weigh it."

"Del'll be real pleased when he sees the bill."

"You can write the whole order down on the book. So Ma'll know what you've charged us for it."

Charles said nothing, but the scars on his face turned red, so she guessed the shot had gone home. She'd always suspected that Ma checked up on him sometimes, and now she was pretty sure she'd been right.

"Next time don't go pawing around," he said, plunking down the wrapped steak.

"Pawing around my foot! If your shelves get messed up, you ought to check up on Miles. Or Julie." She stopped, suddenly remembering. "Where *is* Julie?"

"Gone to the bank. Clear out now, Elsie. I want to close up the store."

"Mercy, I thought banks closed at three. Or am I mistaken?"

Charles had got out the little white quill again and was working around his gums. "You know, you're getting fat, Elsie."

He was looking right at her middle, where the things were.

Elsie spun around, clutching her parcels. "What if I am?" Headed for the door, she said over her shoulder, "I'm pregnant again, if you care to know."

Had he seen anything? Shoot, what if he had? It's all in the family. I'm his sister, anyway.

Worried, she was nearly home before she thought again about Julie. Well, if there were anything going around, Delbert would know. He picked up a lot of gossip in the bank.

❋   ❋   ❋

In June, Starball created its own magic of summer, with high, blue days, cool winds, and a great thrust of green, lush as a rain forest, in the woods along its shores. The salt pond was rimmed with snowbanks of pin cherry and shadbush bloom, beach peas sprouted, and out of the pebbles around the old houses tough little sea forget-me-not put forth its first gray-green velvety leaves. On the Indian shell mound thorn bushes blossomed, a froth of white humming with bumblebees. By day the beach rocks were warm to the touch, pleasant to sit on. Mary Cartwright sat on them sometimes, feeling their age and their smoothness with her fingers. The warmth was comforting; it seemed to come from deep down rather than from the sun overhead, as if the icy core of the desolate place were melting, with grace and friendliness saying, Don't be scared. Things are better. They may be better still.

She had been scared. Since the middle of winter, when things had gone so badly for Chris, she had been scared to death. On the first day, when she had come here with Sue to clean the horrible dead house, the scare had turned into icy fear, clutching at her heart. Chris was so strange; he had grown thin and haggard and silent; it had seemed crazy, moving here, so far away from everything. She would have gone anywhere, unafraid, with Chris, so long as he was the Chris she knew. Anything he wanted she would do, work until her fingers dropped off. And had.

Always before, he had talked everything over with her. This time he hadn't. He had just come home one day and said, "We're getting out. We're going." The only thing he talked about was, she must not write Larry. Larry mustn't know.

"He's all right where he is, on his own. If we write him about this mess I've got us into, he'll come flying home to help out, and what could he do? Be in the same mess we are, is all. Let him alone, Mary. Let him finish school. He might be able to help then, though the Lord knows I ought to be able to pull us out of it before that. He'll know when he comes home in June, anyway, and that's time enough."

Laurance, their son in Boston Law School—he had this year's heavy schedule to finish, and then one final year which would be tougher. He had too much on his mind already. She must not write him about hers and Chris's troubles. Desperately she wanted to—Larry was a rock. Just having him around would help his father. But Chris was right. Once Larry knew what had happened, he would come home.

On the day Chris and George had hauled their things down Starball in the truck, it had seemed to Mary that overnight her familiar world had snapped in pieces and blown away on the wind. In bed with Chris, that first night, she had sensed Chris's body, stiff and straight beside her, as if even in sleep he could not let go. If he were asleep—she couldn't tell. Everybody else in the house was, and George was snoring.

George and Sue and us. Their three kids and our four. All in this place at once, sleeping helter-skelter around until we can think where to put so many beds. And breathing. So many people breathing. She had wanted to scream.

This place. No wonder people had abandoned it. Wild, bleak, and that sound day and night of water moving. *Hissh-hussh*. Pause. *Hissh-hussh* again. Till it got like a sound inside your head. And when it stopped as it mostly did when the tide pulled back over the flats, you heard *rabble-dabble, rabble-dabble*, the brook running, at the end of the beach.

A strange light growing at the window had startled her. Not a fire. It was too white. Some prowler on the beach with a flashlight? No, it was steady. She got out on the floor, silently eased herself between the scattering of beds and cots to the open window.

What a fool! Moonlight.

But it was not the moonlight she was used to in town.

Beyond the cove mouth, across a tremendous flat plate of water, the moon was just pulling herself free of the horizon. Behind her, the huge sky was pallid, ice-white. The cliffs on the far side of the cove reared black and towering, the ledges where they ended dead-black, too, but catching sparkles from the great bar of cold silver, which grew as she watched it, widening on the ocean, thrusting a long finger into the cove, ending in glitter on the wet beach rocks below the house.

Shuddering, she thought, It's so lonesome. It even smells lonesome. But that was foolish, too, because what she smelled was only a chilly small breeze blowing up out of the southeast, heavy with salt. From frozen wild, unhuman places, though, not where anyone warm had ever been, and coming over this desolate-as-a-dead-face cove, where the poor man had drowned . . .

From the bed Chris said softly, "Mary, you'll get your death out there. Come back to bed." And she had been glad to, glad beyond belief that he was awake. She had got in beside him, feeling his warmth and the sheltering circle of his arm.

"What on earth were you doing out there? Freezing?"

"Pretty nearly. I . . . guess I was watching the moon. I never saw it come up out of the water before. I feel like the Ancient Mariner."

"Yeah. So do I. Who's he?"

"Chris—"

"I know. It's a god-awful hole. I wish I could have done better."

"You've done more than better, darling. You've pulled us out of a terrible spot. Here we are, we and the kids with a place to be. Sue and I'll have fun fixing it up. It won't be god-awful then, you'll see."

"If I'd had the sense God gave a goose, I wouldn't have got us into a bind like this."

"Sh-h! You've done wonders and I'm proud of you."

"We could have stayed. Taken handouts. I . . . maybe I ought to have given in, Mary."

"The day you give in, I'll stop being proud. Go to sleep now, honey, you need your sleep."

Relieved, as she felt his tense body letting go, Mary set her jaw. He wasn't going to find out that she was scared. Ever. And the kids weren't going to either. Nobody was.

But by the time June came around, she knew that there hadn't been so much need to be scared. Scared, yes, worried. But not in a panic. They weren't out of the woods yet, but they weren't lost in them either.

Larry would be home soon for summer vacation. Chris was better. A good sign of that was that he was more touchy now than anything else. The grimness, the silence were gone. Work had always been his life, and he was working—George's house was now livable; he and Sue had moved into it with all their things, to Mary and Chris an infinite relief. For while Mary dearly loved them, she couldn't deny that at times they'd been irksome—so many kids around underfoot, and Sue's quick temper which flew out sometimes before she could stop it.

Chris had already started work on the third old house, which was to be Waldo's, though Waldo said there was no hurry about that—a house was for winter. He still slept aboard his boat or around in the woods in a bedroll. Just now he was sleeping over by the garden clearing, trying to keep coons and deer and other night pests out of the vegetable seedlings, and, he said, to be company for Abigail the cow. Chris, he said blandly, as if the matter had been planned and already settled, had better begin on a house for her next. She needed a roof more than he did. But on this Chris dug his heels in.

"That critter's strictly Waldo's business," he told Mary. "He stole her and it's only a question of time before somebody comes after her. If he wants a cowshed, he can build it himself."

Waldo did not take this amiss. What he did take was a waterproof tarp from one of Chris's carefully protected lumber piles. This he arranged in a sheltered stand of trees on the edge of the grass clearing as a roof for Abigail the cow. "Do for summertime," he said. "Keep off rain." Right now he and the kids were too busy building deer-scare around garden, but before snow flew they'd find time to make nice varm shed for Abigail the cow. "Or maybe," he told Mary, "by that time Chris get over grumps."

Mary couldn't help but side with him, and neither could Sue. So far as Abigail the cow was concerned, Chris stood alone. The kids loved her dearly and George loved cottage cheese. Her plenty flowed over the table from meal to meal —milk, butter, cream, sour milk for cooking, buttermilk— the only things in the world, it seemed to Mary, that she didn't have to economize on. If anyone from the Plummer farm came and took away Abigail the cow, Mary didn't know what anybody would do.

Waldo was building a fence around the garden, setting nine-foot poles—not that it would do much good, he said, if the deer took it into their heads to jump in. He had seen one of the damn things go twenty feet in the air once when he had scared it up in the woods. But he was thinking. He guessed he would come up with something.

He did. He scavenged old tin cans and rusty metal from various dumps around town; every night after school he took the kids on a jaunt around-shore to salvage old rope. Quite a lot of warp from wrecked lobster traps could be untangled from seaweed piles, especially in spring after the winter storms had brought it in. The kids were active and enthusiastic; it wasn't long before Waldo had a great coil. Then he constructed a wonderful combination of objects hung to jangle on rope strung crisscross above the garden. He would crawl into his bedroll with a rope's end close by his hand; every once in a while throughout the night, half waking, he would give a great yank. The tin cans were of all sizes, from five-gallon oils down to condensed milks. Each gave off a different musical note, as did the various shapes and lengths of rusty metal.

The first time he used it, the resulting clash-together set birds to singing in the trees and scared Abigail the cow so that she burst loose from her shelter and went ramping off into the woods. He had to get out of his warm bedroll, hunt her up, and spend time soothing her shattered nerves. It was nearly daylight before he got her back together again. After that, until she got used to the racket, he yanked gently, played his instrument—more like, he said, a tune. Then he got really interested and practiced on it and after a while swore he could play "My Country, 'Tis of Thee." Rob, who was generally to be found dogging Waldo's heels, said if you gave it a little scope it did sound like that, though he hadn't realized it did until Waldo'd told him what to listen for. Almost incidentally, the creation served the purpose it had been built for—the deer left the area and no one saw any around the pond all through spring and early summer.

Waldo was always inventing something complicated or strange which either worked or didn't; if it didn't, he abandoned it cheerfully and turned to something else. He was always coming home with stuff which could be used or eaten that he'd salvaged or picked up from who knew where. Mary and Sue were all for it—many a time Waldo's donations had solved the problem of a skimpy meal; but Chris was edgy. He hadn't forgotten the short lobsters lifted out of somebody's traps, and, of course, there was Abigail the cow. Bothering a man's traps, Chris pointed out to Waldo, could end up with a stiff fine or a jail sentence. In the old days, before there'd been so much law in the area, people had got shot for it.

Waldo shrugged and grinned. "Okay. No more. But people got to eat, Chris, dear."

Around the shores, particularly after a storm, there were always traps washed up, some badly smashed, some in fairly good shape. On the quiet, working by himself on one of the islands, Waldo began salvaging these. This was also against the law; even wrecked on a beach, a lobster trap still belonged to the fisherman who had set it. His number, sometimes his name, would be on it. To Waldo, an old trap was an old trap; some he had spotted on offshore islands had to his knowledge lain weathering for weeks. He gathered in all he could find, using the materials from the worst-smashed ones to repair others in better shape. This took time, and he had to be gone from Starball while he was doing it.

When, after the second day, he did not come back, Chris said at suppertime, "Well, I guess Waldo's gone again. He always goes, after a while."

"You mean he won't be back at all?" Mary said. "Why, he must've been here last night. And this morning too. Anyway, the milk was here. Somebody milked Abigail and none of us can."

"I can," Rob said. "He showed me how. I did it."

"Good for you!" Chris said, but he put down his fork and sat looking glumly at his plate. "If he's gone, we've sure got to do something about that cow. She don't belong to us."

Desolation passed over the table in a wave. To lose Waldo was the ultimate disaster, but to lose Abigail the cow, too, was piling it on. They had not only thrived on her abundance, they loved her. With Waldo's gentling she had calmed down. Sudden, unexpected noises could upset her now, but the kids knew about that and were careful. Any one of them could stake her out to pasture, scratch her between the horns. They took turns checking to make sure she was all right—hadn't tangled her rope or anything—and Blob-top's favorite seat was on Abigail the cow's back when she was lying down, and they both watched while the others helped Waldo build a garden fence.

"Chris, we've got to keep her. How can we possibly do without—" Mary stopped, seeing his face.

Paul, the twelve-year-old, stared stormily at his father. "Yes, and you know if we take her back, that crazy man'll shoot her." He glared desperately around the table, and Pete, the youngest, burst into tears.

"Look," Rob said. He had been sitting getting redder and redder in the face, always a sign with him of a great decision to make. "I know where Waldo is. He asked me not to tell. He's doing something. When it's done, he'll be back. So . . . so everybody shut up! And stop howling, you pee-baby!"

"Well, it's Waldo's cow," Chris said. "If he's coming back, he'll have to tend to it himself." He grinned at Mary as the clamor subsided.

And then one day Waldo appeared with a boatload of lobster traps, which he set along the rocky shores outside the cove.

"So ve in business," he told Chris triumphantly. "Now ve git little bit cash, ve need it."

"God, I'm glad to see you, boy!" Chris said. "No short lobsters this time, hanh?"

"Mercy, no. Never touch *them*. Leave them grow up, make big. First haul, ve buy another bag feed for Abigail. Next vun, hot dog, roast meat, doughnut. For kids. You kids get busy now, ketch pollock, sculpin, all kinds bait. For lobster trap. Ve go now, do that." He gathered the entire batch and went off with them in the boat.

Waldo had a way with kids. They were always tagging after him; they would do anything for him. Mary and Sue could not fathom how it was that the dreariest kind of chore turned into a game if Waldo were around, and got done, too, with no whining or digging in of heels. Now that school was out, he would take them whenever he could, in the truck to town, in the boat, or beachcombing the shores around the cove. Things of all kinds washed up from the ocean, some useful, some not; they found old trap heads and bait pockets and warp for Waldo's traps, and everybody had his own pile of flotsam and jetsam, treasures stacked in private and woe betide anyone who touched. Now that school was out, on balmy days when the sea was calm, he would take them picnicking in the boat, off somewhere, off anywhere, and they would forage their own lunches. At first Mary offered whatever she happened to have in the house—it would be skimpy, but then it would be if they'd stayed home. Waldo always shook his head.

"Ve eat, don't vorry."

And they would. They would come back in the late afternoon, sunburned and tired, not even hungry for supper. What had they had? Oh, they had had chowder made out of milk and clams and mussels, or lobsters or fish; Waldo had showed them how to find greens, dandelion and pigweed, in a field on one of the islands. Or he had caught a monstrous great haddock, slit it and nailed it to a board and broiled it over a fire. They had had crackers and bread and butter with with it. On the way home they had had what was left over of everything. And they had brought fish for dinner tomorrow.

Mary wondered wryly what would have happened if she'd put dandelion greens on the table at home, when they'd lived in town. Into the garbage can they'd have gone, more than likely. But the kids assured her that they were lovely greens; everybody had dug lots, so they could bring lots home. Waldo put in salt pork. Besides, they were food for free.

The kids were getting knowledgeable about finding food for free around the woods and shores. Once, when they had come home all but covered with dried mud, Mary found that they had had cattail roots for lunch, among other things. Everybody had helped to dig the cattails out of an island swamp. They had brought some home. They were *good*. Both she and Sue had gasped at the size of the washing-to-be; but the next morning, to their astonishment, the kids were all down on the shore of the pond, each scrubbing mud out of his own clothes, with Waldo superintending the job, even rigging an extra length of clothesline.

"It's a godsend," Mary said to Chris. "Just to have the kids out from underfoot for a whole day at a time. And not even supper to get for a crowd, just for you and me."

They were sitting on the steps of the old Randall house, watching Waldo unload the kids from the boat into his dory. They had been gone since daylight; it was six o'clock and the boat had just chugged in.

"Sure must be," Chris said. "I don't know, though. Sometimes I—" He stopped, watching the laden dory put out for shore, with Rob at the oars. Rob was making heavy weather of it, splashing a good bit, but the dory was moving.

"Why, what bothers you, dear?" Mary asked, surprised. "They're having a wonderful time, and they're getting brown as Indians and growing like weeds. And learning things too. Look at Rob. When we first came here, he'd scarcely seen a pair of oars."

"I know. I'm all for it. Waldo's a heck of a good guy, and I don't believe we could have got along here without him. But, damn it, Mary, he's bringing home a lot of stuff he hasn't bought and paid for. I don't like it. And those kids worship the ground he walks on, especially Rob. Anything Waldo does or says is gospel to Rob because it's Waldo. Rob's growing up. I can't have him thinking that all he has to do when he wants something is to go out and grab it."

"They did it in France. In the army. When they needed food, they took it. People's chickens and"—she glanced at him out of the corner of her eye—"cows."

"Waldo? In the army? I didn't know that."

"He told Rob he was all through the war. Chris, dear, most of the things he brings he's got for himself, like fish. They aren't things he's had to pay for. Maybe it depends. On what people need, I mean." She wanted to go on and say that she herself would steal anything she could find if the children were hungry; but it would only make him feel inadequate again, so she didn't. She watched, with affection, the big man coming happily up the beach with Blob-top on his shoulder. From somewhere in her reading she remembered a phrase that seemed to describe Waldo, and she dredged for it. " 'A picker-up of unconsidered trifles,' " she murmured.

"Yeah, Well, that roll of new hen wire he brought home to fence the garden with ain't a trifle. That cost something. I dunno, Mary, I—" He stopped, as Waldo came within hearing distance, and in spite of himself grinned in answer to Waldo's grin. "Hi, Waldo. Have a good time?"

"Sure, lovely. Ve got awful tired vuns here. They had supper. Oh-h, they eat! They go bed now." He slipped George's staggering youngest from his shoulder. "Ve got six haddock. Big vuns. Dinner tomorrow."

"Who's that?" Rob said. He was looking at the turnaround on the far side of the brook. "There's a car over there."

This was so unusual that everybody got up to stare. No car had been in the turnaround since they had been here at Starball—only Chris's truck. This one had pulled in beside the truck and two young women and a man were getting out of it. The man had turned his back and had opened a rear door. He was apparently getting something out of the back seat, for all they could see of him was his bent back and a pair of legs.

"Oh, I know who one of them is," Rob said. "That one in the pink dress is Julie Plummer. She was a senior in the school this year."

"Plummer, hanh?" Waldo stared, galvanized. "I go milk cow now." With great strides he set off along the beach.

"Go now hide cow," Chris said. "More like. It won't do him any good, if that's what they've come about."

"Oh, maybe they're just out riding around," Mary said hastily, seeing the gathering storm on the faces of the children. "Mrs. Plummer wouldn't send two girls after a cow— Chris! That's Larry!"

Rob let out a howl of joy. He tore along the beach at the head of a line of yelling kids. The young man just coming off the walkway over the brook was overwhelmed for a moment in a flying melee of arms and legs, so that no one could see whether he were Larry or not. There was no doubt of it, however. He had dropped his suitcases and he and Rob were doing a whirling dance on the beach, their arms around each other and yelling.

"Oh, Chris," Mary said. "How wonderful!"

"God, is it!" Chris said. "Thought he wasn't due for a week yet." He went on under his breath, "Well, I guess he had to know sometime."

"He already knows," Mary said. "When I wrote him where to find us, I told him."

Larry didn't seem to be upset, not by anything. He bellowed, "Hi, Mumma, hi, Puppa!" and came bounding along the beach, leaving the others behind and the kids to manage his suitcases, while he tried to hug both of his parents at once. "Gee, what a swell place you found! This is wonderful—you'll never know how it looks to me after the city! Been hotter than a griddle." He stepped back and stared admiringly at the houses. "Gee, Pop, what a beautiful job! Did you go to town on those!"

Mary, all at once seeing the houses through Larry's eyes, realized suddenly that this particular worry had been just that—a worry and nothing more. The two houses in their fresh paint and new shingles were snug and neat. They looked comfortable and lived in, and not only that—they were beautiful.

Chris was looking a little dazed. He stared at the houses and glanced back at Larry; then, to Mary's delight, she saw on his face the almost foolish, embarrassed expression he had always got when he had outdone himself and knew it, and had to listen to someone admire his work. She hadn't seen that look for a long time.

Thank God, she thought. Maybe he's getting through his silly head how proud we are of him and of the job he's done.

"Sorry about my manners," Larry said. He had turned to the two girls who had come more slowly along the beach and had waited tactfully in the background. "These are the Plummer girls, Nan and Julie. This is my beautiful old lady and my handsome old man. We're glad to see each other."

"So it would seem," Nan said, smiling. "Does he ever run down, Mrs. Cartwright? He picked me up on the train and talked all day."

"Oh, I always pick up girls on trains," Larry said. He grinned. "And with this one I got a bonus. I found out we were both headed for Granite Hills, and I was crazy to hear where Starball was and what it was like, and she knew. So then I thought, Ow! Five miles toting two suitcases full of torts, and me still weak in the knees from final exams! When she let drop that she was going to be met at the station with a car, I really flirted with the girl."

"Oh, he was so pitiful," Nan said. "I practically got tears in my eyes, listening to him. But I'd just got through finals myself, so I knew how it was. Ludwig was a terror," she went on, smiling at her sister, who did not respond. "He nearly dumped me, Julie. I'll tell you about it. Anyway, rather than have this man's skeleton found in the woods next spring, I thought we'd better haul him down."

Mary had been wondering about the other girl, who

seemed to be a sulky sort of young person, or maybe just silent and self-contained. So far she hadn't spoken a word.

She said now, "Somebody had to come, sometime. Ma wants to talk to Mr. Cartwright. She's been wondering how to get word to him."

At this there was a sudden stir among the circle of children. They had been standing, Mary realized, staring intently at the Plummer girls. Now the stares had become ominous. The kids glanced at each other with faces like thunderclouds. Then they departed in a body up the steps of the Randall house. Somebody gave the door a good hard slam. In a moment Mary heard the back door close, and Rob went along the beach toward the walkway, not running, but walking with long, fast strides.

Oh, my Lord, the cow, Mary thought. It must be about the cow.

Chris's own face had darkened. He said in the voice of a man not about to give an inch, "What does Mrs. Plummer want with me?"

"She wants to ask you—" Julie suddenly giggled, burst out laughing.

"Something funny?" Chris said, glowering.

"Those are the maddest-looking kids I ever saw. Four windows full. My goodness!" Julie gasped.

Inside the front windows, six identical scowls, six identical thrust-out lower lips were lined up, six faces glared, uncompromising, grim. The only variation was Blob-top, whose nose was hideously flattened against the glass.

Mary couldn't help herself; she burst out laughing too.

"They've been on an all-day p-picnic . . . tired out . . . sc-scatty as a bunch of field mice . . ." But it was no use. She choked and stopped.

The kids, affronted, left the windows, one by one, with great dignity, and Mary's laughter pealed again.

"Oh, Chris, darling, tell them we'll send back that c-cussed cow, and you'll explain."

"Cow?" Nan Plummer said. "It wasn't about a cow, was it, Julie? At least, you didn't mention—"

Julie's puzzled look went from Mary to Chris. "You've got me guessing, Mr. Cartwright. Ma wants to have you re-shingle her big dairy barn and build an addition. For cows, I guess, but that's the only connection. She wondered if you'd have time to come and talk to her about it. Uh . . . she asked me particularly to say please."

On the way back up the Starball road Julie gave her absorbed attention to driving Abigail's car. Nan, delighted to be getting home, to be seeing everybody at last, especially Julie, realized that she was getting very little response to her excited and affectionate talk. When she had got off the train, she had regretted her promise to see that the brash young man got transportation down Starball before she went home; but it would be a chance to see Julie and talk to her before she saw her mother. From Maureen's letters Nan knew that Julie was in trouble at home and at school; she knew about the dance-band project. Earlier, in the spring, she had written to Julie: "Don't be such a little fool. You'll spoil all our plans, you nut."

It had been the same kind of forthright talking to that she and Julie had always given each other when needed. It got no reply.

Then, two weeks ago, she had got an offhand, slapdash letter from Julie, which had worried her a good deal since it didn't sound like anything Julie had ever written her before. She couldn't tell from it whether Julie was upset or kidding; but she had taken a chance and had written: "Darling, I'm up to my neck in finals. I'll be home in two weeks, so hold everything, and when I get there we'll tackle Ma together. Ludwig's being very tough."

In the old days Julie would have understood; she would have waited. Instead, she fired off a scribbled note: "Don't bother if you're busy. I'm making out on my own, thanks. Ma's going to find out she can't push me around the way she does the rest of you. Have fun with Ludwig."

This did worry Nan. She went back to memorizing the Beethoven which was a part of her finals and played it well enough when the time came, but not so well as she might have if she had been able to sleep better nights.

Now she was home and here was Julie—behind a front as hard as glass.

"Julie, honey—"

"Don't talk to me now. This is Ma's gold-filled, simon-pure Model A. I'm trying not to get squashed bugs on the windshield."

"Julie, listen. This is Nan."

"Friend of Ludwig. Whoops!" A branch of alder, where the road narrowed, had slapped against the side of the car. "If that's put a scratch on, I'll hear."

"Julie, I'll talk to Ma."

"Nan, my love, shut your beautiful trap or I'll drive up a tree."

"Julie, I don't know you. You're all jangles and glitters."

"So I am, aren't I? It's all that jazz I play. Ludwig never heard of jazz, did he? I expect you don't care for it either."

"Of course I do. I think it's wonderful. I'm dying to hear you play some. Julie, darling, what *is* it?"

"Are you, really? Well, listen." With both hands Julie began to beat out on the rim of the steering wheel a thumping, syncopated rhythm.

The car lurched toward the side of the road. Nan reached over and turned off the ignition.

"How about that?" Julie said. "Needs a few clicks here and there for the jizzamaroo. Might sound better if I had a class ring on my finger, wouldn't you say?"

Nan's temper flew. "And why haven't you got one? Of all the—of all the damn fool silly ways to get back at Ma! I know you can't stand Mr. Graves, but just one year, Julie! He has such a lot to offer, you could have learned from him and gone on from there, and we could've been together again. It's your own foolish fault and I could shake you!"

"I've been shaken. Plenty. I'm not taking any more of it, not even from you. In fact, I might do a little shaking myself. I'm going to, when the time comes."

"Why? It'll only make things worse. And in the meantime you go rattling around Gilmore's."

"So what's wrong with that?" Julie said. "You used to go there yourself."

"I went once with Joe Baker, and that was it. Gilmore got after Joe and me both, trying to get us to drum up custom with the high-school kids. It made me sick. Julie, let me talk to Ma. I know she's put her foot down about you taking your senior year over again, because you failed it, but I might be able to make her see that if you came with me, you could just as well finish up at a Boston school."

"You're a little late for that. Ma hasn't got the money to send me to Boston now."

"Of course she has!"

"Know what she's done with it? She gave it away. A scholarship for some bright kid from Bristol. Somebody who deserves it. I don't. Absolute justice, that's Ma."

"She couldn't have. I don't believe it!"

"Oh, she does that every once in a while, didn't you know? Anonymous donations to the worthy, and nobody supposed to know."

Nan stared at her. "Then how did you find out? Did she tell you?"

"Not she. I got it from our sister Elsie, who leaks. She got it from Del at the bank. Poor Elsie, she can't help it, she peddles quite a lot of the bank's private business around town. Telling me that was her good deed for the day."

"Julie, she must've made it up!"

"Oh, well, whatever, doesn't matter. I'm not going back to school. Ma can put that in her pipe and smoke it. I've got other fish to fry now."

"I know. Jamie Stetson's band."

"Anything the matter with that?"

"I don't blame you for wanting to play with a band, you know that. It's darned good experience for you, but—" Nan stopped. She had run out of arguments and had got nowhere. "Is it a good band, Julie?"

"No, not very. I'm the best one in it."

"Yes, I expect you probably are."

Julie looked at Nan and her eyes were bleak. "I wish you could have got home sooner," she said, and leaned down and started the car.

Abigail said, "I won't coddle a tantrum, Nan. That is what this is, a tantrum, pure and simple. Julie's not eighteen— what kind of a life will she have if she finds out this young that all she's got to do to get her way is to worry everybody into giving in? She won't find it out at home."

Ma doesn't know about the dance band and Gilmore's. And I can't tell her. The way Julie feels now, everybody against her, she'd hate me forever, Nan thought.

"Ma, it's got to be more than a tantrum. There's something more. I can't find out what it is."

"Well, I'm sorry you can't. I was hoping you could straighten things out when you got home."

"I can if you'll let her go back with me when I go. Please, Ma, I do mean it. She's stubborn, she won't bend—" Nan almost said, "any more than you will," but she did not.

"No," Abigail said. "She's made her bed, she'll have to lie

in it. She's not going to get her own way in this. She's going
back to school next fall."

Maureen said, when Nan asked her if she knew where
Julie might be, "Off somewhere by herself, thank God. Making a nuisance of herself any place but here." Maureen's
wedding was only a couple of days away and she was showing some strain. "I wish I knew what's got into her. She
doesn't like Arthur, and she makes no bones of saying so,
pretty nearly to his face, I might add. She said last night she
was glad you'd got home in time for the wedding, she'd
rather die than stand up with me when I got married to
Arthur Bickford. He was in the porch swing, and I guess he
heard her. He was rucked up about something all evening."

"Oh, dear, I'm sorry," Nan said. "She shouldn't have done
that, Maureen."

Nan herself wasn't too taken with Arthur. He was being
a fussbudget about the wedding and the new apartment; he
was also acting like a son of the house, which of course he
would be, but no need to force it in quite that bossy, pro-
prietory way. It would be cruel, though, to tell Maureen
that. Julie had probably tangled with Arthur over something and hadn't held back.

"Between her and Elsie, I'm going nuts," Maureen said.
"I wanted the wedding to be simple, and Elsie's bound and
determined to build her idea of a beautiful bower out of
greenery and lilacs in the parlor, and Julie's backing her up
with crepe-paper dingle-dangles." Her smile was plaintive
and a little wry. "I wish you'd tie their tails together and
hang them over the clothesline, Nan, till I get married and
gone."

"Well, I will!" Nan said with indignation. "And set them
both spinning too. Don't you let anybody spoil your wedding, honey!"

"I won't," Maureen said. "Oh, Nan, I knew you'd be able

to help." After a moment she went on, "Julie might just be at the store, Nan. She's supposed to be helping Charles, but I haven't seen her there lately."

Charles said, "No, I don't know where she is. It's not worth my time to bother to find out. She's not here, thank God. You're kind of slow coming around to see your relatives, aren't you?"

"I've been meaning to," Nan said. "But I got home so tired out I haven't done anything, really."

"Well, no matter," Charles said. "You see me now."

He stood solidly behind his counter, picking his teeth with his eternal quill toothpick, his face turned slightly away from her. He did this from habit, nearly always, because one of his cheeks was less scarred than the other, or so he thought, and this had been true in the beginning. Through the years his scars had grown much less noticeable, as the surgeons had told him they would, but he still turned his face away.

"How are you and Clarice?" Nan asked. She didn't point out that when he had been in Boston last fall for a final session with the doctors he hadn't bothered to look her up either.

Actually she hadn't minded. Seeing Charles was always a strain, since he didn't seem to like anyone in his family very much. It was as if he blamed them all for what had happened to him, though for years the whole Plummer household had revolved around him, everybody trying hard to help, to make him feel better, to love him, and no one getting anywhere. He would take nobody's love and he would give none back. She remembered the peace which had descended on the household when he had gone upstate to a business school and had been away for a year. He had come back married to Clarice Burney, a girl whom he had met at the school, and Ma had turned the store over to them to run. Charles never went home now, and nobody saw very much of Clarice either, though she was a pleasant, quiet person whom everybody liked.

Charles took the toothpick out of his mouth. "We're all right," he said. "Or would be, if Ma'd keep her nose out of the business."

Well, there was no answer to be made to that.

Nan, when she and Julie had worked in the store, had heard many an argument over that. Charles had always been fiercely determined to use his own methods, his own ways. They were not Abigail's ways.

He could make a profit even in a depression, he said, if she'd stop hounding him about the quality of his goods and cutting corners. Of course you had to cut corners. In business you made what you could, where you could. Everybody did it—how was he any better? Other businessmen in town would think he was crazy if he didn't take advantage of every loophole there was. And why not?

"Your own conscience and dissatisfied customers, that's why not," Abigail had said succinctly.

"What if some hardheads do get mad? Let them get over it."

"Your customers are your real stock in trade, and right now you need every one you've got. I've never had a dissatisfied customer in my life. There's no place for one here." She had then put the stopper in. "Not in my store, Charles."

She was hard to take. Her nose was into everything. She would appear unexpectedly, ask to check the stock and the books. Charles had had to take time to fake a set of books— a nuisance, but it seemed to shut her up for a time. At any rate, she'd seem satisfied. Then she had made him take down a sign he'd put up that he'd thought was pretty funny and which said what he'd wanted to say, as well: *In God We Trust. Others Pay Cash.*

"I've got customers I've trusted for years, Charles. And

they trust me, they know they can. That'll be all of that sign."

"You'll get damn poor pay these times!" he'd stormed. "Every Johnny-come-lately in town's looking for stuff on tick."

"If people are hard up, they need credit."

He'd taken down the sign, but Nan happened to know he had put it carefully away. Both she and Julie had got to know Charles's methods in the store pretty well. He had made their lives miserable, his notion being that Abigail had put them there to spy on him, which she had not, nor had they the slightest inclination to spy. Their one desire was to get out of working for him; they had made his life miserable by plaguing him, so that sometimes at the end of a day they would have him jumping up and down. But they had no intention whatever of putting up with the nastiness and the row that would follow, if he ever found out they had carried tales to their mother.

Charles put the toothpick back into his mouth. "Well, I tell myself she won't be around forever. She's looking pretty tired these days."

"She's worried," Nan said shortly.

"About Pa? How is the old boy? Goofy as ever?"

"I don't know. He doesn't know me, not yet, but Ma says he will," Nan said steadily. "I suppose she would look tired, with all she has to do."

"Yeah," Charles said. He bellowed suddenly, "Hey, what'd you want in here? Go on back out there and stay, like I told you."

"What?" Nan said, startled. "Oh."

Her young brother Miles had started to come in through the annex door. He was in the process of withdrawing as she glanced around, and he grinned slightly at her and winked.

So Miles was having his turn now. Why on earth does Ma do it? Nan thought. Julie and I could take care of ourselves

—we had each other—but I don't believe for a minute Miles can.

Miles was a quiet boy, going on twelve now, with pleasant manners and a sense of humor. His quick grin and the wink, as he'd ducked back through the door, had reminded Nan startlingly of Felix—just as, she told herself grimly as she turned to go, Charles's manners, the way he is now, are a living image of Uncle Jos. Both of them, unbelievable. Something you'd have to hear and see before you could believe it at all.

"Not saying good-by?" Charles asked. "Well, well. You want Julie, try Jamie Stetson's place down by the station. That little slut routs around there most of her time these days."

"Thanks, Charles," Nan said.

One thing, she thought, as she walked down the street, if he thinks Ma's going to wear out, he's got a long wait coming.

Hard work did not wear her mother out; she had worked all her life, not because she had to, but with zest, because she liked it. At forty-nine, her thin body was tough as a slat. She had never had a sick day. The look of strain Charles had so hopefully noticed was worry, of course. She was terribly worried about Felix, who was not getting better now; as a matter of fact, he was getting worse, his spells of confusion coming oftener and lasting longer. Nan could see the change in him in the time she had been away. He was much thinner and very frail; so far he had not recognized her at all.

Ma must see it too. And then, of course, there's Julie.

Ma's changing too. She's harder now, tougher. Maybe she has to be. Hard to talk to, and she never was that, not with me; we could always see each other's point pretty well. Still, about the only thing I've talked to her about since I've been home is Julie. It's almost as if she doesn't hear me. Or, yes, she hears me, but she won't let herself think that what I'm

saying makes any sense, she's dug herself in so far about
what she's sure is the right thing. And it isn't right, not now,
for Julie. Maybe it began as a tantrum, but now it's something Julie can't handle and Ma won't see it. All she does is
say no and get that look on her face as if it was carved out
of marble. . . . Oh, my goodness, is *this* the place?

Jamie Stetson's old railway coach was abandoned and
looked it. Nan eyed the blank dusty windows and the blis-
tered green paint. The step gave spongily under her feet
as she knocked on the door. When nobody answered, she
tired the knob, which turned easily in her hand.

If there isn't anyone here, I'd better not go in, she thought,
and gasped at the scene of mess and disorder inside—un-
made bunks, with gray-soiled blankets and no linen; ashtrays
crammed with old cigarette butts; a helter-skelter of dirty
dishes and stale food piled on the table, on the chairs, on the
top of a rusty oilstove. Something smelled very dead. She
saw what it was—a chunk of raw, reddish-black meat half
out of its wrapper on the floor; some creature—a rat?—had
apparently been gnawing on it. These housekeeping disasters
cluttered both ends of the car; in the middle was a cleared
space for a circle of kitchen chairs and battered music stands,
and an ancient, spinet-type piano.

The dance band . . . they must stay here, four or five of
them, when they're in town. A headquarters, where they live
and . . . and rehearse. So Julie must come here too. Julie,
here?

I'd better go. I'm snooping, and I mustn't.

As she turned to go, the skirt of her jacket brushed over
the keys of the piano. From inside the peeling, banged-up
case a few forlorn wires stirred with a whispery discord. Nan
hesitated, put both hands down, played a few bars, and
turned away. The piano was hopeless; it couldn't have been
tuned for years. Some ivories were missing from the keys;
the ones remaining were grayish, crusted with dirt. Some

keys didn't even sound. What could Julie's fastidious fingers have been doing, what could they have done with this sad, broken, junky wreck? If she had been here at all, for whatever desperate reason . . .

Nettie said at suppertime, "No, I don't know where anybody is. Your father's had one of his bad turns and I been with him all afternoon. Dr. Graham's just been here and your mother's up there now."

"How bad?" Nan said.

"Bad enough. He's better now. He's sleeping."

"Will . . . will he be all right?"

"As all right as he ever is, I guess."

"Nettie, I'm sorry I wasn't around to help. But I've been hunting Julie all afternoon. I can't think where she could be."

"That one," Nettie said. "Who ever knows where she is? I s'pose she thinks I *like* to keep her supper hot, with all the rest there is to do." She started to bang a kettle of hot potatoes into the sink, remembered Felix sleeping upstairs, and set it down gently. "She says Charles keeps her late at the store, but I don't believe it for a minute. Her bed ain't made and I be blest if I'll make it—she don't appreciate nothing and she's got more time than I have. . . ." Nettie subsided into mumbles for a moment, snuffing with indignation, as she put some vegetable dishes on the table. Her indignation seldom meant much; it was an outlet for hurt feelings or worry, or whatever at the moment was stirring Nettie up. If she had not been busy with Felix all afternoon, Nan knew, no bed in the house would have escaped a thorough airing and spreading up.

Nettie sat down at the table with a long sigh. "Well, thank the good Lord in his mercy I can set down at last and eat. Them chops is nice ones. I give Charles a good going-over about the last ones he sent, and I guess he's see the light.

You got some mail, honey, there by your plate. Two letters, one's from that music school, the other's an ad or something, anyway mailed here in town."

The letter from the music school was a report of her finals and a résumé of her year's work. Delighted, she saw that she had done well, had come off with honors. And did she want a job as an accompanist at Berkshire for the summer? The pay was good, the experience would be wonderful, and they'd be pleased to have her.

Did she want it? Who wouldn't? What a chance, and one she'd longed for and had never dreamed would be offered. Some very fine musicians went to Berkshire for the summer.

Without comment, she handed the letter over to Nettie, who was craning, obviously dying to know what was in it.

"Take a look at that, Nettie, old socks," she said, and carelessly slit the other envelope, the plain one, by her plate. The address had been typewritten, but the letter was not; she stared for a moment, bewildered, at Julie's familiar scrawl.

Nan, darling, stop worrying so. I know I've been a bitch to you, but we always did beat each other up when we got mad, and I guess that's what I was doing, and it didn't mean a thing. I've gone to live with Jamie, after all, where else? He's my husband, we got married awhile ago in Bristol. When I talked to you in the car I had a ring all right, I had two and not one of them a class ring, poor me! Maybe all Jamie wants now is a good piano-player and what I want is a dance band to play in, but I expect we'll change some when the baby comes, they say parenthood does wonders. We'll probably name him "Saxophone," we need a good tenor sax player. We have had a wonderful break with the trumpet, a guy named MacPhail, who can get sounds out of said instrument to make cold buttermilk run down your spine, even if he is an awful creep otherwise. He said he took the job with Jamie's band because he heard me play piano at a dance in Bristol and he says that between

us, him and me, we'll make that bunch of tin whistlers go
places, and I guess he's right, because all at once Jamie gets a
contract for the Seaside Inn at Quadrant Harbor, down-coast,
and that's a pretty swanky place with a lot of summer trade, so
we'll get heard maybe by someone who knows what it's all
about, some different from the knuckle-heads in Bristol and
points north, and I may see you in Boston after all, and then
again I may not. Of course, Jamie plays trumpet, too, and he's
terribly jealous of MacPhail, not about me, ha ha, but about
MacPhail's trumpet! Nan, I didn't know what else to do, I
thought I had better get married before I began to show. When
you give your first concert at Symphony Hall, I'll be there
rooting my head off, and sometime I want you to listen to me
play "Night and Day" and hear the words over the music.
Because I am a damn good player of jazz and such and what
I mean by it comes through loud and clear.

All my love
JULIE

"Ma, you have got to listen to reason about this," Nan said.

"I'm trying to," Abigail said. "Reason is something I can
understand, Nan. Julie can't. She's like—" She stopped.

The firelight from the living-room fireplace played on her
face, showing it chiseled and stony, flickered on the white
patch in her lap which was Julie's letter, slightly crumpled
in one hand.

Nan had lighted the fire because she had felt cold to the
bone. Waiting for her mother to come downstairs, she had
cried silently into her hands clasped over her face. It had
been a long wait. She had heard Maureen and Arthur go
out, and Miles's cheerful tramp as he went upstairs to bed—
he had tried to be quiet, on account of his father, and so
had stumbled loudly on the landing. She had hidden her
grief from Nettie, who came in before she went, demanding
that Nan get herself to bed, she must be tired. The sounds
of the house seemed so normal, so everyday, even Nettie's

passionate argument that she couldn't close her eyes "until every last one of you devils is settled away for the night," and Abigail bringing her supper tray in to the fireplace because she loved a fire.

"This was thoughtful of you, Nan," she'd said, settling herself wearily, with the tray in her lap.

Let her eat first, she's tired to death, Nan thought. Aloud, she asked, "How's Pa?"

"Much better, I think. He's had sleeping pills—he'll sleep till morning. What is it, Nan? Why have you been crying?"

And now, Nan thought, she looks as if she had seen a ghost.

Perhaps Abigail had. She had barely stopped herself from saying aloud, "like your aunt Grace," and for a moment it had been as if a ghost, a long-forgotten one, had walked across the room.

I did this to Grace. And now I have done it to Julie. And Julie is like Grace. Irresponsible, stubborn, and that black temper.

Under her breath and not even aware that she had spoken aloud, she said, "I guess blood will tell," and saw Nan start up, staring at her in amazement and fury.

"Ma, do you, for heaven's sake, mean Uncle Jos? How can you? It isn't a time for copybook quotations, this is for real!"

"Of course I don't mean Jos. I was thinking of someone else, someone who died a long time ago."

"Julie's like Julie! She's here and now, not somebody dead and gone who did something years ago you didn't care for. She's got to be helped. We've got to think what to do, not—"

"Hush, Nan. Stop storming at me and tell me what you think can be done. I've tried to think, through a whole year's willful foolishness."

"And pushed her! And it's never been any use, pushing Julie—"

"And has done harm, I know. Tell me what you think we can do now that would be right."

"Not what's right, what's kind . . . what's human."

"Stop and think. Julie's under age—I could have that marriage annulled. But Julie's pregnant by this man. I could, perhaps, force Julie to come home, have her baby here, take care of it. Do you think Julie would? Read her letter."

"She could come with me and have the baby and put it out for adoption. She could be with me, it was what she wanted before—"

"That sounds simple, but you can't duck obligations that way. There's the child to be considered. Julie's child, my grandchild, turned out to strangers? I don't know this man Julie's married, who he is or what he is, but—"

"He's a . . . a creature!"

"—but he is the child's father. It's his business, which you or I can't settle, high-handed, without consulting him."

"So you'll drop her, cold, you'll let her go without—"

"No. We are, after all, responsible for our own. I'm only trying to think what's right to do. I wish you would too."

"I can't think," Nan said. She put both hands to her temples and pressed hard. "I'm so tired."

"Please try. You and I together were always good with Julie. Perhaps I've made mistakes without you."

"And now I can't even talk to you. You don't see that what I've suggested's the only solution for Julie?"

"No, I don't. If that's a headache, Nan, there's aspirin in the drawer behind you."

"Ask for bread," Nan said, a little wildly, "and you get aspirin. If you dance, you pay the piper. Make your bed, lie in it."

"Maybe I deserve this from you, Nan," Abigail said. "I don't quite know. I think you'd better get a night's sleep before you decide. You would like to get Julie out of this in the most painless way possible—painless for Julie, that is.

And, I do have to say this, for you. I don't think your solution is decent or honorable. I'm sorry."

"Are you? You can't see out over your marble principles, can you? Well, I'm not marble and neither's Julie, but our stuff, whatever it is, won't break any sooner than yours will. I'm going to get Julie to come away with me—we'll manage without you. I'm sorry, Ma, but you keep your aspirin."

She turned and went blindly out the door.

In her room, she wrote to Julie.

Julie, lamb, I love you too. I have got the job in Berkshire I wanted for the summer. The pay is good, it'll be enough to take care of both of us for a while if you want to come with me. Here's train fare, in case you need it. I'm taking the midnight tonight and I'll be at my old address in Boston for a few days or until I hear from you.

Maybe you won't want to come, or can't, so then, there's this: If you ever in your life need anything, you come straight to me, because I am the one, you said so in your letter, and I play it loud and clear too.

All my love, and hoping
NAN

She folded the note, thrust it into an envelope with two ten-dollar bills, and mailed it on her way to the station.

So neither Julie nor Nan was on hand for Maureen's wedding, and Elsie, to her infinite delight, had a chance to stand up with the bride.

✿   ✿   ✿

"It's work," Chris said to Mary. "Jobs for the four of us, George and Waldo and me and Larry, if he wants one. Mrs. Plummer's building a new addition to her barn and re-shingling. It'll take awhile. Work with pay! P-a-y, by the God!" He grabbed her around the waist, lifted her up, gave her a hearty smack on the lips. "So what d'you think of that, old girl?"

He hadn't been like this for so long; it was almost as if he had been away and had come home again. Mary buried her face in his chest and hid the tears. After a moment they were gone, wiped away.

"Not me," Waldo said. "I don't vant *no yobs*. I got hands full, right now. I make out."

"Yes, you do, you old loafer," Chris said. "You like cows, so I've seen to it that you'll be wet nurse to a whole barnful for a month while Mrs. Plummer's foreman's away on his honeymoon. I told her what you'd done with Abigail the cow, turned her from a wild moose of the pampas into a nice playmate for kids. She thinks you must be pretty good with animals."

Waldo reared up, his fists doubled. "You tell her ve got Abigail the cow?" he roared.

Chris grinned. "She knows it," he said calmly.

"You tell her ve give back? By yesus, Chris, I flat you out flat! Put foot in mouth, vhere it go good!"

"Aw, come on, Waldo, don't hit me. I'd fall apart."

An expression of great grief came over Waldo's face. "Vell, I go, then. I go this time for good. I don't come back."

"Who'll milk?"

"Milk, to hell and damn! No cow, no milk. You crazy?"

"Abigail don't want Abigail, Waldo. She says the cow's no good to her. If we bring her back, she'll go wild again. She can't be pastured with the rest of the herd and penned up, she'll go crazy, have to be shot. If we'll board her, it'll be a favor, and we can have the milk and some extra cow feed for pay."

"I be damn," Waldo said feebly.

"I didn't tell on you," Chris said. "Not but somebody ought to have, you old rustler. She brought the matter up herself. She's known right along who stole her cow. She had farm-hands out looking, and they spotted Abigail quite awhile ago."

Waldo sat down again. "So," he said, "I don't go. But I don't vant *no yob*. You and that lady, you spoil my fun."

"You could help the poor lady out for a few weeks, couldn't you? She's been pretty nice about this."

"I don't know," Waldo said. "I yust don't know."

But he was not to go to work for Abigail Plummer, nor anywhere else for a while. That evening Jerome Green appeared, with Willy Meader. They arrested Waldo and took him to court. The charge—stealing a roll of hen wire from Charles Plummer's store.

Jerome Green did very little these days but sit at his office desk. He was an old man, feeling his age, and almighty bored with his job. Each year now he thought would be his last one as sheriff; he would be glad to retire and let Willy Meader take over. Willy could get elected and he wanted the job—deserved it too. For nearly five years now he had been doing most of the work. He was a nice fellow—a pleasure to work with—and he could get things done so that Jerome didn't have to worry about work being neglected in the sheriff's office.

There were two or three good reasons, Jerome told himself, why he ought to resign, let Willy go ahead with it; a man seventy-seven years old, it was probably illegal for him to hold the job anyway, but Judge Clawson always laughed that off, said don't worry, if anybody started crabbing or checking up, he, the Judge, would fix it.

"Jerome," he would say, "you and I have had a pretty good thing going. We wouldn't want to be without our little sweetenin', would we?"

Well, no, Jerome wouldn't. He probably had enough laid by to last him out, till the man came for him, but still, it was pretty nice, and kind of a habit, too, to have that little extra coming in every so often. One thing he knew, Willy wouldn't hit it off with the Judge. Willy was an honest man

—too honest for his own good. He'd never seemed to learn that there were times when a man ought to keep his mouth shut, not bite just in case he got bit back. Willy, if he got hold of something, took out after it like a bloodhound, worse than Abby Plummer. Matter of fact, Jerome had said to Willy once, "By God, Willy, if you don't unlatch, I'm a-going to nickname you Abby."

After all, if a man had something going on the side, it was his own business, wasn't it, in times like these when anybody had to pick up a little here and a little there to make ends meet? Most people, if they found out somebody was carrying on illegal, all they'd do would be to gossip behind their hands. They wouldn't start a great clack going, bring everything out into the open and brand a man. Matter of fact, quite a number of them would wish they'd thought of a shenanigan first, been smart enough to get in on the ground floor themselves. Not Willy, though; he didn't feel that way. There was that time at the public meeting with the town council, when Willy had got up and asked point-blank why so much tax money was being asked for that didn't seem to be needed; and Abby Plummer had said in a voice loud enough to hear, "Bigger pockets." She was another one. She hadn't caught up with the Judge yet, and God help all if she ever did. The day she plowed into the courthouse in that hat she wore and with her chin stuck out, quite a number of folks were going to have to fight or run. All except Willy, who'd be right in there rooting her on.

That Swede, Larsen, it wasn't right to jail him on the evidence; he was only somebody Charles Plummer had got sore at. Larsen had had a witness to prove that he'd thought Charles was letting him have the hen wire on credit; but it was only Miles, Charles's kid brother, and the Judge had scared the pants off him, so that he didn't know whether he'd been going or coming. The thing was, Charles had poured some sweetenin' onto the Judge's flapjack, and a little of it had run down onto Jerome's, as was right and proper. Charles and the Judge were pretty thick, anyway. It had turned out to be quite hard on Larsen. Jerome himself had thought at the time that *he* wouldn't want to be anybody Charles Plummer got sore at.

Well, having Larsen in the jail was a godsend for Jerome. Things were pretty slow in the sheriff's department. Except for an overnight drunk or two, Larsen was the only regular, and you didn't often find a man who could play a rattling good game of cribbage. Interesting fellow too. Tending jail was one of the few things Jerome could do nowadays, to kill time; when he took in the meals, he liked to stop and chew the rag, say there was anybody in there worth talking to. He'd spent quite a lot of time with Larsen. Kind of wished the feller was going to be in there for more than three months.

Well, three months was three months. He'd be there that long, unless he busted out. Of course he didn't know it, but a big bruiser like him could likely walk right out through the wall of that jail if he wanted to. Something ought to be done, old place been ramshackle for years. Maybe when Willy got elected, he'd do it.

Miles Plummer was miserable. When he and Charles had got back to the store after court was over, Charles had grabbed him by the back of the shirt and had shaken him like a rat.

"The next time you run off at the mouth about anything you hear me say in this store, I'll knock your head off. Damn you, I wouldn't have you within sight of the place, if it wasn't for one of Ma's crazy quirks. You clear out of here for the rest of the day. I see you around, I'll murder you."

Miles cried. He was scared of Charles, whose scars got red when he was mad and looked awful, and you never could tell how much he was going to hurt you. This time was just a shaking; then he opened the store door and chucked Miles out into the street.

A couple of men going by guffawed and one of them said, "Hey, sonny, what'd he do—catch you into the candy?"

Well, they weren't going to see him cry. He got up, managed a grin, and said, "None of your nose-picking business," and walked away. When he was out of sight of them, he ran.

It hadn't been right. Charles *had* told the Swedish man he'd charge the hen wire. When they were all out in the back of the store, he'd said so. Afterward he hollered that he wouldn't, but by that time the man had gone, or, anyway, he hadn't heard.

Well, I heard it, and that pink-headed old slob of a judge balled me all up, wouldn't let me tell.

It was awful to get balled up so easy. If only your mouth didn't get full of your tongue. At school sometimes, when he knew the answers to something perfectly well, he'd all of a sudden think, My mouth's going to get full of my tongue. And it always did.

One thing was, he'd got a half day off from the store. He wasn't going home, either. Out at the farm the carpenters would be working on the barn. He'd been dying to see what they were doing, and he hadn't had a chance to, because weekdays he'd had to work at the store, and Sundays, of course, nobody worked. Since he felt so bad and mean and worked up, as if he were partly to blame because the Swedish man had had to go to jail, he would do something he wanted to. Maybe it would make him feel better.

At the dairy barn a good deal was going on. The cement foundation for the new addition had been poured, and three men were busy ripping off the board frames which had held it up while it had hardened.

Miles settled himself unobtrusively to watch. He didn't want to bother anybody, but all of a sudden he had a lot of questions. They'd built that high board wall good and careful and strong, too, with wires sticking out—why did they have to tear it down? He edged over to the nearest carpenter, whose back was to him, and said tentatively, "Why are you tearing this nice fence down?"

"The forms?" the man said. "Oh, the forms always have to come off." He was quite a young fellow, about Charles's age, Miles saw as he glanced around, and he suddenly took a second look at Miles and laid down his hammer.

"Hey," he said. "You're the young fellow the Judge tromped all over down at court this morning, aren't you?"

Miles nodded and turned red. He guessed that awful business must be going to follow him around the rest of his life. And probably serve him right, because he hadn't had the guts to open his mouth and say what he knew, no matter what the Judge said. "I couldn't—" he began, and stopped.

"Darn right you couldn't. I was there, I heard it. Damnedest piece of legal jizzarmaroo I ever heard in my life. Well, now, look. I'm Larry Cartwright. That's my father and my uncle over there. And you know Rob, don't you?"

"Well, a little. He's in the high school. I'm seventh grade. I don't really know him."

"Says he knows you, you're a baseball player."

"Yeah, some."

"Now we know each other, how's about you coming and helping me eat my lunch while you tell me what it was you really wanted to say? Something's got to be done about this."

"Could you . . . do something?"

"I might be able to. Hey, Pop, come over here a minute, you and Uncle George."

The whole story came bursting out of Miles. He had been bursting with it anyway, and here was somebody who would listen.

Back in the woods behind the Indian mounds, Rob was rehearsing the kids in what had come to be called The Game.

Paul and Martin were going to fight. Liz would try to stop them, screaming. She could really scream—it sounded like a fire whistle. Ralph, who was nine, would yell and duff into the fight, trying to pull Paul off his cousin. Paul was taller and huskier than Martin. It would look awful, a big guy beating up a littler one, though actually Martin was a year older than Paul. Blob-top and Pete, the youngest of the lot, three and seven, could stand around howling. In case they couldn't work up tears, Rob would have a big fat onion in his pocket. He could probably depend on Pete to yell the house down; but so far as Blob-top was concerned, who could depend on her for anything? He had wanted her to carry an old Raggedy Ann doll, but she didn't like dolls. What she wanted to play with most was an American flag on a stick.

Rob flopped down breathless, having taken the whole crew through the act three times.

"Now, look," he said, eying his two principals. "This has got to be a real fight. You both got to get mad. We can't spend money for a bottle of ketchup, so, Mart, you've got to bleed. When we get ready, you've got to let Paul smack you one, right on the nose. No, no, don't do it now, Ma and Aunt Sue'd have kittens. So he hits you, you jump him, you both roll over and over hollering. We have got to make the loudest noise we can possibly make and it has got to be awful pitiful. If it ain't pitiful, it won't work. And if you don't feel pitiful, you put your minds on what it's like around here now. We'll go through it just once more, that's all there's time for. Everybody remember we have got to do it this afternoon. Liz, you can screech louder than that. I've heard you."

"I'm afraid they'll hear it back at the house," Liz said.

"Yeah, they might. Okay, damp it down. Come on. Ready . . . Go!"

The last rehearsal went pretty well, except for Blob-top.

She wouldn't even try to cry. All she would do was wave her flag and sing, "Brighten the corner where you are."

"All right," Rob said. "When the time comes, Liz, maybe you can fix her up with the onion. I wish we didn't have to take her, but we do. Blob-top, you cry when Liz tells you, or I'll take your flag and chew it up!"

"Come on," Liz said. "They'll be hollering at us to come and eat."

As they came out of the woods, they met their mothers, Mary and Sue, hurrying along the beach.

"Well, thank heaven!" Sue said. "What on earth was that awful screeching about?"

"We were playing The Game," Rob said. "Uh, the cowboys and Indians part."

"We wasn't neither!" Blob-top said. "Rob was—"

Liz gave her a level look. "That was me, Ma," she said. "I was being scalped."

"I know it was you. I've heard that caterwaul before. Aren't you a little old for that?"

"Oh, we were just horsing around, showing the kids. What's for lunch?" Rob said.

"Nothing, till you get cleaned up. What on earth have you been doing to Cordelia Ann? She looks as if she'd been rolled over and over in the saltflats. Somebody's got to lug some water before anybody gets to go to town this afternoon, or I miss my guess."

Blob-top suddenly set up a shrill wail. "Rob told a big fat lie," she sobbed. "He was eating my flag. Damn him."

"Cordelia Ann, let me hear one more word like that out of you and you get your mouth washed out with soap. And you don't go!"

"Well, he was *eating* it," Blob-top said. She gave Rob a look, serene and superior. She could cry if she wanted to. See?

Rob heaved a sigh. That little nut, nobody paid much attention to what she said, but she was probably going to run off at the mouth all through lunch. He wished, with passion, that he could get her to cuss again, because Aunt Sue was a woman of her word. He had too much on his mind to have to cope with Blob-top this afternoon. If just one thing went wrong . . .

He said, "I don't know as I want to take Blob-top anyway. All that jabber drives me crazy. I'm likely to put the truck up a tree."

"Of course you'll take her," his mother said. "She's been promised to go. Come on now, get washed up, while I put things on the table."

"Hah!" Blob-top said. "Your mama says I kin."

"I'll handle her," Liz said. "Don't worry, Rob." She gave Blob-top a ferocious look and Rob felt better. If anybody could handle Blob-top, Liz could.

She did. All through lunch she told a complicated story about an elephant who ate rattlesnakes and could talk and say what they tasted like.

Blob-top was fascinated. "They did *not* taste like oatmeal," she said. "If they did, vhy diddun he eat poi?"

"He didn't like pie. And that's enough of talking like Waldo. The word is 'why,' with a w."

"I vant to talk like Valdo. Vhen he comes home, I'm going to, all the time."

"You hustle and eat, or we'll leave you right here," Liz said.

"Now, here's the grocery list and the money," Mary said. "You and Liz be careful how you spend it, won't you?"

"Sure, Ma. Don't worry," Rob said.

"Of course not. But what are you worried about, son?"

"Me?" Rob said. Something must be showing; he had better pull up his socks. He grinned at her. "Been quite awhile since we've had money for groceries," he said. "I guess I feel responsible, or something."

Well, that was no lie. Thank the Lord, he hadn't had to tell one. She always knew when he did.

What was showing was a drop of sweat which had run down from his hairline across his forehead, though he didn't realize it.

Mary said doubtfully, "Are you sure you don't want me to go too? I could, you know."

"Shoot, Ma, Liz and I'll make out. You take a rest from kids for a while. So long." He turned quickly and tramped off along the top of the beach, the kids tailing out behind him.

Mary stood looking after him. What could be wrong? Something was, she could tell. Or maybe that sweat was from being dressed up in his good blue suit, which was too tight for him. Or maybe it was just the responsibility, as he'd said. After all, the money he had was a goodly portion of Chris's and George's first pay checks in months. Still, she could wish Waldo were on that truck, she thought, watching it pull out. Rob had had his sixteenth birthday earlier in the summer and Waldo had paid for his driver's license. He had also taught Rob a great deal about driving the truck, and Rob was careful. So no worry there, but she did wish Waldo could have been here to go along today. Rob was terribly upset about Waldo—perhaps that was it, going to town alone without him to ride herd on the kids.

It looked as though they'd be without Waldo for quite a while. Larry had been trying to do something—he hadn't got very far. He had gone to see Charles Plummer and had offered to settle for the hen wire. Charles hadn't even listened to him. He'd been trying, he said, to nail that guy for weeks —it wasn't the first time things had been missing from the store. Larry had also been to see the Judge and had come home very thoughtful indeed.

"Got brushed off there, too," he'd said. "The old boy doesn't have much use for lawyers in pin feathers. Well, I've got an idea there's one more thing I can try, and I'm going to." He hadn't said what it was.

Waldo, that crazy fool, he'd probably picked up stuff from the store and ought to be in jail for it. But we're all just as bad as he is, Mary told herself. We used the groceries he brought home, wherever they came from. It isn't any excuse that we desperately needed them. I almost told Chris I would steal if the children were hungry. And I would. It's that darned innocence of Waldo's that breaks your heart— he sees what's needed and gets it, and it's not for himself. Could that be so criminal, after all? Stealing, after all?

She stopped. What's the matter with me? Of course it is. It was stealing, all right. You couldn't get away from it.

Charles Plummer didn't care to have children in the store without their grownups. In these hard times he never could tell which ones might be light-fingered. Not many kids got treats these days—most parents couldn't afford candy and ice cream, and it had been Charles's experience that when kids couldn't buy, they'd take. He kept his candy in a glass showcase, but there were numerous small items lying around, so that he had to watch every minute—and not only the kids, for his money. That damn Swede had somehow got away with an expensive head scarf and two pairs of stockings— probably kept a woman somewhere. Well, it would be quite some time before he'd call on her again, blast him. With bums like that stuck away in the cooler, and the more of them the merrier, you wouldn't have to worry quite so much about the store being broken into at night.

Well, no rest for the weary. Here was this batch of kids, all sizes, six or seven of them piling in through the store door; and two of them high-school age—the worst kind, Charles told himself.

The tall boy said, "Hello," and laid a long grocery list on the counter.

Charles said distantly, "Afternoon." He stared at the list without moving. Hadn't seen these kids before—must be some new family in town. They looked decent enough, all dressed up, but he'd keep his eyes open till he found out who they belonged to. That was a long list, some quite expensive stuff on it. Women, these days, didn't usually buy quite so much all at once, unless it was on tick. If they did, they'd shop for it themselves, not send a batch of kids with all the money it would take.

The boy, waiting, said, "Ten pounds of sugar, please."

Charles stopped reading the list and looked him up and down.

Yeah. Suit too small, wrists sticking out of the sleeves halfway up his arms. Some family, new in town, seen better days. It'd be a credit deal, all right. Charles took out his toothpick.

"That'll have to be cash on the barrelhead," he said.

"Okay."

"And messmellers. I can have messmellers." The smallest child pulled herself up so that her nose barely showed over the edge of the counter. She was a fluffy little thing in a blue dress with frills, and she carried what seemed to be a flag rolled up on a stick.

"No candy," Charles said, "or anything else, till I know if you can pay for it."

"Well, you can't be too careful, can you?" the tall boy said.

Charles didn't like that. He didn't like tall, good-looking boys anyway. They gave him the pip.

"Show the old—show him the money, Rob, and let's get out of here." This was one of the younger boys. He had been roving around, looking at things, whistling between his teeth.

"You'll get out sooner than you want to if you don't look out," Charles said. "I've got no use for fresh kids. And just come away from the shelves there, will you?"

The boy started whistling again, with a sound that just escaped being a raspberry.

The tall boy said, "Shut up, Paul." He pulled out a wallet, opened it, riffled bills with his thumb.

"Well, sure. All right." Charles began filling the order. "Who are you kids anyway? Where'd you come from?"

Nobody answered for a moment. Then the big girl said, "Our name's Cartwright."

Charles stopped in his tracks. "That the Cartwright's working for my mother?" he demanded.

"Yes, it is." She stared back, looking him icily up and down.

She didn't think much of him, he could see that. He didn't think much of Cartwright, either. Fellow had hornswoggled Abigail into building an addition on the barn she didn't need, just for the sake of getting himself a job. Charles had pointed this out to his mother, who, as usual, hadn't listened to him. So he had a grudge against Cartwright. And Cartwright's kids had a gall, coming in here, looking down their noses at Abigail Plummer's son. Staring at his scars too. He hoped she liked what she saw.

Miles, who had been working in the back of the store, came by, headed for the annex. He grinned at the tall boy and lifted a hand at him. "Hi, Rob."

"Hi, Miles, how ya doing?"

"Good," Miles said, and vanished promptly through the door, just as Charles was opening his mouth.

There was a silence.

"*Vhere* izza messmellers?" the small child asked.

Sounded just like that damn Swede. Mop of white hair, too, just like his. What kind of a family mix-up was this? Probably about what you could expect. Might have a little fun with this.

"What's your name? You a Cartwright too?"

"Yah. Blob-top!" she said forcibly.

By God, that was a little too raw, that bum's kid calling him names, making fun of his face. Charles dumped the last of the groceries on the counter and held out his hand. "That'll be twenty-one dollars and eighty-two cents," he said sourly.

The hair, eyes, and nose of Blob-top appeared again over the edge of the counter. "Is zissa messmellers?" She reached politely for a box of soda crackers.

"No," the tall girl said, taking it away from her. "He's charged us for marshmallows and for clothespins, but they aren't there."

Why, that little bitch! She'd been checking up on him.

In a dead silence Charles added the missing items to the order.

"Messmellers," Blob-top said. Blissfully she clutched the box to her bosom. "I got messmellers."

"For a down-and-outer, your pa don't take long to throw away his wages on fool stuff like candy, does he?" Charles said to Rob. "And seven kids. He might better spend his money on a suit you ain't half grown out of."

Nobody said anything. The kids shared out the bags and parcels between them and headed for the door.

"You better be careful how you eat them marshmallows," Charles told their backs. "You'll have a bellyache."

Only Blob-top turned around. "I *will* not!" she said. "So blah! So damn you!"

Cheeky little brats! Abigail was sure going to get told a few things about Cartwright's kids, how they acted in public. Maybe Cartwright would, too, if he showed up here.

Outside, Liz bundled Blob-top headfirst into the pile of quilts and cushions in the back of the truck. Blop-top enjoyed this; the quilts and cushions had been put there to make landings soft for the overflow from the front seat—there wasn't, of course, room enough in the front seat for everybody—and Blob-top landed soft.

"Vasn't he a funny mean man?" she remarked.

"He's a . . . a toad!" Liz said. "Oh, Rob, you did so *well!*
I hope the rest of us did. I was ready to kill him!"

"I could ha' bunged him right in the eye with a can of shoe
polish," Martin said. "He's who ought to get a poke in the
nose, not poor old Paul. I had my hand right on a good old
can of shoe polish and I was all ready to draw a bead and
whango!"

Rob wiped the sweat of fury off his face with his handkerchief. "And I'd sure like to've seen you do it," he said. "Nailed
him, dead center." One of Martin's accomplishments was
that he was a very good shot with a beach rock. "That's the
last time I ever set foot in there," he went on. "Wow! We
did okay, though. He'll remember us, all right. If anybody
gets any ideas about the Cartwright kids, sure, we were
there, grocery shopping and all dressed up. Get set and hang
on now, because here we go."

Out of sight in the woods, at the beginning of the Starball
road, he stopped the truck. "Okay, step on it. Change clothes
fast. Fold up your good ones, nice. We've got to put 'em
back on before we get home and they mustn't be a mess.
Paul, you dig out that can of axle grease and make sure
everybody gets a lot of it on. There's the old duds I raked
up. Some of 'em's Waldo's and some I got at the dump."

Jerome Green was at his desk, resting, and hoping there
wouldn't be any more calls to bother him. There had been
one—a fight down on River Street, and Willy Meader was
out in the police car to tend to it. It seemed funny, with all
the fist and bottle fights Jerome had seen in his time, that
another one down on River Street would set his corned beef
and cabbage to rising up on him, and it probably had been
foolish to eat a whole boiled dinner at noon. That was just
the kind of a twizzled-up mixture that would bring on a
heart attack or a stroke, and Jerome was deadly scared of
either one. Two more good reasons why he ought to resign.

Willy, of course, hadn't minded. He had the years, by God, on his side.

"You go ahead, take a caulk, Jerome," he'd said. "This won't be much. Couple of drunks probably."

"If the phone was to ring, I wouldn't likely hear it," Jerome said.

"Never mind. I'll be right back."

Jerome settled down. A good nap, he'd be all right. His wide leather belt was too tight for him over that damn cabbage, and he unbuckled it, tossing it on the desk with a jangle of keys. He had to wear his keys hooked to his belt all the time these days; otherwise they'd get mislaid like everything else. Then he unfastened the top buttons of his pants and sagged back in his swivel chair, his feet on the desk and his bandanna over his face. With relief he felt the tension begin to ease in his rumbling midriff.

He was having a very good dream about four handsome young women who had to be chased because they had robbed the post office, when one of them turned, came at him, and grabbed him by the foot.

"Wha'?" Jerome said. "Wha'd you do that for? Leggo my laig, dammit!"

He stared wildly around, but he'd either gone blind or slept right on into the night. Everything was blackish-gray. He sat up with a crash. Phew, that was some dream, and—

"Jeezus H. Christ!" he said, his jaw slowly dropping.

While he had slept, the office had filled up with pygmies.

Looked like they'd been landed straight off of Mars. No, there was the American flag, so that couldn't be.

His blurred vision had taken in at first only Blob-top and Pete, who were dressed in grain sacks slobbed and blackened with axle grease. The grain sacks, out of which arm- and head-holes had been hacked, swept the floor, so that neither Pete nor Blob-top appeared to have any feet.

Blob-top had gone a little far with the axle grease. She

had enjoyed dressing up—she felt she looked quite nice and different in Abigail's the cow's feed bag, and when Rob had said to rub on the squidgy stuff, she had done so with enthusiasm. What felt good on the fingers was even better on the face. Her white chiffon hair stood out above her blackened features, out of which her bright blue eyes stared unwinkingly at Jerome with a pleasant female demand for admiration.

When he only swore and looked at her with his mouth open, she said, to remind him, "This is pretty dirt. We got it off a automobile."

Someone said, "Sss-h!" and someone else said, "Yeah, we have to sleep under a truck now," and Jerome came to with a click.

Kids. Six unbelievably filthy kids.

There was a tallish girl, might be fifteen, in a woman's ragged old housedress, black with grease and haggled off at the hem, so that one side touched the floor and the other showed her bare leg to her knee. The dress was hiked up with an old piece of tarred rope and draggled down in folds and bulges. The one foot which showed had on the biggest shoe Jerome had ever seen in his life with a broken-down counter and a flapping sole. There were three boys, odd sizes, in greasy rags—old overalls zigzagged off at their thighs, a pair of black-stained, wet-looking woman's pants. The sweater on one of them came only to a little below his ribs. He had no shirt on; his bellybutton showed, a black spot outlined like a star in the same oozy black stuff.

Jerome stared at him, shocked. "You haul up your pants," he said. "You ain't decent. What kind of a gah—what kind of a cussed minstrel show is this?"

Rob had said, "Don't do a thing unless he wakes up before I get back. If he does and starts to ask questions, start the fight."

Rob had had to revise The Game, because he hadn't

counted on any such luck as finding the policeman asleep with his keys in plain sight on the desk. What he had coached the kids to do had been to look pitiful, say their name was Larsen, that they'd come to see their father. Liz would sob out that they were starving to death and had to sleep under a truck because it was all the home they had now. Then when the jail was unlocked, Paul and Mart could start to fight, the policeman would have to get busy and separate them, and while he was doing that, Waldo could run for the truck.

That had been as far as Rob had been able to plan The Game. He had done everything else he could think of. He had come around a few days ago and had scouted the jail— where the doors were and where was the best place to park the truck. He had known that The Game had holes in it, and that a lot of it he would have to play by ear after he got there. What if the cop wouldn't fall for the sob story, or what if kids weren't allowed to go into the jail? But here the man was, sprawled out dead to the world and his belt with his keys hooked to it under one of his feet on the desk. Rob had grabbed the keys, belt and all, while Liz had carefully held up the foot, and had made off as fast as he could go. His instructions had been brief, and the kids were a little slow getting the idea that The Game wasn't to be quite the same as rehearsals had been.

Liz gave Martin a glare, and he caught on.

"You shut up!" he said. "You say that again, I'll sock you right in the mush!"

Since this was the one with the indecent bellybutton, Jerome had no doubt that this sass was aimed at him. He began to rumble.

"All right, that'll do, mister! I don't take no funny business in here. This is the sheriff's office, and you kids got a gall coming in here like that lugging the American flag, that you're by gorry a disgrace to—"

In the store, when no one had been looking, Martin had scooped up a bottle of ketchup and stuck it in his armpit. It had been stealing, but he couldn't bear the thought of hitting poor old Paul hard enough to make his nose bleed. During the past few minutes he had been stealthily decanting it into his hand. It had come slowly at first, as ketchup, the darn stuff, always did out of the bottle, and he'd aimed to have a lot more of it in his hand. But now was the time. He flew at Paul and slapped him across the face with this handful. The bottle fell to the floor and smashed. The ketchup splattered bloodily, and Paul, surprised because he had not expected ketchup, turned toward Jerome a ghastly blind face from which, apparently, most of the features had been slashed away.

Jerome came roaring to his feet. "Oh, my God, you crazy little devil, you've cut his face off!"

Jerome had seen broken-bottle fights before. There, certainly, was a busted bottle on the floor and two boys, one of them badly hurt, rolling over and over in a mess of blood, pounding each other and everybody screaming and yelling like a kettle of cats. He broke out from behind his desk and found he was wading through his pants, which had started to fall down around his knees. He just managed not to take a header, stooped to grab his pants, and pulled them up. Where in the name of the jeasly was his belt? It had been right there on the desk. He began to ferret around on the floor under the desk and his chair. He was on all fours in the kneehole when somebody hollered, "Okay, beat it, quick!" Feet scampered and silence fell.

Jerome reared up. There was his belt, four inches from his eyes, right on the desk where he had left it, and not one living soul but him in the office either. Before the God, that belt hadn't been there a minute ago. He reached up and slammed his hand down on it before it could get away again.

Had he had a stroke? Or was it the grandmother and grand-father of a bad dream?

But no. As he got stiffly to his feet he saw the broken bottle, red-splattered on the floor, some more red splatters around it. Those kids had been here, all right, and had had a fight, and one of them was hurt bad enough to need a doctor. He had better hustle out and see what he could do.

The office door opened slightly, and Ory Carter, the court-house scrubwoman, thrust in her head. "For the Lord's sake, Jerome! What'd you do? Drop your hamburger?"

Jerome swept past her without comment. He was in full uniform now, an officer of the law, complete with revolver. By the God, he had something on now that would scare somebody.

He hunted around and around the courthouse and couldn't find a soul. And nobody else saw the peculiar-looking outfit, then or ever. It had gone off the map, vanished into thin air. The devil had flown off with it.

Chris Cartwright's dump truck rolled joyously down through the woods on Starball, the kids cleaning up and changing clothes as they went along. Through town they had lain flat in the back of the truck on top of Waldo, who was under the quilts and the cushions. Once out of sight in the woods, he emerged and became part of The Game, and rejoicing broke loose.

Rob had been worried about how they would get the axle grease off, particularly off of Blob-top, but he had assured himself that Waldo would know how, and Waldo did. Among the groceries was a five-pound pail of lard, which he opened and removed a top layer from, carefully smoothing over the surface so that nobody would know it had been touched. There was also soap. Halfway down Starball, in the swamp, and not too far from the road, was a clear boiling spring Waldo knew about. Lard rubbed on and wiped off with the discarded old clothes turned inside out did the job, took the axle grease even out from under fingernails. With good luck, nobody would notice anything. The old clothes Waldo buried in the swamp, lifting up sphagnum moss from a boggy poolside, spreading it neatly down again.

The truck rolled home with a neat, clean mess of children back from a shopping trip in town. Mary and Sue saw them pull into the turnaround and heard Blob-top bawling at the top of her lungs, "Brigh-tun the cowr-nur vhere yow-ar are," saw her standing in the back of the truck in her frilly blue dress, waving her flag on a stick, but by that time Waldo had melted into the woods. Vunce he got in voods, he told them, nobody catch him, and he'd stay nights in the shelter with Abigail the cow.

The worst that came of The Game turned out to be for everyone's benefit, according to Rob's way of thinking. Mary and Sue were shocked to find the five pounds of lard so far short of honest weight and that two cakes of soap, charged for on the grocery list, were missing. Charles Plummer, they decided, was a cheating storekeeper; in the future they would shop elsewhere.

❖   ❖   ❖

The hat Abigail Plummer wore when she went out into town was of plain black straw and shaped like a Dutch oven. Held in place by two black-headed hatpins, it rested comfortably high on her neat pug of slightly grizzled hair. At the time when the jail delivery of Waldo Larsen was going on, she was adjusting this hat and finishing quite a long talk she had had with Larry Cartwright.

The one final action Larry had had in mind to take was this talk with Mrs. Plummer. After all, Charles was her son; she might have some influence with him. They were two vastly different people, Larry had found that out for sure. He liked Mrs. Plummer. She'd been around, off and on, to see how the work was proceeding at the barn. She and Chris had had some arguments that Larry had enjoyed listening to

—both of them, he'd thought, ought to've been lawyers—good, honest, logical minds like that ought to have more scope. They sure could be put to good use down in the Judge's office here in Granite Hills. At the time Larry had still been burned up about his interview with Judge Clawson.

She said now, as she finished putting on her hat and picked up her handbag, "Have you decided where to go when you've finished your lawyer's training, Mr. Cartwright?"

"Haven't got that far yet," Larry said, holding the door for her.

"Why not come here—to Granite Hills?"

"Darned if I wouldn't like to. With something more on my side than—uh, pin-feathers. It'll be quite awhile, though, before I can decide anything."

"You have a year to go, your father said."

"About that. If I could buckle down to it, I might finish in one more semester, but I do some hash-slinging and furnace-tending on the side. Takes time. Are you sure you don't want me to go with you, Mrs. Plummer? The Judge doesn't think I'm much on the legal side, but I could catch you if he throws you out of the office."

Abigail smiled. It was the first time she had, and the smile surprised Larry. As he'd talked, her face had set itself like stone—stone with a face carved on it, he had thought, answering her quick, quiet questions, and wondering with a sinking feeling in his middle just how mad he was making her. After all, this was her son at the bottom of the mix-up. And she could fire the lot of us off the job . . . Lord, maybe I should've kept my trap shut.

But here she was holding out her hand and looking like a different person entirely. "No, thank you, Larry. I won't need help. Besides, I have to see Charles first. Before you think seriously of coming here to practice, if you do, I would go and talk to Willy Meader. I expect Willy will run for sheriff next fall. Jerome Green, the present sheriff, will be retiring, and Willy is the man for you to see."

Be damned, she called me Larry, he thought, and he went to eat his postponed lunch and do some thinking.

Judge Clawson, about to leave his chambers for the day, saw Abigail Plummer's hat rising steadily up the staircase which led to the courthouse's second floor. For a moment he was of a mind to duck back inside the frosted-glass door and turn the key, but it was too late. She had seen him.

He said inwardly, Oh, damn it to hell, and bowed to her with a cordial smile.

He was a dapper man, smaller than average, who, the legend was, had to sit on four volumes of torts before he could see up over the bench. He had, however, a handsome head of stand-up red hair peppered with white, which made him look impressive when sitting in his robe.

"Good day, Mrs. Plummer. I don't often see you in my bailiwick. How are you?"

"Well enough," Abigail said. "If you have a minute, I'd like to talk with you."

"I was headed home, but—certainly. What can I do for you?" He threw open the door of his office. "Come in. Have a chair."

"I won't keep you." She did not sit down. "My son Charles has withdrawn all charges against Waldemar Larsen, whom you have in jail. Will you please see that the man is released at once?"

"Charles . . . withdrawn charges?" He was taken aback. "What did he make them for in the first place then?"

"Charles has remembered something he said which made Mr. Larsen think he had credit for the roll of chicken wire. And people are accustomed to receiving credit, if they need it. In my store."

"H'm. I see. I guess you jogged Charles's memory for him."

"I did. The man is in jail unjustly, without cause."

"Well, er, yes, it would seem so. We'll certainly do what we can, at—"

"Which should be a great deal, I should think." Abigail eyed him. "I understand that the fine he was asked to pay was somewhat larger than is customary in cases of petty larceny, which of course this was not. Why was that?"

"We-el, now, Mrs. Plummer, there are wheels within wheels." The Judge's pencil, busy on a pad in front of him, began to doodle a wheel. "Sometimes those of us who are in charge of the town's morals and, ah, ethics, if we are conscientious about our trust, have to, ah, play things by ear. Frankly, Mrs. Plummer, and of course confidentially, if we have an old offender whom we can't nail on one charge, we try to do it on another. There have been complaints, suspicions, about this man. Other things have been missing from Charles's store. For one thing, an expensive head scarf—"

"You do this with nothing proven?"

"For the good of the criminal sometimes. A spell in jail might help a man to realize he's on the wrong track, before he does something he could get a longer term for."

"I see. And you give a man a police record for some crime which hasn't been proved against him. The charges in this case have been withdrawn. The man thought he had honest credit for the chicken wire. I expect he could sue for false arrest, if—"

"Certainly. Of course. I'll call the jail and let you hear me." He pulled the phone toward him. "Jerome," he said into it, "that bum, Larsen. Let him go. He's in the clear." He listened briefly. "Well, I don't give a gah—a dangblast if he does play good cribbage. Let him go."

"Thank you," Abigail said. She turned to leave.

"Thank *you*, Mrs. Plummer. I'm delighted you came in

about it. A responsible act, and believe me, Mrs. Plummer, we need responsible and humane citizens who—"

"Yes," Abigail said. "We do."

Smiling, cordial, he opened the door for her. "Oh, and by the way," he said, "I've been wanting to see you, was planning to call, one day soon. Do you still plan to develop Mulligan's Mound? I know you once intended to, and of course you have had—er, and there's been this Depression, I mean. Heavens, it can't last forever, can it?"

"I have already begun to develop Mulligan's Mound," Abigail said.

"You have! Why, Mrs. Plummer, I take off my hat! In times like these you are far-seeing enough to see that some-day real estate will be worth something again! If more of our people would have that kind of courage, we wouldn't have depressions, would we?"

"That," Abigail said, "is my opinion." She marched past him through the open door.

"Oh, but just a moment! What I wanted to say was, I'd like to look at house lots up there. When you're ready, of course. The view up there is magnificent. I was up there with Charles last fall, partridge hunting. We were both speculating on where we would build our houses if we had our choice. Charles, I suppose, will inherit his? Not, of course, we hope, for many years, but—"

Abigail did not stop. She was walking away, and he had to step fast on his short legs to keep up with her. "Only," he said, shaking a jocose finger, "you really will have to change the name for real estate purposes, won't you? Mercy, old Mulligan, everybody remembers what he was!"

"Cranberry Mountain," Abigail said, without turning her head. "Anybody is welcome to *look* at house lots there, at any time."

The Judge stood where he was, watching the black hat recede down the stairs. Halfway down it stopped. He craned his neck and saw that she was talking to Ory Carter, the cleaning woman, who seemed to be very much in earnest about something. After a moment Abigail nodded briefly and went on.

Now, what had that been about?

Whistling softly to himself, he went back into his office, closed the door. Yes, he had left the drawers to his desk locked. He had better watch his step, if that damned old war-horse had started her snooping around the courthouse. And a cleaning woman had a fine chance to soak up private stuff that might get left around in sight.

The trouble was, Abigail Plummer wasn't a stupid nosy woman, she was a smart nosy woman. And she had a tongue like a clap hammer. Once she started it flapping, there were people around town who were going to take notice.

Well, he'd given her reason to pause a little. She might be as honest as a pint of her own cream, but she was also a damned good businesswoman. She wouldn't go out of her way to make an enemy out of a possible buyer for some of that real estate.

A lot of people were going to wish they'd been the first to see the possibilities in Mulligan's Mound. As soon as the Depression let up, and it wouldn't be long now—it couldn't be; hard times always got better in time—the summer trade would be back, tail over the dasher, and when it came, that hill was going to be a high-class development. Nice homes, with acreage, for some of the town's substantial citizens, too —space to move around in away from that blasted river, which was beginning to stink too high for the nose of a decent man. The Judge knew exactly the house lot he wanted to buy. It was the most desirable site on the mountain. He had better nail it down before by some chance—life for any-one was precarious—Charles got hold of it and kited the price sky high. He'd see the old girl again, make an offer. Kill two birds with one stone. She was too smart to make trouble for a substantial customer. Darned substantial, he told himself, whistling.

On her way home Abigail stopped again at the store.

"Charles," she said, without preliminary, "the head scarf that was stolen from you—can you remember what it was like?"

"There's one just like it over there on the shelf," Charles said sullenly. He was still stinging from the going-over she had given him earlier. Get Norman Hardwick in here to manage the store, would she? He'd see them both in hell before he'd clerk for Norman. He'd had to give in to her because she'd come at him before he'd had time to think. But wait. Just wait.

She came back with the scarf in her hand. "Have you sold another one of these to anyone?" she asked.

"No. I only had two in the first place."

"I want this for a while. I'll bring it back."

What was she going to do? Give the other one to her Swede boyfriend to make him feel better about going to jail?

"And, Charles, I've been talking to Ory Carter. Please give her credit when she asks for it."

Abigail went on, out of the store. What she suspected was probably true, but she had to be sure. At Delbert Smiley's house she went up the steps and in at the front door.

"Why, Ma!" Elsie said. "I didn't expect to see you. You haven't been here, oh, I can't remember when."

"No," Abigail said. "I thought I'd drop by. Did you leave your pretty scarf at my house the last time you were there?"

"Why, no, I don't think so. Let me check. No, here it is, with my coat on the hook. Why? Ma, what's the matter?"

"You forgot to pay Charles for it the day you bought it, didn't you?"

"Why . . . why, no, of course I didn't." Elsie hustled the scarf back into the coat closet, shut the door. She turned around and saw Abigail's face. "Well . . . perhaps I did.

There, now, what a fool, it's this baby coming, I get so forgetful . . ."

"I expect you had better go around to the store and pay him," Abigail said. "Hadn't you?"

"Oh, yes, of course I will. My goodness, I—"

But Abigail had closed the door and was going quietly away.

Now how did she find that out? Elsie thought, furious. Well, that's the last time I ever go around to her house and show her anything new I *ever* buy again.

"Now, Abby, I've lit the fire in the parlor," Nettie said. "I want you to go in and set by it and not do one livable, nameable thing this evening. You look tired to death."

"Well, I am, a little. But I've got paper work to do, Nettie. You run along and don't worry. Paper work always rests me."

"Hmf, 'twouldn't me. All them decimal dots and fractious, and who's bought buttermilk. I'm a good mind to tell Zeke to go off to the dance alone. He wouldn't have no trouble finding himself another girl."

"He'd have trouble finding another one as nice," Abigail said, and was pleased to see Nettie turn quite pink. "No, you go, Nettie. You've had a day, running up and down stairs. You need a little fun."

"Fun, nothing! I'll have plenty of time to rest my feet while you and Fee are in Boston. If he's able to go tomorrow, Abby. I don't know . . . He ain't ate good today."

"I know," Abigail said. "Well, we'll have to see tomorrow morning. Dr. Graham's coming in, first thing. He thinks Fee can make it all right. You go now. I won't sit up long."

Nettie went off, grumbling. Her young man, Zeke Peterson, was a friend of long standing who had once had hopes which now, according to Nettie, were dying away. He had proposed several times without success and now, as she put it, was "looking." "But I guess if I can catch him, I better," she had told Abigail not long ago. "If they was any kids routing around the house, I wouldn't think twice about it, let me tell you. That Zeke ain't got a red penny and never will, and I seen the day when I had enough of that kind. Looks as though if I want kids around, I better have some of my own before I grow into my changes."

She had been making remarks along this general line ever since Miles had gone down to stay, on weekday nights, with Charles and Clarice in their rooms over the store. Poor Miles, he had a terribly hard time getting up in the morning, as no one knew better than Nettie—the worst cross she had to bear was getting him out of bed, getting up an hour earlier herself to do it too. He had to be at the store in time to sweep out and get the morning chores done; by staying there nights he could sleep a whole hour longer. Abigail had suggested it, thinking to make things easier for them both; but the moment the matter was decided, Nettie dug her heels in. She flew straight up in the air. He was not to go, she said. It would make work for Clarice that she, Nettie, was good and well used to, frigmentation though it might be, and Miles spent enough hours in that place without having to be there nights as well, and the house without him was going to be a cemetery tomb, and . . . and . . .and. She had only given in when Abigail pointed out that perhaps it might be better for Miles to be out of the house for a while right now.

"Until we get back from Boston, Nettie," she said. "Perhaps they'll tell us there if anything can be done."

Even under sedation lately Felix had been having terrible nightmares, the sounds he made sometimes dreadful, waking the house. Dr. Graham doubted whether anything more could be done in Boston, but Abigail had made up her mind not to give up unless she had to. And in Boston, several times before, Felix had been helped.

She did not want to go in and sit by Nettie's fire. It would remind her too much, she knew, of the last time she had sat there. With Nan. Nan had left without a word and she had not written. But Nettie knew where she had gone, and Maureen and Arthur on their way home from their honeymoon at Niagara Falls had stopped in Berkshire and had seen her. And Maureen, bless her, had written all about it. Abigail herself had sent a letter to Nan at Berkshire, but had got no answer.

> Nan, my dear,
> Nettie has told me about your honors at the school and I am proud of you, and glad you have got the job you wanted. Please believe me, I can't in conscience interfere with Julie. When your summer session is over, you must stop this silly nonsense and come home.
> With love,
Mother

She must not think, tonight, about Nan and Julie. She could not afford to, with all she had to do this evening and tomorrow. There was paper work to be done, business things to be settled before she left for Boston. Rest awhile first, perhaps; she did seem to be terribly tired. A fire was a comfort and should not be wasted.

I cannot coddle myself this way, she told herself, and went in and sat down by the fireplace, leaning back, watching the flames creep up the logs. Yes, it was cheerful, a help for doldrums. She must make herself think of other things, not of problems she couldn't handle. At least not now.

Let's see. What is there left, before I go?

The work of clearing slash on Mulligan's Mound had already begun. She was leaving it, she felt, in competent hands. She had asked Chris Cartwright to recommend a man to take charge—would Waldemar Larsen be interested—and Chris had said, Great Scott, no, he didn't think so, but he'd ask him. Chris, it turned out, had been mistaken. Waldemar would.

"Don't know what got into him," Chris had said, looking puzzled. "But he said to tell you he'd be glad to. He'll not only take the foreman's job, but he'll pick his own crew, and you won't have to think about the work till it's finished. He'll do a bang-up job, too, Mrs. Plummer. He's a darned good man."

"I have always thought so," Abigail had said.

So that was settled. Joe Crawley, one of the farmhands, would manage the dairy barn and the cattle until Arthur got back—Arthur and Maureen were due home at any time now. The check for Laurance Cartwright's necessary expense at his law school had been sent to the bursar at the school, a splendid use for the rest of the income from Jos's legacy. She had never used a penny of it for herself or for her children, and never would. Charles, perhaps, could someday be told where what he had always considered to be his share of it had gone. He had never forgiven her, she knew now, for not letting him have it. Charles . . . well, there was nothing to be done, at least not tonight, about Charles. She must not think about him. There remained the paper work. She would begin it . . . in a little while.

How still the house was tonight—as if, itself, missing the sounds which had flowed through it for years. Sounds of children, of people moving, of voices in the rooms. Only a soft fluttering from the fire which did not crackle, now that the softwood kindling had burned away and the flames had taken hold of the maple logs. Maple made such good firewood; only apple wood was better, but hard to come by, unless an apple tree blew down, or some fool had no better sense than to cut it down. This fireplace was the only one in the house now, where once there had been a fireplace in every room. Grandmother Julie had had them all bricked up when iron stoves came in—even this one in the parlor, which Abigail herself had had opened. How the children had always loved the stories about Grandmother Julie . . . the time she got down on her knees and thanked God, prayed in front of that first cast-iron stove, when it was new.

"Oh, thank you, God, for no more lame backs, cooking over a fireplace!"

Abigail could see the small faces turned up, golden in the firelight. She could hear her own voice.

"Your great-grandfather told her that maybe God was to be thanked for seeing that the vessel got through the line gale all right, but he and Fred were the ones who'd bought the stove and brought it home from Boston. And they were the ones who were going to have to brick up the fireplaces when more stoves came. All that work. So she said she knew it and thanked them, too, but if they thought she was going down on her knees to them, they had another think coming . . ."

Too many people had lived in this house for it to be so silent now. A procession of ghosts. Grandfather Charles and Grandmother Julie. Father and Mother. Felix and I and all our children. . . .

I must stop this.

Strange how your mind, no matter how much you disciplined it, twisted and turned, brought you back by devious ways to what lay in the dark at the bottom. There was one whom she had not named. Because when you thought of Grace, you thought of Julie.

I can't do any paper work tonight. I'm too tired and wrought up. I can't afford to be wrought up. I had better go to bed and rest.

It was time, anyway, to make sure Felix hadn't waked up, wasn't trying to go to the bathroom alone. She put up the fire screen, climbed the stairs.

Felix was lying on his side, still sleeping, as she had seen him when she had first come home at suppertime. Odd he hadn't moved—he was a restless sleeper, turning, throwing his arms about, tossing off covers. Perhaps he had moved, had come back to his first position. As usual, the covers were off, his arms and shoulders out. She leaned over to tuck him in for the night. Her hand, in midair, arrested itself, dropped gently to his cheek.

"Fee? Felix?"

His cheek was warm, but he was not breathing. He had died here, quietly and alone, not asking for anything, not making any fuss.

Felix. Dearly loved. Lost, a long time ago. No. Not lost, because never had.

I was always too much to live up to, you said if I would just once be wrong. But somebody had to be trusted. There had to be somebody you could trust. Somebody anyone could trust.

Almost by themselves, her hands moved on the covers, as they had done all his lifetime, tucking him warmly in.

❊   ❊   ❊

Once outside the store, Miles ran. He was supposed to go to the bank with Charles's deposit. Instead, he hurled the canvas bag bulging with coins and bills as hard as he could at the store's front window, heard with satisfaction the crash of glass as he took to his heels. His eye stung and ran water blindly; he held his handkerchief over it as he ran. That skunk had hit him. With his fist, too, knocked him flat. Even if he hadn't, though, Miles would have quit. He wasn't staying there, not after what Charles had said to Clarice about Ma.

Charles had come back from Pa's funeral and had opened up the store, just as if today had been like any other day. No customers had come in at first—nobody expected the store to be open—so the three of them had been there alone when Charles started in. He was, it seemed, boiling mad.

"That damned old moneygrubber, she's got every cent and every square inch of property tied up in her own name," he spouted. "Not one of Pa's kids is going to get even a look-in.

By God, we're entitled to a third of it under law. I'm going to get it too!"

"How?" Clarice asked.

"Take it to court, what'd you think? I'll bet it could be proved that she waited till Pa was incompetent and couldn't defend himself and then she had everything transferred on the q.t."

"She'd know that wouldn't be legal," Clarice said. "You know she's too smart to do a fool thing like that, Chuck. And I think she's too honest too. I don't believe she ever did."

"Oh, shut up! What do you know about it?"

"Well, I went to the same school you did, remember?"

This was surprising. Charles often forgot that anyone else ever knew anything. Besides, she'd never talked back to him, not that Miles had ever heard. Charles didn't pay any more attention to her, though.

"Well, I'll get her on something, see if I don't. For one thing, I think she's crazy as a loon. I'll bet Judge Clawson'd go along with me if I tried to get her committed too."

Miles was staring at him with horror. What was he saying—that Ma was crazy, ought to be put away . . . that was awful, that was a lie.

Miles had been holding a quart bottle of mayonnaise, about to put it up on a shelf. Instead he slammed it onto the floor as hard as he could. Glass and mayonnaise flew everywhere.

"You're a liar!" Miles yelled. "You're the one, you're crazy, you ought to be put away yourself!"

And Charles had hit him. As he lay on the floor, he'd thought Charles was going to kick him, but he didn't. Clarice said, "Chuck, stop, you've hurt him enough," and got between.

"Okay," Charles said. "If he didn't have to get that cash to the bank before it closes, I'd write my name on him. You get along with it, you little s.o.b., and then you hustle back here. You'll clean up that mess if it takes you all night."

Miles ran. His blind flight took him out past the dairy farm, where the new lumber on the barn addition shone pale gold in the sun and smelled good—he got a whiff of it as he went by. No one was there—the Cartwrights had been at the funeral and had stopped work for the day, as anybody decent would have. He ran on, crossing the big pasture where the cows were already bunched by the gate waiting for milking time, and didn't stop at the smaller enclosure where the big square Guernsey bull spent his time. He was halfway across it before he realized that the bull was there, and interested; for a moment he wished that the great lumbering thing would come at him and kill him, get him rid of this choking black lump in his throat that kept reminding him that Pa was dead, and Nan and Julie, whom he loved more than anyone, hadn't come to the funeral, hadn't cared enough about anyone at home now even to show they were somewhere in the world and cared a darn. . . .

But when he saw the bull lift one front hoof and claw along the ground, slow and easy, as if he had something in mind, Miles put for the fence. The thing looked just like Charles. He wasn't going to get himself killed by anything that looked like Charles.

He ran on, into the woods, found himself on an overgrown cart road going uphill, no matter where to, just so it was out of sight of everybody and he could run. He ran till he was winded, walked, ran again, finally brought up short, barely saved himself from crashing into an old wooden fence with a high, falling-down metal gate.

Randall's Hill. That was where this was. Out in there was the old cemetery where all Ma's folks from back along had been buried a long time ago. He'd sure had enough cemeteries for one day, but he'd have to get his breath before he could go away from here. Sweating and panting, he hung on the fence. After a little he straightened up, stepped gingerly through the sagging gate.

It was nice in here. Place was full of big old maple trees. Their leaves made a soft, whispery, fluttery sound. Cool. Quiet. In under one of them whose nobby base spread out to make arms almost like a chair, Miles sat down.

Gee, his eye hurt! Swelled up, too, and puffy. Felt like an old soapy sponge. This was a good place. Anyway, nobody could find him. He could stay until he made up his mind what to do. No matter what, he wouldn't go back to the store. There was that busted window—maybe Ma'd make him go back and work, anyway, till he'd paid for it. She'd be sure to. She always thought you ought to pay for things you broke, especially if you'd got mad and done it on purpose. Maybe he just never would go back. All these old gravestones said "Randall," thirty or forty of them, and he was a Randall, too, Miles Randall Plummer. He'd just stay here with the rest of them. His name on one of these old black stones'd look as if he belonged with them too. Looked like they always put on everybody's middle name. That one, that skinny tall one, that had the guy's middle name, John Constant Randall, and a lot of words carved under it. Who had he been? Miles leaned closer, read the inscription:

JOHN CONSTANT RANDALL
1750–1820
A Soldier of the Revolution, Sea Captain and Pioneer.
Born in Gloucester, Massachusetts, he first settled
this town and was lost off the ship ELIZABETH RANDALL
in the Amazon River, South America. His soul to God
and his body to the sea. May he rest in peace.
A GOOD MAN IS AN HONOR TO HIS COUNTRY
AN HONEST MAN IS A BLESSING TO HIS PEOPLE

Miles suddenly stood up straight. Charles, that skunk, that cheat, that liar, ought to read that. These are our folks, our family, and look what they said about this one guy, so everybody'd know what he was, what they thought of him. Gee, so even I could read what they thought of him!

He ferreted around for a while trying to find some more inscriptions. There were some, but none of them anything like the first one. He'd have that to remember.

He'd go back down the hill and talk to Ma. Tell her why he wasn't going back to work for Charles. He'd find himself a job and . . . be darned if he'd pay for that window, though, or anything else belonged to that guy.

He was coming out of the cemetery when he smelled the smoke. He stopped in his tracks, pointing like a bird dog, and sniffing. Smoke up here meant just one thing—a woods fire. How could that be? Nobody came here any more. Still, some nut wandering around might have dropped a cigarette butt. A woods fire wasn't something you just went off and left, if you found one starting. You stopped it if you could, or you went tearing off and got some help. Which had he better do? The smoke was coming from the east—the wind must be that way. One thing, there wasn't much wind, and the woods were damp; it had rained yesterday. He might be able to stop the fire. But to get to where it must be, he'd have to go down the wild side of the hill. No road down there, and not too long, either, before the sun set. Which?

He tried to make his feet go one way or the other, but they only moved up and down in place. Couldn't make up his mind. Just like Pa. No good. Charles had told him, often enough.

No. No, he wasn't. And he could too!

Miles turned, tore back through the cemetery, vaulted the fence, and plunged into the alders and ferns, the slash and blowdowns on the wild side of the hill.

Waldo had worked all morning with his crew of men on Mulligan's Mound, but in the afternoon he let everyone go, because of Felix Plummer's funeral. Waldo himself stayed on the hill. The crew had burned slash and undergrowth in the morning, but at noon some of the fires were still alive with embers. He didn't think there was much danger after yesterday's rain; you never knew, though. No sense to take chances, in case the wind breezed up. He told Rob to come back for him at suppertime.

"Bring lots supper," he said. "If vind blow, ve stay here all night, so bring bed stuffs too."

Mostly it was a chance to sleep out, wind or no wind.

Rob was late getting back. He had had to milk Abigail the cow before leaving Starball, and she was having what he described as a "spizzle." He had had to chase her around some.

Waldo nodded. He'd been expecting it, he said. "She vant hoosband. She get over. Maybe next time ve fix."

Rob was proudly on Waldo's payroll, on the hill. He was doing a day's work with an ax and his appetite had grown with his muscles. Supper, which he had bought in town—not at Charles Plummer's—was lavish, all the things he and Waldo liked. They had it cooking over the coals of one of the slash fires, when Waldo lifted his head sharply, listening. "I think ve got deer in bushes," he said softly.

"I don't hear anything." Rob cocked his head. Yes, he did. Something, a ways down the hillside, was thumping and crashing around in the undergrowth.

"Not deer, annyvay," Waldo said, getting up. "Somebody. Some man. Vhat he do down in there, must be lost." He put back his head and let go with a wolf howl that raised Rob's hair. "Hoo-oo!"

The crashing sounds stopped.

"H'm," Waldo said, after a moment's silence. "Scared him, I guess. Thinks it's vild critters up here." He called again. "Who you are, come this vay, to fire. No volfs, people."

Miles came slowly out of the bushes. He stood, staring

wildly, his breath grating in his throat, his eyes rolling in his head, one of them blacked and half-swollen shut. He had lost his cap somewhere; his jacket had been ripped in two up the back, and half of it, including the sleeve, was gone. His pants were torn down the side, the pocket hanging inside out. He was soaked to the skin.

These two men, what were they doing? All these fires, three, four fires. That one there, that big one, was Larsen—the one . . . the one Charles had arrested. He must be sore at Charles; he's trying to burn up our woods. What'll he do to me, now I've caught him?

Then Rob said, "Holy cat, Miles, what's happened to you?" He got up, jumped across the log he had been sitting on, caught Miles around the shoulders. "My gosh, he's all in, Waldo. Wet, too. Gee, come over by the fire, Miles, quick!"

Relief had weakened Miles's knees. He stumbled, straightened up, and made it to the fire. The big fellow put out a hand to steady him.

"Take easy, you fall into fry pan. You okay now, don't be scared."

Miles found his voice. "I'm not . . . scared. I just thought . . . I thought the woods were afire. I was over on . . . Randall's Hill . . . I smelt smoke."

It was all right. Rob was here, and Larsen was okay, not mean, the way Charles said he was. What they were doing, they were cooking supper, hot dogs and hamburgers. A big loaf of bread. Coffee bubbling in a pot on the coals.

"Rob, you bring blankets from bed stuffs," Waldo said. "Get this feller varm. Then we eat. That alvays help."

Rob got the blankets. He held them over the fire until they were good and hot and Miles even caught a whiff of wool singeing. Snug in them, with only his head showing and all his wet clothes spread out on a log to dry. Miles felt his shivers and shakes stop; he began to wonder if he didn't look pretty foolish to these two, tearing around through the woods like that, and, after all, here were these fires. "I guess you think I lost my marbles," he said. "I smelt that smoke, though, and you know how it is when you smell smoke in the woods."

"Sure," Rob said. "Didn't you know your mother's having the slash cleaned off the hill? We've been working here a week, a whole crew. Waldo and I thought we'd better camp out here, tend fires."

"Oh," Miles said. He thought bitterly, Then I do look like a fool, anyway a baby, not to know about a big thing like Ma having the hill burned off. They don't ever tell me anything, Charles, and not even Ma. They just say do this, do that, as if I was a big hunk of nothing, not worth telling anything to. He stared blearily at the fire, winking away water that wasn't only from his hurt eye.

"That eye hurt you, I guess," Waldo said. "I fix that, little bit." He scooped a wad of raw hamburger from its wrapper lying open on the log, pulled out his bandanna. "We tie this on, make feel better."

Leaning over Miles, getting a closer look, Waldo suddenly began to rumble. It was a low sound, deep in his throat, and Rob hadn't heard it often, but he knew when he did hear it that Waldo was getting mad. What was that about—couldn't be sore at Miles, could he? Probably most of what ailed the poor little devil was his father's funeral, and Waldo sure knew about that.

Waldo tied the bandanna gently around Miles's head, came back to his seat, sat down. "Now you look like Pirate Joe," he said. "You ever hear about him? Real mean feller, bang vith pistol, vickety-vickety vith big sharp carve-knife, off goes ladies' heads. How you get that bad eye, son?"

"Must've run into a tree," Miles mumbled. "It was pretty thick down in there. Getting dark too."

"You know, Rob," Waldo said, "this quvite a feller, this

guy. Run five miles, down, up, Randall Hill, this von. How you get through big svamp down there? Svim?"

"One place I had to," Miles said.

"My gorry, I be scared my death of. Go in there daytime, maybe. Dark night coming, nossir! You hear that, Rob?"

"Sure do. Me, too, I'd think twice. Golly, Miles, I wouldn't do it for a million!"

"You hungry?" Waldo asked "How 'bout samvich?" He had been busy while he talked. The result was everything, because he liked everything. Miles smelled hamburger, onions, ketchup, mustard, chopped pickles inside the two slabs of buttered bread that Waldo handed over.

"Pirate Joe," Waldo said, "man fix him, whango, vith jug molasses. Real mean guys get vhat's coming, sometimes. That eye feel better?"

"Mm, some," Miles said, through his mouthful. He felt a lot better all over. Warm as toast, and maybe that had been quite a trick, getting through that swamp. Some of those deep, muddy places . . . Br-r. He hadn't thought about it at the time, though, he'd been too scared.

"That an awful vallop," Waldo said. "Somebody hit you, hanh?"

"Yeah," Miles said. What did he care, after all, if somebody knew Charles had knocked him down? Besides, this guy was nice.

"I go hit him over head with jug molasses," Waldo said. "Who done it?"

"My brother, down at the store. He got mad." Sure'd be swell if somebody was to whang Charles over the head with a jug of molasses.

"Vhy?" Waldo said. His voice was quiet, quite low, and Rob glanced over at him.

"He said my mother was crazy. He was going to have her, I guess he meant, put away. So I banged a big glass jar of . . . of stuff, onto the floor. So he hit me. You want to go conk

him with a jug of molasses, or anything else, it's all right
with me."

"So," Waldo said. He began to eat. For a while nobody
said anything. "Have more samvich," Waldo said at last.
"Have hot dog, cake, pie, coffee, everythang."

Over his third piece of cake Miles fell asleep.

Waldo scooped him up, carried him over to the knoll where
the bedrolls were spread under a tree.

"He sleep with you, Rob. Ain't room vith me."

"Sure," Rob said. "But what about his folks? S-pose anyone knows where he is? His mother'll worry."

"Time somebody vorry about this boy."

"You sound awful mad, Waldo."

"By yesus, I am. Sure she vorry, she better."

He got into his bedroll, yanking the blankets up to his
chin. For quite a while Rob could hear him thumping and
rumbling around.

"She don't put tin ear on that son-a-bitch, I do. I make him
two pieces. Maybe more."

Just before Rob went to sleep, he heard him say, "Vell, I
take cow, she don't care. Maybe I take this boy too."

Neither Charles nor Abigail missed Miles at first. Charles
supposed he had gone home and was staying there. Abigail
had no reason to suppose he was not still with Charles and
Clarice.

As for Miles himself, he was having a wonderful time helping to clear slash off Mulligan's Mound. Daytimes he spent
with Rob, wielding an ax or tending magnificent bonfires.
He ate with Waldo and Rob—hamburgers, onions, steak, hot
dogs, cooked over open fires. On fine, dry nights when the
fires needed tending, they all three slept in bedrolls under
the trees. On wet nights he went home with them to Starball.

The Cartwrights didn't seem to think it was anything out
of the way, his coming to be with them.

Waldo said, the first night, "This Miles Plummer, he vork vith us now, come visit Rob, okay?"

And all they did, they made him welcome. Mrs. Cartwright put something on his eye that was smooth and cool, and it got better fast. She gasped over his ripped-up clothes —"Boys get fierce sometimes, vorking in voods," Waldo told her—and lent him a change, overalls and a jacket of Paul's, which Miles returned the next evening, with thanks. She had no way of knowing that he had not been home for the new work clothes he had on, or that Waldo had bought them uptown, paying for them out of an advance on Miles's wages. For Miles was now on Waldo's payroll too.

It was then, during that first week, that Miles fell in love with Starball. In the time to come, in the war, on Iwo Jima and later on the mainland of China, when he was sick for home, it was Starball he thought of, the *hussh-hussh* of water along the beach, the *rabble-dabble, rabble-dabble* of the pond brook; nights when he slept aboard the boat with Rob and Waldo; of Mary Cartwright and of Blob-top, who said from the first that she loved him.

❊   ❊   ❊

Maureen and Arthur were settling into their new apartment. They had got home barely in time for Felix's funeral; up until now there had been no time for anything. Maureen was feeling her father's death deeply; she tried not to show her shock and sadness, and Abigail could not help but admire the way she met, and went along with, Arthur's continual outgoing good spirits. He had been—Abigail supposed you had to call it—sanctimonious, in a way that had been hard to listen to. It hadn't helped either her or Maureen to be told that they shouldn't grieve for Felix. "He's better off where he is. He's had a long, hard trial, and nobody could wish different for a man who had to suffer so." This they already knew. Abigail did not blame him; he was only saying what he felt ought to be said, what people did say; but she was glad when he lapsed into telling about his honeymoon. He had gone exactly where a newly married man ought to go—Niagara Falls and New York City—and he was full to the brim of both. On the way home they had seen Nan, and, he went on, after some hemming and hawing, they had stopped off in Quadrant Harbor and had seen Julie.

"Oh, Arthur!" Maureen said. "You know I promised."

"Sure, you did. But I didn't," Arthur said. "Now, look, Moreen, it won't hurt a thing for Mama to hear." He stopped and glanced sideways at Abigail. It was the first time he had called her "Mama," but he couldn't tell from her face how she was taking it. "I mean," he went on defiantly, staring at Abigail over Maureen's bent head, "well, I'm their brother now, I'm in the family, and Ma—Mama's got a right to hear where our sisters are, what they're doing. You might say she takes an interest, Mo-reen, as much as we do."

"Of course," Abigail said. "How are they? Are they all right?"

"Oh, sure, seemed to be. Of course, Julie took us to kind of a funny back-street restaurant I had my doubts about." Arthur's doubts showed in his face, the concern of a responsible man. "About womenfolks going there, I mean. And Julie had a man in tow, wasn't Stetson, wasn't her husband, a fellow plays in the band, name of MacPhail. I asked Julie where Stetson was and she said not to worry, Jamie was frail, couldn't cope, and MacPhail was a big bruiser, he could handle anything that was likely to turn up at this eating place we were going to."

"It was just a Chinese place." Maureen said faintly. "The food was awfully good."

"Well, it was if you like them funny-tasting Chink dishes," Arthur said. "I'd rather have a good plate of hash any day. I kept an eye out, but I couldn't see anything out the way, not while we were there, anyway. I felt jumpy as the deuce, though, all the time. Julie said she was in hopes of showing us some excitement, maybe a good stabbing fight, and that fellow, that MacPhail, said yes, you could expect one if you stayed there long enough. But there wasn't one."

Oh, Julie, Abigail thought. The sadness, the blankness hiding Julie had shifted a little. Here was a Julie she remembered well. The scamp, she ought to be spanked. Poor Arthur, sitting there, expecting murderers with knives to come leaping over the tables at any moment.

"It wasn't a place I was any too pleased to see Julie in," Arthur said. "And that dance hall where she's playing in the band seemed kind of splashy to me. But both the girls looked fine, Nan, too, you be glad to know, Mama."

"Yes, I'm glad to hear," Abigail said. She turned toward the door. "I expect you two'd like to be by yourselves for a while, wouldn't you?"

"Oh, wait a minute, Mama, don't run off yet. Mo-reen, where's the present we brought for Mama from New York City?"

"In the other suitcase, I think, Arthur. I haven't got to it yet."

"This one, is it?" He clicked open another suitcase, began ransacking eagerly. "Little yellow package, it was. Don't seem to be here. But oh, yeah, look, here's something else I want you to see, this book I bought in New York City for Mo-reen and I. This is some book, Mama, tells everything about how to raise kids so they won't run wild. I and Mo-reen, we figure to raise ours the right way."

"Arthur," Maureen said, "here's Ma's present."

"Okay, okay, but I wanted her to see the book."

He held out the fat black tome. Abigail took it and riffled the pages.

"It looks very good," she said, handing it back. "I expect you'll find it extremely helpful." She took the yellow package from Maureen, leaned over and kissed her on the cheek. "Thank you both," she said. "And now I do have to run, I've got a million things to do."

"Never hardly looked at it," Arthur said. Disgruntled, he

sat down with his book in his lap. "And don't she care what we brought her? Never even opened the package, for cramp's sake!"

"She was brought up to believe it isn't polite to look in front of people," Maureen said.

"Well, I don't believe it says anything about that in this book," Arthur said. "If it does, I ain't found it yet." He began rapidly turning pages.

Well, she certainly had a son in the house, Abigail thought, a little wryly. Bearing down hard on the "Mamas" and the "sisters" and the "family." She couldn't help but be touched by it, because she could see so clearly what was behind Arthur, pushing him now. He had only been trying to let her know that he—the hired boy who had married Maureen —was responsible, a man of worth and character. He had no intention in the world of instructing her with his book on child-raising, or even to make any comparisons. If anyone had told him that he'd put his foot in his mouth, nobody would have been more appalled than he. That was the one thing that would keep him from being a disaster in the house —there was no guile in him. His conceit, his ego, whatever it was, was blind.

He'll have all the help I can possibly give him, she thought. But, oh, I hope Maureen understands what ails him too. If she doesn't, she's going to have a long, hard pull with Arthur.

When Miles did not appear for Saturday noon dinner, as he was supposed to, Abigail called Charles. If Miles were late, it meant Charles was keeping him, and she had, from the beginning, had that out with Charles. Miles worked hard all week. His Saturday afternoons and Sundays should be his own. Besides, she wanted him at home.

"Charles, are you keeping Miles overtime? Please send him home."

"Why, he left here quite awhile ago," Charles said. That

was no lie. He'd left, as a matter of fact, last Monday, but what was the little snot-nose up to? Did she think he was still working at the store? Apparently she did.

"What time? We're waiting lunch for him."

"The usual time, I guess. I didn't notice, I was busy. Maybe he went out to the farm, said something about it."

"Oh. Well. Thank you, Charles."

By gum. The little devil! He must've been leaving home every morning, telling her he was going to work, and then never showing up. Didn't know he had it in him.

Charles went back to his work, which was, at the moment, replacing the smashed store window. He had had some trouble getting a piece of plate glass from Bristol—the first one had arrived with a crack in it and he had had to send it back. The whole thing had been a royal nuisance for him and had cost a lot. Besides everything else, he had had to explain to every nosy fool that came in asking, how some kid had put a rock through it. No point in starting a lot of yak, saying what had really happened. In the end Ma was going to have to pay for that window, and for his time, too, but right now he was going to lie low, see what she came up with. He'd been expecting her all week to come roaring in to give him hell, madder than a hornet because he'd beat up her pee-baby. She must know he had by now. The kid probably had a righteous and holy black eye.

He'd been relieved when she hadn't come, and if she wanted to know, he was tickled to death she hadn't sent Miles back. It was the first time since he'd been running the store that she hadn't had someone in there to check up on him.

Well, well, well. Turned out she didn't know a thing about it. That kid must've lied about his black eye, too, or she'd have said something. What d'ya know, thought he was all Pa, but maybe he did inherit a wild hair or two from Uncle Jos. Too bad more of Pa's kids hadn't. Of course there was

Julie, but she wasn't anything but a slut. Not worth any-body's second thought.

Ma could think what she wanted to about Uncle Jos, but he had been one hell of an up-and-coming fellow, who took the neatest way there was in his day to make money, and left a lot of it behind him, according to Delbert Smiley.

And a good wad of it belongs to me. Well, wait. Just wait.

No one, passing by, would have thought, seeing Charles puttying away at his window, that he had anything at all in his head but sincere good will for all the world.

Abigail drove out to the farm, wondering why on earth Miles hadn't let her know he wouldn't be home for lunch. It wasn't like him. Besides, he knew that she and Nettie alway planned especially good meals—all the things he liked—for Saturdays and Sundays. Probably he'd had a reason. She'd know when she caught up with him.

It would be a chance, too, to talk with Chris Cartwright, find out how much more work he had to do before the addition was finished, and if he had any prospects of work when the job was done. With all his responsibilities he would need it, she knew, and she had been racking her brain, but she had not been able to think of anything. She had been to the farm only twice since the funeral—Arthur had been carrying on the work out there—and neither time had she felt like seeing or talking to anyone.

The shingling job, at least, was done, she saw, as she drove up beside the barn. Chris and George were on the roof taking down staging.

Chris saw her and swung off the roof to the ladder. He looked a different man already from the black-visaged enemy who had come storming into her office last spring. He had put on weight, the strain was gone from his face; he might have been ten years younger.

Decent, she thought, watching him stride toward her. Responsible. He wants to work, to build. And what he's managed to find is only a stopgap.

"Nice to see you, Mrs. Plummer," he said. "We've missed having you around."

"Thank you," Abigail said. "I've missed coming. The roof looks nice, Mr. Cartwright. You've finished, I see."

"Just about. About a week on the addition, and then we're through here. I expect you've been wondering how long it would take."

"Certainly not. I'm surprised that you've done it so fast. I thought it would take much longer."

"George and I don't hold back. And, of course, we've had Larry."

He sounded quite short, almost touchy. He couldn't think she'd come around to jog his elbow, say hurry up, you're making the job last too long. Some men would have done that, she knew. She had seen it happen. Not Chris. The idea would never have entered her head.

She said, "I'll be really sorry to see your plaque go up, Mr. Cartwright."

That was enough. And he would know what she meant by it. She had better say what she had really come for and be on her way.

"By the way, is Miles around? I thought I'd ride him back home, if he is."

"Well, he was. He worked this morning, but this afternoon—" Chris grinned. "I guess the good weather was too much for Waldo. He took off, took all the kids fishing. Larry went too. And Saturday afternoon . . . you'll find it on the time sheets, Mrs. Plummer."

"Miles . . . ?" Abigail began. "I don't quite see . . ." She looked at Chris, bewildered.

"We sure have enjoyed having that little feller with us this week," Chris said. "My wife says send him again, any time, she'll be glad to have him. It's done him good, too, you'll be glad to know. He feels a lot better and his eye's healed up fine."

"What? His eye . . . was he hurt? Mr. Cartwright, what on earth has been going on? Miles—at least I thought so— has been staying down at the store with his brother, working there. He's been coming home only weekends, so I haven't missed him until today. Now you say he's been with you. What's happened? I don't know anything about his hurting his eye."

"I can good and well see you don't," Chris said. "I thought you did. Waldo and Rob brought him home—" Chris choked suddenly. "Waldo!" he said. "That cussed Waldo!"

"Tell me," Abigail said. "For goodness' sake, Mr. Cartwright!"

"I sure will. Mary and I thought you knew all about this. If you don't, you'd better. Miles's brother laced into him down at the store last . . . last Monday afternoon. The kid ran off into the woods. I guess he got lost. Waldo and Rob came across him up on Mulligan's Mound, after dark. He was in bad shape. His clothes were half torn off his back and his eye was out on his cheek where that . . . that guy hit him."

Last Monday afternoon, Abigail thought. After Felix's funeral. She had wanted Miles to come home with her then, but he hadn't seemed to want to. Perhaps, she'd thought, he'd feel better if he didn't, so soon after . . . The house had been so lonely then. And still was. But if I had only made him come . . .

Chris was going on. ". . . So when he came back with them the night after, he had his work clothes and shoes and his eye was bandaged and he had some salve for it—we supposed he'd been home to get his stuff and that you'd taken him to the doctor. That was the word we got, anyway. And that you'd let him come with us because he wanted to. He's—all right now, Mrs. Plummer. Working, if that's what you want him to do. Helping Waldo, up on the Mound. On the payroll. Worth it too. Waldo said—" Chris stopped. "I'm sorry about this, Mrs. Plummer. I know the man is your son. But I had to talk Waldo out of going over there and . . . and giving him as good as he'd dished out. Had a time doing it too. I've never seen Waldo so mad. He'd probably have killed —done a lot of damage, and he's been in trouble there before. Larry said no one would believe it wasn't because of that."

He saw she had gone very white, but her voice was steady.

"I have to thank you for that, Mr. Cartwright. I've seen in my lifetime what violence does. My son Charles is . . . is the result of it. He was very young when he was exposed to it, and we have tried for years to . . . I expect what we tried was wrong. I have been—" She paused, then went on, her voice crisp. "Perhaps Mr. Larsen's method would be better understood. But I can't have him fighting my battles, getting into trouble, that kind of trouble. I'll drive down now and tell him how much I appreciate his looking after Miles. And explain to Miles, if I can, that I haven't known what was going on. I hope you'll believe that too."

Chris followed her as she went back to her car. Funny stiff way of talking, he thought. But maybe it's because she's holding on. You could see she'd been hard hit. He opened the car door for her.

"Mrs. Plummer, if you want me to, I could drive you down."

"Oh, no, thank you, I'm all right. Unless I can give you a lift home?"

"Well, George and I've got a little more staging to come down before suppertime. Plan to stay to supper, Mrs. Plummer. Mary'd be tickled to death to have you."

"Thank you. Perhaps I will."

"That's quite a gal," Chris said to George, as he climbed the ladder to the barn roof.

At Starball, Abigail parked her car in the turnaround and got out. All the way down she had dreaded this part of it—the getting here, seeing the place again. No sensible person, of course, could believe that any place was evil, in some way responsible for tragedy, for ill-luck, for destruction, and she did not. It was not superstition that was making her heart-sick, cold to the bone. It was not the past of a quiet cove, a peaceful beach, the sound of a small wind in summer trees. The remembered past was greed and guilt and violence, selfishness and arrogance and mistakes—her own mistakes as much as anyone's, her own unawareness and, yes, stupidity. If you chose to believe in ghosts coming out of years ago to haunt the present, you had better pick the ones you could fight, not some poor lost shade from under a tombstone.

She walked across the turnaround and stopped, seeing Starball as it was now. Over on the beach, two of the sad old houses had been repaired—rebuilt, one of them—and the yellow gleam of new lumber, studs, and collar beams showed that work on a third was under way. New paint shone white and glossy in the sun. The beach was swarming, like an ant hill, with children dodging in all directions—some kind of a game. There were a couple of half-grown boys. Neither of them was Miles. The sun getting down in the west had already shadowed the western shore; the cove was without a ripple except for a slight *hussh-hussh* of rising tide along the beach. Its pale water reflected sky. The brook under the walkway was nearly full, running into the pond without a sound.

As Abigail crossed it and walked along the beach, Mary Cartwright, who had been sitting on her doorstep, got up and came to meet her.

"Hello," she said, smiling. "Are you—did you want to see Chris?"

"I've just seen him," Abigail said. "Mrs. Cartwright? I came down to fetch Miles home, if he's ready to go."

"Oh, you must be Mrs. Plummer," Mary said. She held out her hand. "I've been hoping you'd come to see us."

"I've been meaning to," Abigail said, taking the hand. "I do want to thank you for having Miles. I hope he hasn't been a trouble."

"Of course not. We've loved having him. I think he's had a pretty good time too. He feels much better, Mrs. Plummer."

"I'm sure he does." Astonished, Abigail heard herself saying, "I think I would myself, if I stayed here awhile."

"Please do. It would be a way we could thank you for letting us use your house. Of course, we squatted in it, but—"

"Never mind." Abigail glanced at the houses, smiling. "You haven't done it any harm, have you? Please feel welcome."

"I guess, illegally, we do," Mary said. "Will you stay to supper? Everybody went fishing this afternoon with Waldo, and they brought back enormous masses of fascinating fresh things. Miles is looking forward—I hope you won't take him away before he's tried fried lumpfish. It's dreadful, really, but Waldo likes it, and whatever he likes, the kids all think is heaven."

"Why, thanks, I'd like to try it too. If one more won't be too many—you seem almost to have your hands full."

"Of course not." Mary turned. "Hi, one of you kids go find Miles and—for goodness' sake. Where'd everybody go?"

Over Mary's shoulder, Abigail had seen the children, one and all, duck around the corner of the house, where a shrill, squalling rumpus suddenly started up.

"Now, look!" Mary called. "Whoever's on top of Cordelia Ann, get off. And go tell Miles his mother's here."

The squall ended in a dying fall, and Blob-top, somewhat

rumpled, appeared around the corner. "So blah, you!" she said, glaring at somebody behind her. "Go fry a kite! I go talk vith lady."

The intonation was definitely Waldo's and so was the accent; there was also the silvery pale mop of hair.

Abigail said, "Is this youngster Mr. Larsen's?"

Mary laughed. "Might as well be," she said. "The kids all track around with him from daylight to dark, when he's here. Some of them are getting to talk just like him. They're pretty mad with you for giving him a job, so he can't play every minute of his life. No, this is Cordelia Ann. She belongs to George and Sue."

"I *am not* mad," Blob-top said. "You Abigail the lady? You vant my can?"

Blob-tops' flag-waving days were over; her familiar, now, was a tin can, gold-colored, with a hole in the top just the right size for small pretty rocks which she collected, filling it four or five times a day and dumping it in a secret place she knew of. She held it out and Abigail took it.

"Thank you," Abigail said.

This Blob-top had not expected. The gesture had been a false one indicating social approval. She had heard about Abigail the lady and had looked forward to seeing her, the only drawback being that she was all lady and not part cow. Never in the world had Blob-top meant to give away her can. Stricken, she stared at it in Abigail's hand.

"You know," Abigail said, "I really don't have a place to keep this. So I expect you'd better take it back for now."

"Blob-top, you're a big fake," Mary said. "You go tell the kids to find Miles."

"Kids gone," Blob-top said. She was making off, discreetly, around the corner of the house, the can held behind her back. "All run off in Injun voods." Her voice came back as she vanished. "Miles over help Waldo milk cow."

"Oh, so that's where," Mary said. "Well, you go find the

kids, then, and tell them that pretty soon I'll have a word to say about manners. Let's walk over there, Mrs. Plummer. It's by the garden, just a step beyond the bridge."

Waldo, in fact, was teaching Miles to milk. He had sent all the other kids except Rob back to the beach, because Abigail the cow was flighty with Miles. She had a good memory and anything she had ever seen at the dairy farm reminded her of unhappy times. She had already taken two hefty kicks at the milk pail, denting it, and Miles, too, was flighty. He felt she didn't like him very much. He had felt the wind of both of those kicks, and even with Rob scratching her head and Waldo trying to calm her down, he doubted if he could concentrate. Milking was a tougher job than he'd ever thought it would be. Watching the farmhands at home, he'd always considered it easy and pretty uninteresting. Turned out it wasn't either one.

"You go on now," Waldo said. "Try easy, Miles. She come better."

But the sight of Miles was nothing compared to the sight of Abigail herself approaching through the alders with Mary. This recalled a really dreadful day. Abigail the cow reared up behind; her flying hoof caught the pail dead center, sending it spinning, and Miles ducked back ten feet.

"Abigail!" Waldo said. "Vhy you be such damn nut? You keep big fat stern down, or, by yeezus, I *kick!*"

But she was beyond reason. The rearing up became front as well as hind; she broke loose from Rob's soothing clutch, snapped her tie rope, and took off, fishtailing, into the woods.

"Vell, I be goddam!" Waldo said. He stood staring after her in amazement. "Vhat get into her? Loco in cow feed? Maybe I give too much—" Catching sight of Rob's face, he spun around, his voice dying in his throat, as he saw who was standing behind him. And for how long? Who knew?

He said, "Oh, yeezus!" and his face reddened with dismay from shirt collar to hair.

"How are you, Mr. Larsen?" Abigail said.

"Oh, I . . . Oh, God, not good," Waldo said. "Hello, there. I go ketch cow, she get lost." With dignity he strode into the underbrush, plunged, crashing, behind the first clump of bushes he could get to.

Mary glanced at Rob and quickly away. He was standing with a glazed look, his jaws clamped so tightly that she could see the little lumps of muscle on his cheeks. Bless him, he's trying, she thought, and I must, too, because we don't know her very well, we don't know how she'll take this, but I *am,* I am going to break up—

Abigail burst out laughing and laughed till the tears rolled down her cheeks. The only difference was, she stopped first.

"Tell him," she said, "if he hasn't run out of the county— Oh, dear." She stopped, mopping her eyes with her handkerchief. "Tell him I take it as very pleasant that he's named the cow after me. Miles, would you like to come home?"

Miles, who had been staring at his mother in astonishment—after all, Waldo had sworn something fierce—now looked at the ground.

"I see you have new work clothes," Abigail said. "Did you buy them out of your wages?"

"Yeah. I did. Waldo did, that is. I paid him."

"Good for you. If Mrs. Cartwright can have you, would you like to stay here? If it's handier to your work, I mean?"

Miles's head came up. She wasn't going to make him go back to the store then.

"We'd love to have him," Mary said. "He's nice to have around, Mrs. Plummer."

"Thank you, I have always thought so. If you stay, Miles, you'll need some of your things. Will you stop by, or shall I send them down?"

"No, I better come home, Ma."

Gosh, he wanted to anyway. His own things again. And his toothbrush. Rinse all you wanted to, you couldn't get rid of that funny taste. Besides, he'd been worried about her all week, if she were all right, and why she hadn't sent for him to come home. He said, "Well, gee. Well, gee, I sure can use my toothbrush." He stopped. "I guess that's down at Charles's."

"I'll pick up your things there tomorrow. And tell Charles you won't be back. If I had known anything at all about this, Miles, I would have done something before. You see, all week I've thought you were at the store, as usual."

"You *have?*" Miles stared at her. "Didn't Charles tell you . . . ?"

"Charles told me nothing. I see Mr. Larsen has found his cow. I expect if we go away, he'll be able to tie her up again."

Waldo, who had been peering out from behind a bush, hastily withdrew his head.

"Yes," Mary said. "And I hear Chris's truck. He and George will be roaring for supper. You and Miles will stay, Mrs. Plummer?"

"Thank you, yes. I'd like to try—what was it?—lumpfish too."

"But, Ma . . ." Things weren't cleared up. She'd have to know before they would be. "I busted the store window. I chucked Charles's old moneybag through it."

Abigail reached out a hand and touched the bruise, faded greenish-black now, on the side of his face. "This is better, isn't it, thank goodness? Well, Miles. I'm not sure what I'd have done myself. But I expect any self-respecting person, with spunk, would have thrown something."

*   *   *

Dumbfounded, Charles stared from his mother to the legally sealed and stamped deed on his desk.

"What do you mean, a new store? And Norman Hardwick to run it? Why not me to run it? I'm your son!"

"I am giving you this one, Charles. As it stands, lock, stock, and barrel. It will be yours, to run in any way you like."

"Good God, you must be crazy! What's the use of my owning this old rattletrap, and you with a new grocery market two steps up the street? Three-quarters of my customers'll come over to you and you know it!"

"Perhaps you ought to think why, Charles."

"I know why! Because you'll carry half the deadbeats in town on your books. You'll buy the best you can get and keep prices down. Hell, you can afford to. If you lived in the world instead of up there on that fat cloud of dough you've got stashed away where no one but you can touch it, you'd realize that in business you've got to grab what you can or you're sunk. People think you're nuts if you don't! Everybody else does it, why shouldn't I?"

"Perhaps some people—"

"Everybody with any sense. Why are you doing this now?" He thrust a finger under the edge of the deed, flipped it away from him. "If you'd done it when I started in here, let me tell you, I'd have it made, right now. But no, you've got to have your nose into everything. You even stuck your stinking kids in here to check up, to spy on me."

"No, Charles. That wasn't the reason. It was a mistake, I know now, and a stupid one. I'm sorry for it, more than you know."

"It wasn't the first mistake you ever made, was it?" Charles's scars had turned red; he was clutching the corners of his desk.

"No. Nobody has spied on you. No one told tales. Even Miles didn't when you half killed him the other day."

"I wish I had killed the little snot. Going around smashing windows—"

"I'll send you a check for your window. Because it is your window now. Meanwhile, I'm going ahead with a new grocery market."

"You know damn well it'll bankrupt this one!"

"Yes. It probably will. If you would like to change to hard-ware, I'll finance your stock without strings. People do not need hardware, they can get along in a pinch without it. Food, in hard times, is a different matter."

"Why, you damned old hypocrite!" Charles said. "There you stand, telling me it's crooked to make money selling food. What's milk, for godsake? Food for babies. You've made a mint out of it, and got plenty of people over a barrel to do it, too, if the truth were known!"

"I have ethical objections to getting anybody over a barrel. It may be true, as you say, that the men you know in busi-ness follow each other into dishonesty like a flock of sheep into a turn field. And it may be true that a successful man honors himself and the world honors him whether he's crooked or not. I haven't, myself, ever made money by hik-ing prices in hard times or refusing credit to needy people. You have, Charles."

"How do you know I have? You've had your nose into my books—"

"I have known from the beginning about your fake books. Any competent bookkeeper would."

"You're pretty lily-white, aren't you? Jesus, don't talk to me about being crooked. I'm an amateur compared to you. What about Uncle Jos? You not only killed him, you stole every damn cent he left!"

"Jos left me his money. Legally, Charles. As a joke, to show me how much better his way was than mine. I have never touched a penny of it."

"You'd damn well better not! We were in that together, and the whole kit and kaboodle of that belongs to me. By God, I'll get it out of you too!"

"You can't. It's a foundation now. The interest—the in-come from it goes to help young people who need college expenses. It's not to be touched, used for anything else."

Charles half rose from his chair. "That's what you think," he shouted. "I'll live a damn sight longer than you will, and don't you forget it."

"Yes, I expect you will." She went on quietly, "I meant in the beginning to give you the store. When you and Clarice were married, you remember, I offered to finance a store, a business, whatever you wanted, in Bristol or wherever you wished to go. Anything I could do, I thought—"

"Yeah. Anything you could do to get me out from underfoot! So that every time you looked at my damn face you wouldn't be reminded of Uncle Jos and Pa, and that a big wad of what you've got socked away belongs to me!"

"I didn't know that was why you refused, Charles."

"Damn right it was why I refused! And I'm not being chucked out now. I'm sticking around under your nose till I get what's coming to me."

"Charles, let me finish. I thought if you went away somewhere, with Clarice, on your own—away from our heartbroken household—you might forget Jos, his money and his things, boats and cars and hunting gear to drive a boy out of his mind with wanting till he gets, gets, gets, no matter how. Because you did break our hearts, Charles. At home you were dearly loved. We tried for years to show you, to do what we could to help. All of us. Having the children come here to work was part of it, trying to say, We're trying, we're hoping, please come back, be one of us again. Anything of mine you could have had—"

"In a pig's eye!" Charles said. "If you aren't lying your head off, how about letting me have it now?"

"—but not anything of Jos's. He left you enough, more than enough for any boy to handle, the part of himself that rots away decency, sinks its hooks into anybody, anything, regardless of who gets hurt. He wasn't a man who should have had power over anybody, and he did have. And I know you are not to blame for it, Charles, but—" She stopped and looked at him. Two tears formed in her eyes and rolled silently down, unnoticed, for she did not wipe them away. "But neither are you now. Not even the power to say who shall have credit and who shall not in a small-time grocery store."

"My God, I think you're crazy," Charles said. "You've spent your time hating Uncle Jos till you've gone off your nut. I could have you committed—"

Abigail picked up her bag and gloves. She went toward the door, moving almost briskly. "Dr. Graham will be interested," she said.

Charles, too, got up and kicked back his chair, which fell over behind him with a crash. "Well, I'm not taking this lying down," he shouted at her straight back.

"I should take it standing up, if I were you. I should put in hardware."

"Talk about hooks! You can sure sink yours in, can't you? Into me and—and into Uncle Jos, the poor old devil! All he had when you got through with him was a tombstone. It's a wonder he got away with enough of his money to buy it, but by God, he did and it's a good one, the best one out there! And I hope I live long enough to see you buried right next to it!"

"That," Abigail said, "you or anyone else will never live to see. And if I were you, I'd take a long look at the man and not at the most expensive monument in the cemetery."

Julie

Julie fought off her morning sickness—if that was what it was. It came at other times of day besides mornings. One moment she would be feeling fine, laughing and kidding, the next she'd be all but knocked out by dizziness and nausea. Jamie was put out with her about it. What if it happened sometime when the band was playing at a dance? He made her go to the doctor in Quadrant Harbor, who said it was morning sickness, ha, ha, young lady, lectured her about late nights, and gave her some pills which didn't help. Something about their aftertaste made her sick all over again. After a while she flushed them down the hotel toilet and didn't mention to Jamie that she wasn't taking them, not that he'd have noticed whether she was or not.

Jamie was absorbed in his band; all his interest was focused on it. He would have been equally concerned, Julie knew, about any other player who didn't feel well, would have insisted on a trip to the doctor in just the same way. She didn't blame him; she felt like that too. That is, now she did. She'd thought at first he might be kidding when he'd said he was going to latch on to a good piano player while he had a chance, so they'd get married. Besides, if the band got out-of-state engagements, he didn't want to be fouled up with the Mann Act. He hadn't been kidding.

249

If that was the way it was going to be, so what? Julie wouldn't be staying with Jamie forever. The band, except for herself and MacPhail, wasn't good enough. Before Mac-Phail had joined it, it hadn't been good enough to suit the manager of the Quadrant Harbor Inn and Jamie had come within an inch of not getting a contract there at all.

Jamie dearly wanted that contract. The inn would be jammed till Labor Day with summer trade—out-of-state people, some pretty wealthy and important folks, he said, who'd know a good band when they heard one. One of their regulars, he said the manager'd told him, was Gil Kirkpatrick, a big restaurant owner from Boston. Who knew what might happen?

"Anything," Julie'd said, "if you haven't been to too many movies."

The trouble with Jamie was that he had rosy dreams which he sometimes didn't hesitate to translate into reality. You never quite knew, with him, which was which.

"So what's the matter with you? We might get a contract for Boston."

"The band's not good enough."

"It better be! I'll lick it into shape. . . ."

But the band was still on trial the night MacPhail came easing up out of the crowd between dances, carrying his trumpet case and asking if he could sit in for a few numbers. And that night Jamie got his contract. He also signed one with MacPhail.

Jamie had his doubts about it, which he mentioned.

"We already got all the trumpet we need," he said, meaning his own. "I do solo trumpet myself."

MacPhail grinned. He said, "Uh-huh."

"Well, then, d'you want to—"

"You need some more sax. A lot more sax."

"You play saxophone too?"

"Uh-huh."

Julie didn't think she'd ever forget the next practice session, the first time she'd heard MacPhail's saxophone.

The melody took off in all directions, seemed almost to climb the walls. Like a scared rabbit, Julie thought. She, along with the rest of the band, was left plugging a couple of beats behind.

MacPhail stopped, grinned at her over his mouthpiece. "Come ahn, come *ahn!*" he said. "Cut out the kitten on the keys."

"Bag of tomcats, sounds like to me," Jamie said. "What *is* that, Mac?"

"That's playing. You're gonna have to learn how, Buster."

Jamie didn't like that. He considered he played pretty good trumpet. His trouble was that he owned too many phonograph records of big-time trumpet players; sometimes his imitations embarrassed everybody.

"Sounds lousy," he said. "Take that over again, boys." He tapped with his baton on the music stand.

"You seddown," MacPhail said. "Le'me and your girl here put something in the cookpot. She'll know what it's all about, I've heard her."

He didn't wait for an answer; he leaned over Julie and put his hands on the piano keys—too close, so that she moved away. "Look," he said. "This."

The savage beat that came out of the piano was nothing like the sticky sweet that Jamie always called for.

"Okay," Julie said, shrugging MacPhail away. "Get off my back and pick up your whistle."

"Atta girl," MacPhail said.

The thing grew, crescendo, threaded around and over by MacPhail's insolent pattern, a sound clean as glass, but bragging, conceited, creating rivalry to be met on its own terms, paid back in its own kind. Julie made it to the end, but she felt wrung out and a little dizzy. She was pleased to see that MacPhail was sweating; and Phinney, the trombone player, said, "Eeow! That ain't decent!"

MacPhail leaned back until the flimsy chair under him creaked with his weight. He was a big fellow, MacPhail. "Well, what about it, Jimmy? Going to pull up your socks and come along?"

Jamie was in a sulk. "Who in hell's going to like it?"

"They like it in New York," he said. He got up and started putting his sax back in its case. "They don't dance to 'Just a Song at Twilight,' that's for sure."

Jamie sputtered. "I never—I never played that in my life! What the hell? Here, come on back, let me—"

But MacPhail was leaving. "Your girl's tired," he said. "When she's ready, I am." He called back over his shoulder, "'Let Mr. Gershwin come to me.'"

From then on, Julie knew, she and MacPhail had carried the band. Everybody had learned something, but it was MacPhail's breaks and, after a while, hers that the crowd waited for. If she had felt better and he had kept his distance, it would have been magnificent fun. But she seemed to be getting more and more tired. Mornings began to be awful. Usually she could sleep until noon, and had. Now the sickness started early. And always, at practice sessions, in the dance hall between numbers, there was MacPhail, leaning close, putting his hands one on each side of her on the piano keys, breathing on the back of her neck, blowing smoke from his cigarettes. She was grateful to him for what he was teaching her and she told him so; but, "Move back, Mac," she said. "That smoke's strangling me."

"Have one," he said, pulling out his pack. "Great, if you don't feel good."

"I'd heave."

"It's only a pick-me-up. Try one."

One day, in desperation, she did try one, thinking, If I

pass out at the piano tonight, at least there'll be an excuse I can mention.

That night, at the piano, she felt wonderful.

Mac was delighted. "Hey, hey!" he said. "We were a couple whiz bangs tonight, huh? You're getting better all the time. One of these days we'll have us a real job."

"Kirkpatrick?" Julie asked.

Jamie had been talking a lot about Kirkpatrick, who was now here at the inn, a little roly-poly short man, bald as a button, who danced flatfooted and kept calling for numbers. On his head the dance-floor lights would glint in different colors as they changed. You could spot him by that, if you looked, in the crowd.

"Him?" MacPhail said. "Chamber music and easy chairs for the Beacon Hill bewjois?"

"Jamie says—"

"Nuh. Not for me. Not for you, either."

He had no conversation at all. To talk to, he was dull, dull, dull. He had black, dusty-looking hair and little black eyes, like pieces of coal. He was always looking, or rubbing against, or patting, making an excuse to touch. If Julie was a little afraid of him, Jamie hated him. Jamie was jealous of the weird, wild, wonderful sax, which made his own trumpet sound like a tin whistle. As Mac did not hesitate, on occasion, to mention.

But Jamie was in a bind. Because of Mac in the beginning, and now Julie, the band was getting known. People were coming from all over to dance at the Quadrant Harbor Inn. The floor was always crowded; on Saturday nights sometimes customers had to be turned away. The inn manager had already mentioned to Jamie a contract for next season —provided he kept the same players for sax and piano. Kirkpatrick, Jamie said, was pricking up his ears—sure, he'd talked to Kirkpatrick, a couple of times, and the old boy hadn't said no.

Of course, come fall, Julie would have to be out of it for a while; and what they'd do with a kid, Jamie didn't know, unless they could leave it with her mother. He wished now that he'd put his foot down in the beginning, made her get rid of it. Now it was too late. She'd have to go through with that and be away from the band for however long it took. He'd have to hang on to Mac at least until then. But by the time Julie got back, Jamie firmly believed he'd have his own style polished up and rolling—already, he could see, he was better than some of the big-time guys on the records. He had had to give up his trumpet solos, because the crowd always sat on its hands or hollered for Mac. But this fall, when he got that contract with Kirkpatrick settled, and Julie was back, he'd tell that son-of-a-bitch to go peddle his toot elsewhere.

* * *

"You seem cheerful, Mr. Cartwright," Abigail said. "Is it because the job's done?"

"Well, not exactly," Chris said. He had been whistling as he packed up his tools to go home. He had been thinking about Rob's new blue suit for school this fall, which Rob had bought himself and was proud of; that Waldo's job on Mulligan's Mound would last until October; that when Rob left to go to school, he, Chris, if he hadn't found work by then, would take Rob's place with Waldo, clearing land. He had been thinking that, whatever happened, he wasn't going to lose courage again. "I'm sorry the job's done," he said, "but I can't say I won't be just as busy at home for a while. Waldo's after me to fix the roof on the old ruin down there he's picked out for a barn. He's got his winter's hay stacked under my lumber tarps, and if I want them back, I've got to get it under cover."

"For Abigail?" she asked, smiling.

Chris grinned. "That cow's saved our lives, Mrs. Plummer. I guess we gave it the nicest name we know."

"Thank you. When you get that done, could you undertake another job for me?"

Chris jumped. "I'd sure be glad to. Anything I can do—"

"You can surely do this. For a number of years I've considered building a new store. I've a parcel of land at the north end of Main Street, which I bought with this in mind some years ago. Growth of the town is toward the north—I suppose it has to be to get away from the river, which is getting a worse and worse smell, I'm sorry to say."

"Sure is. Low tide down there, you can't get your breath on a hot day. Too bad. It must've been a nice little stream once."

"Yes, it was. My ancestor, John Randall, built his house on the riverbank when he came here. He was the first to settle in these parts, though I understand he didn't stay here long, being a wanderer. I've some old papers of his, telling how pretty it was down there when he came. Wilderness to the water's edge, he wrote, and his house was in a grove of oak trees. All gone now, of course—cut when the lumber mills and shipyards were built along the river. Now they are all gone, too, and the river's a sewer, from the Bristol mills."

This was a great deal for Abigail to say. In her talks with Chris before, she had been mostly brief and businesslike, about the job in hand. He wished he hadn't helped her get sidetracked. She didn't look very well—her face was white and strained—and all this talk was unusual enough to make him wonder if she felt all right.

How big a building? When could he start work on it? Work for pay wasn't going to stop, and what a thing to be able to go home and tell Mary. Why get het up about the river? People had always used one to dump trash into, and if the Bristol mills had got a natural, God-given sewer to let go their stink into, they weren't going to do anything else, so long as it saved them time and money; and who else could? It seemed impolite to interrupt her, though, and he said, "There ought to be a law."

"Of course there ought to be a law. Some good stout fines would cut down that smell in a hurry, Mr. Cartwright."

"Well, you'd have to crack some local knuckles, Mrs. Plummer. Quite a lot of folks down on River Street heave their garbage out of their back doors. There's one feller got a pigpen down there that's a scandal to the jaybirds. Got twenty or thirty half-grown shoats up to their hocks in muck. Smell's enough to knock a man down."

"That's outrageous! The S.P.C.A. could stop that, you know, if his neighbors would complain."

"They do complain—to each other. So Larry says. He was ferreting around down there the other day, Lord knows why. He says the feller is Sam Greeley, and people put up with him because they don't want their buildings burnt down."

"Mm, I see. Sam Greeley. Well, Mr. Cartwright, I have a tentative sketch for the building . . . here, somewhere . . ." She fumbled in her bag, held out a square of paper. "It's very rough. A general idea only. If you'll drop by the office, when you can, I'll show you the land and we can discuss costs and estimates."

Her hand must be shaking a little—he could see the tremor in the paper, and he took it from her quickly, so that she wouldn't see he was noticing. It was, he saw, quite a practical working plan, for a beginning.

"Concrete foundation," he said. "Mm-hm, I see. I'll take this home with me tonight. You know, I might see you tomorrow?"

"Certainly, if you have time, Mr. Cartwright. About ten?"

I hope she's all right, Chris told himself, watching her climb stiffly into her car. I wouldn't want to undertake a job like this for that bastard of a son of hers. The thing was, he wouldn't. He'd take handouts first.

❖   ❖   ❖

Back in her office, Abigail reached thoughtfully for the telephone. She called the sheriff and got Willy Meader.

"Jerome's home sick," Willy said. "At least he says he is. He says he's really retiring this time, Mrs. Plummer."

"Is he, at last? What finally brought this on?"

Willy chuckled. "Well, I'm not too sure. A number of things. Could have been Larsen busting out of jail. Jerome hasn't really been the same since."

"Larsen . . . Mr. Larsen? But he was let go. Legally, wasn't he?"

"Oh, yes, sure. But when Jerome went in to let him out on the Judge's orders, he found the cell empty, door unlocked and swinging. He was all tore out about it. Said it couldn't have happened, he'd had his keys hooked to his belt all day, and nothing out of the way happened, except a gang of hoodlums staged a fake fight in his office with a bottle of ketchup. I would've thought he'd had a bad dream from the way he described it, but I saw the ketchup all over the floor. Anyway, whatever it was, it shook Jerome. So he's retiring."

"Well, Mr. Meader, it's your turn now, isn't it? Are you going to run for sheriff this fall?"

"I'm going to run," Willy said. "I don't know's I'll beat anybody."

"What makes you think so? Isn't Jerome backing you?"

"He was, but he's hedging. Seems Judge Clawson's against."

"Didn't you expect that?"

"From the Judge, yes. Not from Jerome. I guess the Judge got to him. You know Jerome."

"I have for a long time."

"Well, he's old," Willy said. "And he and Clawson are somewhat closer now than they used to be. They've dug up Harley Crawford as opposition. I don't seem to have much of an organization behind me."

"Harley Crawford? Oh, my goodness!" Abigail said.

"Well, he's a nice, accommodating man. He's already told me I can stay on as his deputy, if I lose. I'm likely to lose, Mrs. Plummer."

"You aren't giving up, are you?"

"No, ma'am. I am not."

"Good," Abigail said. "Neither will I. Do you know about a pigpen owned by a man named Sam Greeley, down on River Street?"

"Sam," Willy Meader said, "that pigpen is one of the nastiest messes I've ever seen. You can smell it from here to back again."

Sam Greeley took his pipe out of his mouth and ran a hand over his ginger-whiskered chin. "What you smell down here, and you know it," he said, "is that damn river."

"That's right. But I smell pig too. And so do your neighbors."

Sam stared at the river, which now at ebb tide was revealing grisly secrets—nameless masses of slime and garbage, old buckets and cans, rusted chunks of iron, automobile tires, and, fairly recently dumped, a load of manure and straw from somebody's horse barn.

"Ain't that horrible!" he said. He sniffed deeply. "I d'no what they do up to Bristol, my tongue ain't foul enough to say. Them old spilins down there c'lect up all the guts and gizzards that float down, big clunks of it every day. 'Tain't my fault if the town ain't got the foresight to git 'trid of them spilins and that old hulk over there on the mudflats. I bet they's ten thousand rats holed up in there, come night, along with some boys and girls courting."

He swung around on Willy, pointing with the stem of his pipe. "You know what vessel that was?"

"I can't say I do. Now, look, Sam—"

"That is what is left of the *Mary T. Randall*, by God and by Jeezus, built right here on this river, down where them

old spilins is all that's left of the yard. She broke the record,
New York to Liverpool. My gramfather was aboard of her
when she done it, A.B. first-class seaman. I got his picture
over my mantelpiece. Them Englishmen took it, along with
the skipper and the rest uv um. Look at her bow, you look
at it and remember it, ain't another one like it you'll ever see
on God's green earth, ain't ever going to be. She ought to
be set uptown next to the bandstand in a new co't of paint,
is where she ought to be, as a mem'ry of what was, not laying over there on the flats full of rats and condoms and saying to herself, 'For chrisesake, what kind of people live here
now?' Who squawked about my pigpen?"

"The S.P.C.A. You can't nail it down to any individual."

"Abby Plummer!" Sam said. "Someday someone's going
to haul that hat of hers down over her chin. By the judast,
maybe it'll be me!"

"I'm not the one to tell, if you plan to bother anyone,
Sam. You'll have to clean up here, or the Board of Health'll
see you do."

He reached for the key to start his car, but Sam came over
and stuck his head in through the rolled-down window.

"The world," he said, "has got some old poison when a
man can't raise his own pigs without some nosy old flop-
doodle shoving their clop into his business." He shook his
pipestem under Willy's nose. "And that goes for the Sisspee-
oodle or whatever else it is Abby Plummer's the head of.
And for you too. And," he went on, warming to an old griev-
ance, "for the entire You-nited States Governmint, a goddam mess of Democrats if I ever see one. I pay taxes. Taxes!
So as to pay the wages of someone to come around and tell
me how to raise my pigs. I ask you, Franklin D. Meader, is
them my pigs, or is them not my pigs?"

"Your law too," Willy said. "So don't break it, Sam."

"You can tell them sons up to the courthouse they can't
arrest me for a stink them old spilins c'lect and that smells

like sweet roses of springtime compared to the courthouse. Tell 'em that the other day them spilins c'lected a body."

"Did?" Willy said. "Why didn't you report it?"

"Hell, I thought 'twas Judge Clawson. Then I see 'twan't nobody I knew either, so I let 'er go, down the river. You running for sheriff this fall?"

"I expect to."

"Good, I'll vote for ya. Carry the Amurrican flag, if you want me to."

"Thanks, Sam," Willy said. "I'll sure need someone to."

Independence was all right, he thought, as he drove away. Once upon a time it was what had settled the country. You had to admire a man who had it, but if it didn't stop short of somewhere, the law's job was tough.

❖   ❖   ❖

In September, Elsie had her baby, another fine bouncing boy, whom she named Randall. She had had quite a time deciding what to call him, poring over lists of names copied from newspapers and movie magazines, and the columns of names, both boys' and girls', in the back of the dictionary. She had specialized at first on girls, because, after all, she'd had one boy already, and she could just see her and Del's little new baby, dressed up in pink, lace and frilly things. So pretty it would be. But none of the girls' names seemed right. Either they sounded nice when you said them and looked horrid on paper, or they were like, oh, "Constance," easily turned into some common nickname. Connie, ugh! Boys' names were better; so after a while she stopped mentioning in her prayers that she wanted a girl and asked God for a boy.

"Galahad" she considered for a while because of what it said in the poem:

My strength is as the strength of ten,
Because my heart is pure.

She had dearly loved that poem ever since she'd learned it and spoken it at a grade-school entertainment. Just to say it made you feel stronger all over. And "Blessed are the pure in heart" too. It said that in the Bible. But when she told Delbert her choice, he hit the ceiling and swore.

"Goddammit, Else, no! Don't be such a nitwit! You saddle the poor little devil with a name like that, he'll get kidded all his life!"

Elsie froze. It seemed to her her whole spine went to curdles, right up to the back of her neck. "Delbert Smiley! You stop that swearing in front of me at a time like this— you'll mark the baby! For all you know, you already have marked him. Oh, dear, whatever shall I do now?"

Delbert comforted her as best he could. It took time.

A pregnant mother and her baby were *one*, she sobbed, so the mother ought to keep calm and never tore out, and there was that woman, Daisy Hutchin's great-aunt, who stepped on a strawberry and thought it was a mouse and when her baby came it had a strawberry-colored mouse right on its collarbone and she was lucky it wasn't on the poor little thing's face; and if Delbert didn't think of her any more than to curse and swear where that helpless baby probably heard it just as plain as she had, and no knowing what kind of a dreadful stain a swearword would leave and show on a baby . . .

Delbert tried to think of something. He ought to have known better. He'd have to think fast, too, or the poor kid would sure as hell get named Galahad. He finally said, "Your own family was the first family around here for a good many years, settled the country and all. How'd you like to call him Randall? Randy, that's dignified and cute too." .

That was certainly something, his going so far as to let on her family was better than his. He'd always insisted that the Smileys had been the first people to settle the country, and she'd had to give in before when he'd wanted to call Delly

Delbert Smiley, the second. Still . . . Well, she wasn't going to let him off easy.

"Oh, those old antique pioneers! Igerant as Indians, there wasn't one of them ever went to school. If you said a nice name like Galahad to them, they wouldn't even know it was in the Bible."

"Well, I don't know as I do, either," Delbert said, and checked himself. "What if he gets nicknamed Gal? Sounds like a grocery bill."

"It does not!"

"To one gal. molasses?"

"Well, if I can't call him Galahad, I don't know what else there is." But she was thinking. After all, Randall, the first family . . . And of course every common person in town would say "Gal."

"If you're still hankering after chocolate creams, honey," he said, "there's a box in my overcoat pocket."

"Oh, dear! I did hope you'd bring home shrimps today."

Delbert grinned. "In the icebox," he said. "Mix 'em. Shrimps and chocolate creams on toast. If that don't mark Galahad, nothing I ever say is going to."

Randall came and he was Randy, never anything else. He was fat, beautiful, and perfect, except for a small pink mole beside one ear.

"'N there!" Elsie said. "I'll bet you anything that if you hadn't swore at me, he wouldn't have that witch-tit, Delbert Smiley."

Lying in bed after her delivery, she decided it didn't matter in the least, it was actually kind of cunning. She contemplated him with pride and pleasure, and thought, Here she was, two up on Maureen who wasn't even that way yet, or if she was she didn't show it. That was Arthur's fault, of course, who really must have something wrong with him—never had connections before he was married, not that Elsie thought that was a nice thing to do, but from the way the boys in high school had acted and the way Delbert had acted, it seemed likely that most men did unless they were undescended.

She thought of a joke to play on Maureen that would poke fun, in a nice way, at the situation, and as soon as she was up and around, she baked a gingerbread man, complete, wrapped it carefully in a box so it wouldn't break up, and mailed it to Mrs. Arthur Bickford, signing no name. The box would take overnight in the mail. She'd plan to be over there tomorrow, with both babies, just to see how Maureen took it.

She was walking along the street pushing the new two-passenger perambulator—and wasn't Delbert going to cuss when he got the bill from the furniture store!—when she saw a woman just turning the corner ahead of her who looked as though she was going to be one or maybe two up on somebody and in the not very far future. Tch! she told herself. If I ever looked like that, and I never *did*, not even with Delly! Who could it be?

She came to the corner herself, glanced curiously down the street—though naturally it couldn't be anyone she knew, one of the girls, or she'd have known before this. There was the woman, heading into the alley, the narrow short cut that came out by the railroad station, which wasn't far from River Street. Oh, of course, somebody from down by the winnega works; you'd think they'd stay home when they looked like that.

The woman—girl, it was—turned then and glanced back. Elsie saw, with a sudden gasp of amazement and shock, that she was Julie.

Elsie called, "Julie!" in a voice that didn't seem to carry very far—at least the girl didn't stop—and then half-heartedly, "Hoo-hoo," which didn't have any effect either. She hustled the perambulator around the corner and down to the mouth of the alley, but she couldn't see anybody. Whoever it had been had gone out of sight, and the alley was rough cobblestones, kind of muddy—Elsie wasn't going to push her new perambulator in there, get the wheels dirty.

Probably hadn't been Julie anyway. The Lord knew there were plenty of Plummers and Randalls, too, all over the county; must be one of them with a family resemblance. Well, there! If that hadn't given her a turn! Made her late, too, because Maureen would certainly have got her mail and opened it by now.

❅   ❅   ❅

The summer season and Jamie Stetson's contract at the Quadrant Harbor Inn ended with September. Julie managed to last out the final dance, but when it was over and the band was packing up to leave, she told Jamie she was through; he would have to find a new piano player. At least until after the baby was born and she was back on her feet, and then she'd see. After all, there'd be the baby. Wouldn't there?

"I'm tired to death," she told him. "And I'm lumpy. People notice."

Jamie didn't see it that way. "What do you care? We'll get you a hatching jacket. All the lunks'll be fascinated."

The "lunks." That was what he called his local audiences now.

"No," Julie said. She knew what a hatching jacket was—a hideous sort of chopped-off-below-the-hips Mother Hubbard that pointed to, rather than hid, what you looked like now. Julie hated what she looked like. Already she had had to take comments about it; for her to appear in public from now on would be ridiculous, and she said so.

"Well, what'll you do then? I've got these hick engagements till Gil gets back from Europe." Gil was Kirkpatrick. So far as anyone knew, there was no contract with him, but Jamie was sure there would be. Gil had said this; Gil had said that; and Jamie was already headed for big things. "I can't carry dead weight around with the band, if I have to hire a new piano player. There'll be hotel bills."

"I'll go to the cozy little home you've provided," Julie

said. "The Pullman coach with the chem toilet and the sink spout that drips on the ground outside the bedroom window."

"For godsake!" Jamie said. "Did I ask you there in the first place? That old coach was good enough for me when I couldn't afford different. I can now, and so can you. You've had full wages all summer. Even if you are my wife."

This was a very sore point with Jamie. A man hadn't ought to have to pay his wife wages, and she'd threatened to quit unless she got hers.

"Why don't you go to a hotel?" he went on. "Or make it up with your mother and go home till it's over? She'd pay your expenses and take the kid, so we can get rolling again. You've got to be somewhere where there's a piano, unless you plan to sit on your hands and let your style go to hell in a hack."

Julie was sick of the sight of him. Her temper flew.

"You can go roll your hoop," she said. "I'll take care of myself from now on. If I've got this baby, I had plenty of help from you and don't you forget it, Buster. You can quit being Airy Fairy Lillian, as if you didn't have a thing in the world to do with it."

"For all I know, I didn't," Jamie said, in a dudgeon. All he had taken in was the word "fairy," a deadly insult. "I'll stay away, all right."

He did, for a while. After she moved into the railway coach, he got himself a room at the hotel. Then he came around to tell her that he had a string of local engagements and to find out if she'd had any mail.

"Mac hasn't either," he said. "I didn't know but where Gil was so interested in you two, he might write you first." Well, he wouldn't be around much for a while, he'd be traveling with the band around the county. If she heard anything, here was a list of the places where he'd be. Would she call him?

"Collect," Julie said.

It was a good thing she'd saved most of her wages, she thought. It looked now as if she were going to need them.

She didn't hear anything from him for nearly three weeks, and then one afternoon MacPhail came around.

MacPhail looked quite different from usual. He had shaved and put on a clean shirt, and, for him, he seemed quite talkative.

"Nuh. I've quit," he said, when she asked him if Jamie was back in town. "Everybody might as well. The way the big shot's lurching around, he's fixed his wagon with all the so-called 'lunks' in this part of the country."

MacPhail went on to tell. Seemed it had got to be anybody's guess whether Jamie would keep an engagement or not. If he didn't feel like it, or had a hangover, he wouldn't even bother to let the people know the band wasn't coming.

"Bought himself a lot of fancy new suits and a hell of a great big shiny gold-colored horn. Stands up and tootles it loud and clear, whatever big-time phonograph record he's listened to last. It's a museum piece," MacPhail said soberly. "Oh, God!"

It seemed Mac had countered this phenomenon in his own way. He showed Julie. When Jamie was through, and bowing, Mac would blow three or four flat blats on his sax. Then he would pick up the melody and play it, and the crowd would get the point with cheers and hoots. "Makes him mad," MacPhail said.

Julie would think it might. "Why don't you let him alone, Mac? You don't have to, why do you?"

Mac shrugged and disregarded the remark. He was flashing around some himself, he said. He'd bought a secondhand Model-A for seventy bucks. He'd parked it a few blocks away —didn't want to ruin Julie's reputation.

"You aren't going to be around here long enough to ruin anything," Julie said. "I'm tired out of my life and all I want to do is sleep."

Mac said, "Okay," and went. The next day he was back. She came in from a walk to find him with a set of borrowed tools tuning the ancient relic of a piano.

"What are you doing?" Julie said. "Listen, Mac. Nobody's going to practice here on that old mouse nest. You go somewhere else if you want to work. Go hunt up Jamie's new piano pounder, work with him."

"No new piano pounder," Mac said. "No band, either, for a while. The Horn's gone on vacation. Fishing, northern part of the state. O'Donnell's—where the baseball stars and bandleaders and movie boys go. Baby doll, you should ha' seen him climbing on the train! Fancy fishing rods, creels, high-price canvas pants. Flies!" Mac put back his head and roared. "The guy never cast a fly in his life!"

Julie stared at him. In all the time she had known him, she had never heard him laugh out loud.

"Funny he didn't let me know where he was going," Julie said. "He told me to call him if any word came from Kirkpatrick."

"Somebody tipped him off that Kirkpatrick was up there," Mac said. "Can't think who. You know, Julie, Kirkpatrick ain't going to send any messages to Jamie. Jamie hounded the poor guy all summer till dear Gil told him anything he could think of to get rid of him. Kirkpatrick offered a contract, yes, but not to Jamie. To me and you. I told him we wasn't interested."

"You had a nerve!" Julie said. "Who do you think you are? If I believed a word you say, I'd say mind your own business, let me make up my own mind what I want to do."

"Make you mad, does it?" He ran his fingers along the piano keys, made a wry face. "Them wires in there just about gone to hell."

"Mac," Julie said, "I told you, I'm tired. I wouldn't care right now if somebody offered me a job on the moon to play dance tunes to the angels. So will you please go away?"

"No," Mac said. "I'm sticking around."

Julie's heart sank. How could she get rid of him, anyway, if he wouldn't go? She thought wearily, I can't throw him out. When he does go, I'll go out somewhere and buy a bolt for the door. So far as she knew, the place had never had a key.

MacPhail surprised her again. "I ain't rushing you or anything, Julie," he said. "What I mean, work with me or without me, whatever you feel like. I won't bother you either, if that's what you're worried about. But I ain't leaving you alone in this joint to sull around till you go nuts without anything to do. If you want to work, there'll be this piano, and if you want to work with me, I'll bring my sax. The time's coming when you're going to need somebody, too, and I plan to be within call."

"What's come over you? You sound human, for a change."

"Yeah. I surprise myself."

He didn't bother her, as he had said he wouldn't. He came around once a day from his rooming house, stayed when she didn't ask him to go, did errands, offered rides in his car. Mostly he worked on the piano, absorbed, swearing under his breath at the hopeless old wreck, paying Julie no attention. He tinkered for nearly a week, until she thought the *plink-plank-plunk*, especially when he got to the treble wires, would drive her out of her mind. But after a while she found she was looking forward to his coming. He was someone to talk to, and now that she was getting over her exhaustion, the railway coach was lonely beyond anything she had ever imagined it would be. Dull, too. A terrible bore, nothing special to do. When MacPhail said one day, jerking his head toward the piano, "Try it," she did.

"It ain't much," he said. "Only thing that'd really help it'd be a hatchet. How's about if I bring my sax around?"

"It would be a way to kill time," she said.

But try as she would, she couldn't play very well. Her fingers felt stiff, lumpy; she couldn't concentrate. Her mind

kept jumping around. At the first session MacPhail was patient. Then, after two or three, when she didn't improve any,
he got mad.

"For chrisesake, Julie!"

"Well, I can't. It's this awful piano."

For answer, he took the piano himself and brought out
of it an astonishing rhythm. "See? All you got to do is try,
get going."

She crashed both hands down on the keys. "I won't. I'm
sick to death of it. Will you get out of here and let me alone?"

"Sure." He began putting his sax back in its case.

Julie screamed at him. "Play, Julie, get going, Julie . . . all
you think about. You, Jamie, all you slobs! Play, Julie, so we
can get us better jobs, so we can ride right up into the
bright lights on top of your piano! You don't care anything
about me, myself . . . when I'm half crazy having this . . . this
awful time, you don't even think it's awful."

"Women have kids," MacPhail said. "You ain't different."
He shoved his case under his arm and made for the door.
"Quit yelling. I'm going."

He was going. He wasn't going to try to comfort her, say
it wasn't so, or anything. She snatched up the coffee mug she
had been drinking out of and bounced it on the floor as hard
as she could. It smashed. Dregs of coffee splashed and a
single sharp splinter ricocheted into Mac's face. He stopped,
pulled out his handkerchief, and dabbed his cheek, glancing
down at the small spot of blood against the white cloth.

"If that had gone into my eye, I'd have killed you," he said.

The look on his face terrified Julie. She backed away.

"I ain't going to touch you," he said. "What the hell kind
of a prima d'you think you are? Look, when I run into you
first, you weren't nothing but a small-time pounder, like all
the goddamned rest of Jamie's bunch. I ain't riding your
wagon, you're riding mine. Someday, you and me, we might
get a job in what you call the bright lights, but it ain't going

downhill on roller skates to get there. You gotta work. Like other people, remember? Because, baby, you got an awful lot to learn."

He went out, closing the door behind him with a quiet click. Julie grabbed a chair and braced it under the door-knob. She *would* get a bolt. A good strong one, keep him out of here! The big, overbearing slob! Tell me I'm no good without him. I can play circles around him any day. I'll show him. If the time ever comes when I can *reach* the damn piano!

How long would it be? Soon, it had to be. She didn't know exactly; in the beginning she hadn't worried about the time. Now she wished she had. She lay down on the bunk, trying to remember.

Come on, get born. Get it over with, the sooner the better, she told the baby, and sat up, for a moment panicked, be-cause she thought she had felt it move. Would getting mad, stirred up like this, make it come before it was ready? No, don't be silly. You had to have pains first, then it came. This wasn't anything—no more than she had felt it move before.

Mac had left his cigarettes on the piano. One had dribbled out of the pack where he had tossed it. Those got you out of the dumps. Maybe they would this time, though she guessed she had never dumped as low as this. She got one, lit it, lay down on the bunk again.

It wasn't a half-bad piano. He had really done a job on it, and you could get some good stuff out of it if you wanted to.

Someone was knocking on the door.

Him, she thought. Well, he can wait till I get ready.

The knock came again. Then footsteps. He was going away.

Julie got up, pulled the chair out from under the knob, opened the door. "You've got pretty genteel, knocking—" she began, and stopped, her voice dying in her throat.

It wasn't Mac. It was her mother, halfway down the walk, going away.

"Well, Julie," Abigail said. "It's been a long time. May I come in?"

"Do," Julie said. She stepped aside. "This is where I live now. Not what you're used to."

"No," Abigail said. "But never mind that. What I came for was to see you."

"Not much use to clean it up," Julie said. "Whatever you do to it, it's still scrummy. My husband likes it, though. Too bad you can't meet him. He's away."

"Does he leave you here alone?" Abigail had not even glanced around the place. She was looking at Julie.

"Oh, he's busy. The band, you know. Gone for days sometimes."

"Julie. Please come home?"

"Oh, you wouldn't dream of putting up with me now, Ma. I'm not a problem child any more, I'm worse. I swear now and take a drink, if I want to, and my cigarettes have got something in them to make me feel wonderful when I'm low. Won-der-ful. See?"

"Julie, honey, you always were a flitterbug, but it's no use trying to make me believe you're wicked. Never mind all that now. Come home and let Nettie and me make you comfortable and quiet till you've had your baby. I'm sure your husband wouldn't mind—he could come and see you there when he wanted to, and I'm sure it would do a great deal for his peace of mind to know you were all right while he's away—"

"Jamie's peace of mind? Oh, baby doll!"

"Then after the baby comes, you could do what you wanted to—stay with me, or go. It would be your business and his."

"I'm sorry, Ma. I don't want to come home. I'd go nuts."

For the first time Abigail's gaze went slowly around the inside of the railway coach.

"If I go to Boston and talk to Nan, will you listen to Nan?"

"Isn't it a ducky place?" Julie said. "All the comforts. Even a piano. Want to hear me play it?"

"No, thank you, not now. I have to catch the train at four. You won't change your mind?"

"Not me."

"You ought to have decent care, Julie. I would be glad to see you got it. And we love you there."

She turned and went slowly down to the street. Peering from the window, Julie saw she really was headed for the station.

Let her. Let her talk to Nan till her tongue falls out. I need her peace and quiet like I need a new head.

But seeing the tall, straight figure pass out of sight beyond the station door, Julie wavered.

Oh, God, I do need a new head, this one's all out of whack. I need her and I need Nan, and pretty soon it's going to be night and I need light, not that damn old kerosene lamp. And somebody to come, not be here alone.

Nobody was coming.

After a while she went back to the piano and began playing again. If this was all the company she was going to have, she'd see it was good enough to fill up the time. Her fingers slammed down on the keys. The rickety piano vibrated to the floor; she could feel it through her whole body.

Shiver and shake, she told it. So you fall apart too.

She did not notice when the after-sunset twilight began to creep into the coach and she did not hear MacPhail come in and sit quietly down behind her. A thundering chord ended in a bass twanging sound; the snapped wire jangled away somewhere into the interior of the piano. So that was that. That was it, baby.

"Which one was it?" Mac said. "Sounded like low B."

Julie jumped. "What are you trying to do—scare me to death?"

But he was already at the piano, opening the top, peering in. "Yeah, low B. Hell, I can fix that."

❖   ❖   ❖

Abigail had written to Nan that she might be coming to Boston. The letter had not been answered, but it had not been returned by the post office, so Nan must have got it. At her last year's address, however, her name was not on the list by the mailboxes. Abigail checked twice before ringing the bell marked "Janitor."

The woman who answered was pleasant and helpful. Miss Plummer—oh, yes. She had moved out sometime in . . . let's see, June, it was. She had left a forwarding address. Just a minute . . . yes, here it was. "But I expect you'd be more likely to find her at the school, this time of day."

Abigail had already thought of this. "Yes," she said, "I have been there. She seems not to be in her classes today."

"Perhaps she's stayed home for some reason. I would try there, if I were you."

"Where would this street be?" Abigail asked. "I'm afraid I don't know the city very well."

"I think it's on the back side of Beacon Hill, I'm not sure just where. I'd take a taxi. The man'll know."

It was a place of steep streets and ancient, run-down buildings two and three stories high, made into cheap apartment houses. Nan's name was on her mailbox. Abigail rang and rang. Nobody answered the bell.

After a long time she gave up and went wearily down the steps to her waiting taxi. She had not been in the city since she had brought Felix for the last time to the clinic. Two? —three years ago. The rush and racket had confused her then and it seemed much more confusing now. She sat for a moment, trying to think what to do next.

The cab driver said, "Where to now, lady?" and she gave

him the name of her hotel. With four walls around her, out of all this noise, she would be able to think.

It would have been better not to come, better to have written, because Nan would surely have read a letter. If I had not written at all, had not named a date . . . she may be doing this because she does not wish to talk to me. I must find her. And talk to her. Because it's gone beyond misunderstandings now, people being angry with each other. It's urgent now. If she could see Julie, talk to her, she'd realize how urgent. . . .

If I only knew who Nan's friends were here; perhaps one of them would know where she is. I will phone the school from the hotel.

Back at the hotel, she put through the call and, after a short wait, got a pleasant, eager young voice on the line.

"Nan Plummer? She's not here today. Wait a minute. Hi, anybody know where Nan went?"

A moment's pause. Voices. Then, "Sorry, nobody seems to know. Why don't you call Larry Cartwright at the law school? He's usually not very far behind her. Oh, certainly. You're welcome."

Larry? Did he know Nan? Yes, they had met once, at least—Nan had mentioned coming home on the train with him. If the acquaintance had bloomed, thank God. If only he could help her find Nan . . .

She called the law school, left word for Laurance Cartwright to phone her as soon as he could be given the message.

For quite a long time she sat by the phone, which did not ring, before she realized that she had not stopped even to take off her hat and coat. The room was stifling and stuffy; they kept these places much too hot, and whoever had stayed here last had been smoking an unusually rank cigar. The hotel people should air out, before renting a room to another guest; they certainly charged enough to be able to manage

that inexpensive small comfort which merely involved opening a window. If there were one which would open.

There was, and she opened it, just as the phone rang.

"Mrs. Plummer? Larry Cartwright. You're in town. Where?
They only gave me your phone number."

"Larry, do you know where I can find Nan? She isn't at
home and she isn't at the school."

"She isn't? Oh. Why, yes, I think I do know, at least I can
find out. She's got two or three private pupils she's giving
lessons to—I expect it's one of them. Let me do a little phon-
ing and call you back. Doesn't she know you're in town?"

"I came in a sort of . . . hurry. Tell her I must see her,
Larry."

"Sure will. I'll call back."

"Thank you."

She hadn't, she thought, said "Hello" or "How are you?"
to him. Never mind, he hadn't missed it. He had, apparently,
sensed her anxiety and had gone straight to essentials, first
things first. That was a good, clear, logical mind—she had
found that out this summer.

There was nothing to do now but wait. She took off her
hat and coat, hung the coat on a hanger in the closet, put
the hat on a shelf. She had had nothing to eat since morning,
a sketchy breakfast on the train. Perhaps it was late to order
lunch. She tried and found it wasn't, but when the food came
she could not eat it. She tried to read the newspaper she had
brought in and could not read.

Why didn't Larry call?

Finally she sat down by the open window and let the afternoon drag along.

The room was fairly high up in the tower of the hotel. Its
windows looked out over a jumbled mass of roofs and chim-
neys bleak with shadows under a murky-gray sky. Somewhere under one of those roofs was Nan, dearly loved, in
some ways the best loved and certainly the most trusted of

all Abigail's children. Nan, as clear as glass, honest as rain, her judgment blurred where Julie was concerned, as it always had been. She knew Julie's tantrums only too well; in anyone else she would not have put up with them, not for a moment. She had always been able to see the difference between discipline and blaming, as Julie never could.

I have never blamed too much; it is too easy to destroy a child's dignity by stupid, foolish blaming. But where I have had reason to, I have fought. When I have had to.

This city is built the way most people have to build their lives. You put out what you can with what you have, like a monkey-puzzle tree. And in the end you are what happens to you, after all.

Charles, with his broken face, his brain of a grown man, his ethics of a dishonest child. Elsie, the dishonest child, without the brain. Julie . . .

Manners I tried to teach them—not just "please" and "thank you" and how to use a knife and fork and don't chew with your mouth open. There is more to manners than that. They are what you must have to fight the world with. Perhaps I was foolish to think I could teach something that maybe has to be built-in from the beginning. Maureen will do—her stubborn courage will survive Arthur; and Miles isn't scared of his own shadow now. He will be scared, in his lifetime—everyone is—but not of his own shadow.

From somewhere, almost as if it were in the room with her, she heard Felix's shaken voice saying, "I am myself but indifferent honest"—not making fun, only stating an undeniable fact, to which the answer, if she had known enough then to make it, should have been, "I know that. And I know you cannot help it."

The phone rang, a single startling peal.

"Mrs. Plummer? This is Larry. I—can I come and talk to you?"

"You haven't found Nan?"

"No," he said. "I can't. I've been trying. I've phoned around and done some looking—it's why I'm so late calling. Finally I went around to her place. She's not there. But sometimes when she has to break a date with me—we had one tonight for dinner—she leaves me a note in her mailbox, lets me keep a key. So on the chance, I looked, and there was one. I don't know what . . . she says she's away. It doesn't say where or for how long."

"And that's all?"

"Mrs. Plummer, I wish I could say it wasn't. She couldn't have known you were coming. Gosh, I'm sorry."

"Never mind, Larry. It's not your fault. When you can reach her, you must give her a message. Tell her Julie needs help. She is very near her time and she is living in Stetson's old railway coach. Nan knows where that is, what it is like. I have been to see her and she will take nothing from me. She is there alone. Will you tell Nan that and tell her that she must come home, because she is the only one Julie will listen to, now?" She stopped, feeling her voice start to slip out of control.

"Lord, yes, anything I can do. I'll keep on hunting. Someone must know where she's gone. And I'll leave a note in her box."

"Thank you. Tell her it's . . . urgent. So urgent that I can't wait to see her. I am taking the night train home."

MacPhail did not appear the next morning. Julie did not expect him. He had said he'd be going to Bristol after new piano wire, wouldn't be back till afternoon. She was glad he was gone—she hadn't slept much during the night, and when she finally did drop off toward morning, she had a series of ugly dreams. At daylight she got up, chilled and exhausted, and lighted the oilstove. Last night she hadn't been hungry; she doubted if she'd ever feel hungry again. A hot drink might help—not coffee, that would keep her awake; besides, the coffeepot was dirty. There wasn't any milk, but Mac had brought in a carton of cream for his coffee last night. She heated that and managed to choke some of it down. Oddly enough, it did the trick. She fell asleep almost at once. She was just up and dressed when Mac got back from Bristol at four in the afternoon.

"What's trouble?" he asked, glancing at her. "Didn't you eat?"

"Oh, sure." She hadn't, but what was the use of going into that? "How would you expect me to look?" she asked resentfully.

Mac ignored it. Watching him go to work again on the piano, she thought, He'll be lucky if I don't yell the house down. *Plunk-plunk*. Pause. Then, *plunk*. It would probably go on for hours. She was rested; she might as well clean up the place a little.

First things first, she told herself. In a minute he'll be hollering for coffee. She washed the coffeepot.

She was stacking dirty plates beside the sink when Mac hollered, but not for coffee. "Julie, will ya quit that damn clinking? I can't hear myself think."

She had some things to wash and a couple of dresses that needed pressing. She left the dishes where they were and lighted the stove to heat up the flatiron. There was only one, an ancient sadiron which the boys had dug up from some secondhand store and had used to press their uniform pants in the days when they had stayed in the coach with Jamie.

It was getting dark before MacPhail finished and sat back with a grunt. "New wire," he said. "Damn thing keeps stretching. You want to try it now?"

"I can't," Julie said. She had been lying on the bunk, reading the newspaper Mac had brought in, until it had got too dark to read. Now she was just lying there.

"Ah, here I've worked my head off all day. Come on, Julie."

"Mac, all I can hear is that *plink-plunk*, for heaven's sake!"

That made sense to him. "Yeah, I guess so. Well, we better eat then. I'll go get some stew from the restaurant."

He had left his cigarettes on the piano, as usual.

How long could you take glumps and dumps? All day was long enough.

By nine o'clock things were rosy again. She felt as if she could go on playing forever.

"Atta girl," Mac said. "Give 'er hell, Julie. Let's go. Take it from . . . Who's that?"

Steps were coming up the walk, heels smacking flat down on the boards, hollow-sounding, *thump-thump*. Whoever it was didn't bother to knock.

"Be damn!" MacPhail said, grinning. "Mr. Abercrombie and Fitch himself, back from the wilderness. What hit you? A moose?"

Jamie looked as if something had. A moose was as good a guess as any. His expensive camping clothes were filthy and ripped; they bagged on him as if he had lost weight. A week-old straggly beard framed his lank face, making it look longer and lankier, somewhat like a billy goat's. A fine ripe smell of whiskey had come with him into the coach, was spreading around him. He glared at MacPhail with considerable unfriendliness.

"So that was why, you stinking wife-stealer," he said.

"What'd you do up there in the wild woods?" Mac asked. "Wander off after the pipes of Pan? How does he play *his* whistle?"

"Let him alone, Mac," Julie said. "He's drunk, can't you see?"

"What'd ya mean, drunk?" Jamie said. "Sure, I had a couple on the train. You two should talk, smells like a hop joint in here."

"It is," Mac said. "Julie and I are working up some numbers. Us musicians can't take time off. We might lose our lip. If we had one."

"All right, bud, that's it! Damn you, you clear out of here, or I'll—"

"You'll what?" Mac stretched his legs, leaning back in his chair. "A couple on the train, my God! You're the tail end of a week's binge, if I ever saw one. It's a wonder your own wind don't knock you down. What was it? Didn't you find dear Gil up in the pretty woods camp?"

"You know damned well I didn't! You knew it when you told me. You lied your head off, said you saw it in the newspaper. What newspaper, hanh?"

"Why, the Boston *Evening Transcript,* where else?"

"Mac, shut up!" Julie said. She was beginning to be scared. She had never seen Jamie so drunk, and nobody ever knew what Mac would do, if it came to a fistfight. "Will you both please get out of here, I'm so tired I could—"

"Yeah, I bet you are! You and Mac, in on it together. Send me off on a wild-goose chase, so the two of you could—"

"Jamie, go to the hotel, sleep it off. Maybe," Julie said in desperation, "maybe you've got mail there. I—I haven't checked—"

"He hasn't got mail anywhere and he ain't likely to have, and we know it. Want me to tell you?" he said to Jamie.

Jamie stared from one of them to the other. "Who's heard?" His voice went shrill. "Who's heard anything?"

"Julie and me heard last summer," MacPhail said. "Both of us turned down Kirkpatrick's contracts way back when. When the old boy said he wouldn't touch you with a ten-foot pole, bag of Limburger on the end of it."

"That's a lie! Damn you, you made that up!"

MacPhail started slowly to get out of his chair. "So now you clear out, buster," he said. "You're the one to put foot."

"Mac, don't!" Julie caught at his arm, missed, watched him move, almost as if in slow motion, down the floor.

Jamie backed away until the stove, behind him, stopped him. The sadiron which Julie had left to cool on the turned-out burner was still there; he snatched it up, threw it with all his strength at MacPhail's head. It missed as MacPhail coolly inclined his head to let it go by, struck Julie on the diaphragm, just below the heart.

"Oh, my God!" Jamie sagged against the wall of the coach, stood watching as MacPhail lifted Julie from the floor, put her down on the bunk. "Is she . . . ? Oh, my God!"

"She's breathing," MacPhail said. He raised his head from Julie's chest, leaned down again, listening. "But that's about all. Go get a doctor, or she won't be."

"I can't . . . I'm sick . . ."

"Get a doctor," MacPhail said softly. "Or I'll kill you where you stand."

"I didn't mean to—"

"You don't get the chair in this state. You get the rest of your life in jail."

Jamie gasped. He lunged for the door. His flying footsteps thumped on the boards of the walk, went on, out of hearing.

MacPhail got water in a cup. The only clean cloth he could find was one of Julie's freshly ironed handkerchiefs. He used it to bathe her face. She lay unmoving, the shadows under her eyes darker against her pallor; looking at her, he thought, My God, what's the use of this?

He set the cup on the floor, dropped the wet handkerchief into it. It wasn't helping, and the faint sound of her breath he had heard—he couldn't hear it now. So that was that. He turned away from Julie, picked up his saxophone, put it into its case.

Morrie MacPhail was in too much trouble already in New York City to get wound up in a murder in this hick town and sent back there. The guy would be back with the doctor any time now. If the kid wasn't dead, they'd know what to do. He didn't. And if she was—and God, she was; nothing moved there—he had better not even be seen walking away.

He went to a back window of the coach, the one, he knew, that would open. To get to it, he had to push past Julie's washed and pressed clothes, which she had hung on a line to air. They had that slight fragrance Julie always had had, which had turned him goofy; but not goofy enough, the told himself, to take a chance on this. He opened the window; the fresh air coming in blew the fragrance away.

He managed to squeeze his big frame through the opening. He reached inside and carefully lifted out his sax in its case. Through beginning rain, the soapy-feeling weeds at the back of the railway coach, the dumps, the ashcancluttered rear of buildings, he walked the few blocks to where he had parked his car, to where he had always parked it, just in case, climbed in, and headed up the state highway, out of town.

Oh, God, the poor kid. The poor little kid.

The nearest telephone was at the railway station, and the station was open for the ten-fifteen westbound train. Dr. Graham's number didn't answer; Jamie listened to the far-away jangle until the operator stopped ringing it. "Two-nion-nion does not answer."

Jamie hung up and tore frantically through the pages of the phone book. What other doctor was there? Must be one, he couldn't think. His head felt stuffed with wool; he was dizzy, couldn't read the names. Maybe Timmins, the station agent, would know—he was there at his wicket, mildly looking out.

He knows me, he's seen me. If I ask him, he'd know what I'm after. If she's dead, they could connect me up with it . . . I'd better get going . . . get out . . . get right away.

The ten-fifteen. It was due. And pretty soon. He could get on it, get off at some hick stop, take another train headed the other way. Keep changing trains till he got good and lost, nobody would catch up with him. Get to Canada . . . some place . . . God, did he have enough money left? Turning his back on Timmins, so the guy couldn't see what he was doing, Jamie checked his wallet.

He had, thank God. Plenty. Wow, thought he'd drunk it all up!

Quietly, in a dignified way, so that no one could ever say he had been running away, he crossed the station floor to the outside platform, gazed fuzzily and blearily up the track. No sign of the ten-fifteen. His blood curdled. What if it was late? What if he got caught here, a sitting duck, waiting for a train?

Across the triple tracks a long freight train stood on the siding. He could see the black outline of an open door in a boxcar. Quite a ways up ahead he could see the engine. Steam up. They were waiting for the ten-fifteen to go through, they must be; and that one *was* headed north. At the north junction he might be able to switch trains, and by morning he could be in Canada.

Hands in his pockets, whistling, he walked casually past the station agent's lighted window. Just a passenger, pacing the platform, waiting for a train. Once past, he ducked down, raced across the tracks, pulled himself up into the grateful blackness of the boxcar.

Could've looked in the classified pages. Could've asked the operator. Never thought of it. Too late now, he felt sick. Couldn't possibly make it. Sweating and gasping, he stretched out on the floor of the boxcar. Shock and his week's binge caught up with Jamie. He passed out, cold.

He did not hear the ten-fifteen go through, or the crash of the boxcar door when a brakeman came by and, seeing someone had left it open, slid it shut and locked it. He did not hear the freight train pull out, or the boxcar begin on what, for Jamie, was to be a long, long journey. For the locked car was headed home, by various railroads, routed nonstop, to Oregon.

In the pale light of early morning Abigail got off the train. It had rained in the night; she had heard it for a long time

rattling against the sleeping-car window. The railway platform was wet, and as she crossed through the station, she
saw that there were puddles in the street reflecting a clear,
yellow sunrise.

Timmins, the station agent, had come out of his booth and
was standing in the street door, watching something so intently that she had to touch his sleeve before he moved to
let her by.

"Excuse me, Mr. Timmins."

He glanced around and turned sickly white under his
peaked cap. "Mis' Plummer! You just get off the train?"

"Why, yes," Abigail said. Puzzled, she wondered if he felt
all right and was about to ask, when he burst out in a half-
hysterical spate of talk. "If I'd only known when that crazy
feller tore through here last night, I ought to known, the way
he acted, something was wrong, but I never knew one nameable thing till I come down before daylight and heard that
screaming. I done what I could, Mis' Plummer, I don't know
nothing about a woman having a baby. I got Graham here
and he took one look and said call the Bristol ambulance,
and him and Meader's over there now—"

"Let me by," Abigail said.

He stood staring after her as she walked across to the railway coach where Dr. Graham's Ford and Willy Meader's
police car stood beside the curb. As she went up the walk,
Willy opened the door and came to meet her.

"Abby," he said heavily, "I wish I didn't have to tell you.
I wish to God I didn't."

"Julie," Abigail said.

He nodded. "Graham says she didn't have a chance. Her
heart . . . he says it's a wonder she lived long enough to . . .
we—he's saved the baby."

Seeing her face, he felt the sweat start under his collar,
half raised a hand to steady her in case she needed it. "Anything I can do," he said helplessly.

She said, "Yes, thank you. There may be something, Willy. If the baby is . . . all right, I must get it home and cared for. I would take it neighborly if you would drive me there in your car."

"So I drove her home," Willy said to Larry Cartwright, some days later. "I bet I sweat two quarts doing it. She set there with a face like a rock, holding the baby, and it squalling its head off, and about then people was starting out for work, craning their necks and looking, and she never batted an eye. She'd just been into that railroad car—that was the worst mess I ever saw in my life, must've been a hell of a fight in there, and that flatiron still on the floor. All she done, she went over and put one hand on Julie's cheek, brushed it like. And then she asked Doc Graham what needed to be done for the baby and he told her. So she picked it up and come away. That is one tough-hearted—minded—woman. I don't know . . . whatever it is that's tough, it's tough. It don't wobble around."

"That's right," Larry said.

Nan, too, he thought. He had come home with Nan to Julie's funeral.

The night Abigail had left the city, Larry had gone down to the northbound train. He had waited by the gate until he had seen her coming through the station and then had quietly lifted her suitcase out of her hand.

"Larry, how kind of you!" she had said. "You haven't any news for me?"

He had had to shake his head. "I'm afraid I haven't. I'm sorry. She hasn't got back. I thought I'd come and see you off. It seemed like—" He'd been going to say, "It seemed like a pretty lonesome journey," and had changed his mind. No need to make things rougher for her than they were. "You didn't give me a chance to talk to you," he went on. "And I honestly do have something to say."

She glanced at the station clock. "There's time," she said. "What is it, Larry? I'm sorry to have had to involve you in my . . . difficulties."

"I hope you'll think I've a right to be concerned. Nan and I have been seeing a good deal of each other since we both got back to town. I want to marry her, Mrs. Plummer."

He had been surprised by the warmth of her smile. "Does she . . . ?"

"Yes. She does."

"Good. I was going home thinking that there was nothing in the world that would comfort me. You know we have quarreled?"

"Yes. People get over quarrels, Mrs. Plummer."

"I hope so. I hope so with all my heart."

"I'll get her home as soon as I can, Mrs. Plummer."

She laid her hand briefly on his arm. "I'm sure you will. She really must come, Larry."

"You have to go," he said. "They're about ready to pull out. What's your car number? I'll put you aboard."

She said, as they walked together down the long platform, "I'm very glad, Larry."

"Thanks," he said. "Me, too. And—Lord, I wish we had more time! Another thing I wanted to tell you, when I come home for Thanksgiving, I'm going to have a talk with that fellow you mentioned in the sheriff's department—Meader, you said his name is—about my chances in Granite Hills."

So here he was, talking to Meader, unexpectedly, quite a long time before Thanksgiving.

Tough-hearted, tough-minded, whatever it was, it was tough. He had seen Abigail at Julie's funeral; he had sat with Nan. She had already gone back to the city. So far as Larry knew, she had not gone home; she had stayed overnight at the hotel, and without telling even him she had taken the morning train alone.

"Well, it don't give an inch, anyway," Willy went on. He stared down at the blotter on the desk in front of him. "She never even turned her head when I stopped for the traffic light in front of Delbert Smiley's house. I had to—one of Fairleigh's big delivery trucks was coming through—otherwise I wouldn't have stopped for nothing, let alone there. Elsie Smiley was on her side porch hanging up didies. She took a look and let out a blart you could hear all over the neighborhood. 'Delbert, for heaven's sake, look! Nan's had a baby in Boston and Mama's come lugging it home!' She's a fool. I don't run off at the mouth like this as a usual thing, but I guess if you're intending to be Abigail Plummer's son-in-law, it won't do any harm for you to know the score."

"Never hurts to," Larry said.

"Well, now about the rest you've been asking about, I'm a candidate for sheriff, in November. I might win, I might not. If I don't, the sheriff'll be Judge Clawson's man, Harley Crawford. They'll work together. If I'm still here and you come here to practice law—in January, you said?—you won't have any trouble seeing how it's done. Then"—he grinned wryly—"you know what'll happen to you?"

Larry grinned back. "I'll get slapped around?"

"You'll work a year, maybe two. You'll get just about enough cases to get by. Then you'll be asked to run for county attorney."

"I will? Well, gosh, I might have that in mind eventually, but not until I've had some experience. Why will I?"

"That's just the goddammed point," Willy said. "The county attorney around here is always a kind of a young man and wet behind the ears. It makes the state's cases easy to beat, if you see what I mean."

"I'll be darned." Larry sat taking this in. A slow grin spread across his face. "You know, Mr. Meader, I wouldn't be surprised if in time I might be a pretty good county attorney."

"Nor I," Willy said. "If you was to stay long and knew

what you might be up against. Clawson's been around quite
a time, and so've the one or two old boys who get most of
the legal work. Know all the dodges. Been through the mill.
Which you ain't."

"No. Not yet. I guess I will be seeing you in January, Mr.
Meader."

"Hope so. Call me Willy."

"Thanks. A lot."

"Oh, sure," Willy said. "No charge."

Nice idealistic young feller, he thought, as the door closed
behind Larry. Head in the clouds. Well, they come and they
go.

That crazy Stetson guy seemed to have vanished off the
face of the earth. He hadn't, so far as anyone could find out,
been on the ten-fifteen train. He'd be caught up with, sometime. If he was caught up with soon, it might help out with
the campaign for sheriff. But if a man couldn't get elected
on his past record in a town, it didn't seem much use to try
to get elected at all.

Tough-heartedness, Larry thought, as he walked down
through the streets of the town to take the shortcut along
the river that led to the road down Starball, is that the rock
Nan and I are going to split on?

He had quarreled with Nan last night, and it had been
bad. Stupid, too. Any fool could have seen she was in a state
of shock—that it had been a rotten time to talk plans. But
he had hoped to stir her a little out of the lethargy of grief
that was shutting her away from everyone—her mother, himself—at least try to. He hadn't intended a quarrel; but ever
since the news of Julie had come, she had been rigid and
silent, a Nan he did not know.

Like a sleepwalker. Shock, of course, took time to wear off.
Anybody but a fool would have kept his big mouth shut.

She had turned on him as if he had been some kind of an

interfering stranger. "If what I do has anything to do with you at all, I'm never coming back to this town again. I'll never set foot here as long as I live."

"Nan, darling, why? Why would you—even if I came, had a job here, you wouldn't?"

"I won't talk about it, Larry."

"We always have talked about things—"

"If you talk about this, I'll leave now. I can still get the night train." She turned away from him, went to stand by the window.

After a moment he tried again. "Nan, somebody here is paying my law-school expenses. There was a letter which they didn't let me read because the donation was anonymous, but they read part of it to me in the bursar's office. 'In the hope'—I'm quoting—'that he will come to Granite Hills and open his law office where it is most needed.'"

"Somebody," Nan said without turning. "Aren't you stupid not to know who."

"I don't know that I am. Do you know?"

"If there's a string to it, you can't mistake it. My mother has thrown hooks into people all her life."

"Your mother?" He stared at her. "It was?"

"Yes, it was. And she's going to lead you around by the nose for the rest of your life."

"Nan, darling . . ."

"And I'm not marrying you if you let her."

"Nobody leads me around by the nose. Not your mother, and I'm sorry, Nan, but not you either."

"So that's that."

"Yes. It is. I want to come back here. There's a job here, a dandy. Something I can get teeth into. I could run errands in some big law firm in Boston—there've been a couple of offers—but who wants to? That talk about hooks and strings is—isn't right. You'll recall what the letter said was 'in the hope of.' It didn't say do it or else. All I can think about your mother, it was decent of her."

"The money she gave you," Nan said softly, "was Julie's money for the conservatory. Julie didn't get it because she wouldn't lick back into line. So it went to someone who deserved it—"

"For God's sake, Nan, are you blaming me for something I didn't know about?"

"You know now."

"Yes. I know now." He went on heavily, "I'm glad I do know, Nan. This would hang over us forever if I didn't."

She didn't answer him.

Shut up, he told himself. She isn't making sense, and no wonder. She has to have time.

Nan said, "So you had better stop, Larry."

"All right," he said. "You and I've come quite a way being honest with each other, Nan. What we've had to say, we've said. Had some fights, too, remember? But we haven't ever slammed each other around for saying what we think. I think the way you feel about your mother is mistaken, but—"

"She does what she thinks is right," Nan said.

"And I think it must have broken her in two, this time, to do it."

"And it isn't just off the top of her mind, it's a considered rightness, a matter of principle. It doesn't change, because the principles don't change. As she sees them, they don't change. Julie's made her bed, she'll have to lie in it, she said to me. Well"—Nan's voice grated in her throat—"Julie's lying in it."

And so, this morning, without telling him, she had gone back to the city.

So where does that leave me? he thought. Do I give in?

He had been walking at a great rate along River Street, without paying much attention to where he was going. Now he had come to the end of the quarter-mile or so of decrepit buildings which lined the street—old shacks and sheds, dwelling houses long lived in and long abandoned—which it was hard to tell; all were unrepaired with paintless walls and rotten porches. A nose-puckering whiff from the river informed him that the tide was out, and he stopped for a moment, looking down at the mudflats, the slime-covered nubs of pilings which marked the site of some long-forgotten wharf. He had been here before, last summer. There was the same rotting hulk of an old vessel out in the flats, and here was the same noisome and outrageous pigpen. Phew-w!

As he turned to go, away from the smell, the door to a nearby shack opened and the owner of the pen came out. He carried an ancient shotgun, which he proceeded to load, silently shoving in two shells and clapping to the breech with a rusty snap. He said succinctly, "Git!"

Astonished, Larry said, "Sure, but why? Am I bothering you?"

"No, and you ain't going to. I ain't having no truck with no law."

"Then don't eat fire at me. I only stopped a minute to look at that old hulk over there in the river."

"You better take a good long look at her, sonny. You and all the rest of them lice running the town up on Maple Street. She may be a sick old vessel that stinks of her sickness, but it's a honest stink, by God. They ain't a one of them that ever done as clean a day's work in their lives as haul a load of turnips to Boston, or beets and beans, either, after old Randall got clubroot into his fields and couldn't grow turnips no more. You can tell that crowd of burgulars up there to the courthouse that I ain't done nothing about my pigs, and if the goddamned Board of Health shows up here, they will get the pants shot off of them. When they clean up the courthouse, I'll clean up my pigpen and not before."

"Okay," Larry said. He walked on, feeling crawly between

his shoulder blades, until he was out of range of the shotgun. The old man's eyes had looked pretty crazy.

What he'd said had made some sense, though. Combine it with what Willy Meader had implied this morning, it made quite a lot of sense.

So I come here and hang up my sign, and I'm wet behind the ears. And I bang head-on into whoever it is that's sitting pretty. I get my skin burned off in chunks. And I could lose Nan.

Perplexed and troubled, he walked on, turning into the footpath that led across a field to the Starball road.

❊   ❊   ❊

All through October the wind blew. Northwest, straight from Canada, day after day, the cold air raced across the countryside, snapping clotheslines, spinning leaves off the trees before their time, causing thunderous profanity among the coast fishermen, who hauled gear in boats that jumped like frogs and who spoke of the wind according to custom. At Starball it was pretty weather ashore and in the lee. The cove faced south; Waldo tended his traps in comparative comfort, sheltered by the cliffs on the eastern shore. With great relief he had gone back to his peace and quiet after bossing a crew of men on Mulligan's Mound for most of the summer. That job was done and done well. The trash growth and slash were cleaned up and burned; for the first time in years a man could walk standing up anywhere on the Mound without having to fight his way through jackstraw piles of dead limbs and three-inch sticks from topped trees, laced together with hardhack and running blackberry.

It was a good place now, Waldo thought. He had walked all over it on the last day, checking the job. Hardwoods would come up here now; some were already starting, quite big. Leaves from them were lined out in the wind, blowing off the top of the hill, gold color against the sky; if you had eyes to, looking out there, you could see across the ocean.

Now he was free to worry about the winter at Starball, which wasn't going to be easy. Worry wasn't exactly the word; in a way he looked forward to the winter. Lots of work, lots of planning, things to make. He already had plans for a wooden V-plow to go on the front of the truck, in case of deep snow along that gravel road to town. Getting the kids to school would be a problem. He hadn't quite figured out how to hitch the snowplow to the truck, but he was on the way to it. Think little bit, things came.

Chris and George had work anyway till snow flew, maybe longer. Waldo was glad he'd put foot down about going to work with them. He had plenty without that. He and Chris had had quite a hassle about that, nearly parted company. Waldo had finally agreed to take time to register to vote in November, since Abigail the lady had asked them all to, and he wouldn't mind seeing Willy Meader get sheriff's job—old man up there was rotten cribbage player. But that was it. No yobs, he said firmly. He had all, all to do. Everythang.

Part of the hassle had been over Chris's idea of moving into town for the winter. Starball was too rough on the womenfolk, he'd said; rough on the kids; he himself wasn't in love with wrassling five miles of snowbanks to get to work every weekday morning. He'd find a place somewhere, where they could stay till spring.

Waldo couldn't see why anybody would be scared of winter. Winter was good time, unless a man was cold and hungry, didn't have tight roof and stuff put away in cellar, and they did have.

"What for you think I haul vood down Mulligan Mound all summer?" he bellowed at Chris. "Trees ve cut, good vood for fire, vicked vaste not to bring home for vinter. Got enough, too, ten, 'leven cord, who vants better?"

"I know you've got wood to patch hell a mile," Chris said. "That don't worry me—"

"I bust my head down-cellar all summer! Vhat you think

for? So I bust it again, two thousand, three thousand lump, big as a aig, the yelk, haul all that stuff out, cart to town? Easier cart you and kids than all them apple, potato, turnip, deer meat, vhen I git deer, and you shut up big trap, I git one big buck tomorrow."

"No, you won't, by God, you'll wait till the hunting season opens! Somebody don't hold you down, you'll end up in jail. For keeps, this time!"

"Now look, you two," Mary said. And she came into the argument squarely on Waldo's side. "Waldo, you stop plaguing Chris. You know we've used up all our jars, and we don't have any way to keep deer meat until the cold weather. And Chris, honey, Sue and I and the kids don't want to move to town. Leave all this that we've got here and that you've built? The kids would die, you'd have to lick everybody, and I don't know but I'd die, too, at the thought of all those lumps on Waldo's head going for nothing."

In Jos Plummer's old booze cellar under the house, shelves were jammed with filled jars. Mary and Sue had canned everything from the garden that put out a leaf or a pod; they and the kids had scavenged the woods back of the pond for raspberries, blueberries, blackberries. Any man who hadn't been too tired of an evening had got hounded to put up shelves in the cellar; George and Chris had made out fairly well, but a man as tall as Waldo couldn't stand up straight. He would come up through the kitchen-floor trap door cussing and with tears in his eyes, pointing to another good-sized rising on his crown. Lumps or not, he said, it was worth going down there just to smell. Root vegetables in boxes of sand, cabbages hanging from beams, barrels of potatoes; apples, salvaged from the abandoned orchards over on the far side of the pond. They weren't very big apples, and some of them, right now, were as hard as rocks. The trees of course hadn't been tended for years; but old-time men, Waldo said, had had to know how to plant keepers.

Nodheads taste best, them little dark-red vuns, couldn't put tooth in now, but February, taste vunderful. Bellflowers, yellow, red spots, they took time, too, but vait. Go crack when you bit, joose run down chin, mm, God! Kings vell, these vuns little, but if he cut dead vood off trees, took care, King apples be big as bowls next year.

"And pay rent, in town, any old place?" Mary said. "Chris, this is *home*."

Chris gave in, and that day there was rejoicing on Starball.

PART FIVE

Abigail

"I tell you, Judge," Charles said, "I'm really worried. First, she goes all out to bankrupt me, and that's pretty strange, on the face of it. We've always been so close, my mother and I. If I could see any reason . . . I tell you, I've been pretty down in the mouth about it."

"She owns the land," Judge Clawson said. "She can build anything she wants to on it—grocery store, dwelling house, whatever, so long as it doesn't create a public nuisance. You can't do anything about that, Chuck."

"No," Charles said. "That isn't quite my point, Judge. I know that. It's my mother herself I'm concerned about. This running around town campaigning for Meader for sheriff, wearing herself out, it doesn't make sense, and she's in mourning, Judge. She hasn't been the same since—well, you know what our family's just been through."

"An awful thing!" The Judge shook his head. "A terrible thing! We're leaving no stone unturned to catch that degenerate who did it, and when . . . we . . . do . . . he'll be lucky if we keep him out of the clutches of the townspeople. Your mother still in a bad state about it, is she?"

"Worse than that, I think. Now, I'm her son. Her eldest son. Bad as I hate to, I've got to take responsibility."

"Naturally, Chuck. Naturally."

"I thought I'd drop by and have a word with you, kind of off the record. As an older man and a lawyer. I've been reading up on paranoia. Seems one of the symptoms is turning against the people you care most about. Bearing them a grudge."

"That would be for a doctor to say," the Judge said, with a certain caution. He knew Charles quite well, and by reputation. The word was, watch for a rat to smell. It seemed unlikely that Abigail Plummer was going crazy, not that there'd be quite a few around who'd be relieved if it could be proved she was. Better listen to what Chuck had to say. If anything should happen to her, he'd be quite a wealthy and important man around the town. "Still," the Judge went on, "shock is a very unpredictable thing."

"That's just my feeling. We always planned to build this new store together. Now she comes in, out of a clear blue sky, gives me a terrible going-over, says she's building it herself and going to take all her old customers with her when she moves out. You know these mossbacks around here. They've dealt with her all their lives and they'll keep on with her. So I'm sunk, good and proper. First time in her life she's gone back on her word. It isn't rational. Another thing, this going overboard for Willy Meader, what's that all about? Stumping the town for him, hanging out in his office . . . You know, Judge, women . . . at a certain time of life, just about where she is now, her age, I mean, sometimes they go a little whacky about sex? And this shock she's had, about my sister's going the way she did . . . I think she's out of her mind."

By gum, the Judge thought, if this guy don't think of everything. Nosing around to see what it would take to get his old lady committed, on evidence that'd give the haw-haws to a child of ten, who wouldn't have to be much older to figure out what he's after. She's using up what she's got

You said, lay it on the line. How much would it cost me, all things considered, to have her committed?"

The Judge raised his eyebrows. When he spoke, his voice was heavy with shock, but he was grinning. "Do I understand you? That you're trying to bribe me to give you what legal help I can in setting up this thing?"

Charles grinned back. "That's one way to put it, Judge."

"You realize, don't you, there are pretty heavy penalties for trying to bribe a judge? You actually want to do this?"

"Quit kidding, Judge. You know I do."

"I advise you, young man, to go home and slow down. I'm going to have to look into this, and you'll be hearing from me. Now, clear out of here." But his eyebrows were still up; he was still grinning.

"Okay, Judge, I—"

The Judge waved a jaunty hand. "That's all, Chuck. I'm disappointed in you and deeply saddened. So young a man—"

Charles waved back and grinned as he went out and closed the door.

Judge Clawson's grin did not fade at once. Oh, the fool, he thought, the big, flatfooted fool!

He pressed the buzzer on his desk for his secretary, and she came in from behind the closed door of her small office, next to his.

"You get the whole of that, Sadie?"

"I certainly did. And I heard you read him the riot act too. He had it coming, if anyone ever did. That nice woman —and his own mother, too—"

"Well, you get it transcribed right away, Sadie, and bring it in, will you?"

The door between his office and Sadie's generally stayed closed, for clients' privacy; but the large picture of Abraham Lincoln behind his desk concealed a small open grille with a wooden slide which could be closed, depending on

salted away, and quite fast, too, which must be a grinder t
a touchy fellow like Chuck. I'll bet he's lying awake nigh
wondering how much'll be left by the time it gets to him.

"Have you talked this over with anybody in the family?
he asked.

"Well, nobody but Art Bickford. I guess I left him think
ing, but all he's concerned about is that she's out getting
votes for Meader all over the area, when she's in mourning
and ought to be home knitting. He don't think it looks nice."
Charles's opinion of his brother-in-law showed on his face.
"Be hard to convince him that she's being anything but
foolish, wasting her time when you and Green have got the
county papered with Harley Crawford."

"No, we aren't overly concerned. Aren't lying awake
nights," the Judge said. "Now, Chuck, let's lay it on the line.
What I understand is, you think your mother's insane and
you've come to me for legal information about a committal.
Is that right?"

"That's right."

"A committal is a very serious thing. I would go slow, if I
were you. Your mother's well-known and liked. She's got a
lot of friends and Dr. Graham is one of them. Another thing,
in the case of a committal where money and property are
involved, a legal mind might point out the question of self-
interest, particularly since, as her eldest son, you'll doubtless
be called on to administer her property. She's got to be crazy
and show it to somebody besides you. Under the circumstances. You realize that? Your story about her could be
looked into. A smart lawyer could point out that her store
was started, the building was begun, before your sister died."
He held up a hand. "Now, wait. You've got to think of these
things, unless you're pretty sure she needs, uh, medical as-
sistance."

"All right, Judge, thanks. All this stuff I need to know.

whether the Judge wanted an interview witnessed or taken down in shorthand. Knowing Charles Plummer, he'd thought it might be a notion to have a copy of this one, and he'd been right—he'd come up with pure gold.

There wasn't anything in that insanity notion. The old girl was eccentric, was all; but she was a town institution. You might as well try to put away the Congregational Church steeple or the bandstand on the village green. Let Chuck peck away at it awhile. He wouldn't get to first base. Didn't matter. Anybody's life was precarious. Who knew? Chuck hadn't learned yet that in this world you had to wait, usually, for what you wanted to get. He, Harold Clawson, had. When Chuck inherited, later—or sooner?—he'd find that a man's grin didn't show on a transcript and that the cost of suborning The Law really was quite high. Could be a prison sentence; or it could be a wad of that inheritance; or it could be whatever slice he fell heir to of the fancy real estate on Mulligan's Mound . . . Cranberry Mountain. Abigail Plummer's boy then would be over a barrel.

Day after day, through October, the indomitable Dutchoven hat, the decent black dress, the unmistakable straight figure had been seen around the town, visiting house after house, plodding along River Street, turning down muddy back lanes where even a Model-A could not go. To some the sight was remarkable, a seven-day wonder when you remembered what Abby Plummer had just been through and realized the courage it took to do what she was doing. Others were shocked—this was not suitable for a woman in mourning. Elsie was one of these and so was Arthur Bickford, who remonstrated with Abigail, but only once. Word spread from somewhere that Charles Plummer was worried about his mother's mind; the strain, the shock, had sent her a little over the edge. Nobody believed this; it was taken for granted that the people who were plugging for Harley Crawford for sheriff would put out a lot of bushwah, anyway, and except for a few of that particular crowd, nobody thought Abigail Plummer was funny. One thing about her, if she said something was so, then it was. You could depend on it.

Catalysis in chemistry is predictable; obediently, in the stable acid the sugar turns to glucose. This, too, you depend on. But who can say what, in the minds of men, the catalyst may be? The coast towns, for years, had been flattened under depression, most people discouraged and poor. The bottom of stable things had dropped out. What could you do? What did you have to do with?

Well, you had a brain and a vote. If you used both, you might get nowhere at all in the end, but at least you'd have tried to throw out of office the shady politicians who were robbing the town funds blind. It wouldn't cost you a penny, and you might win. On the other hand, if you wanted to keep on paying them to swindle you, you could do that too. It was your tax money.

It would be oversimplification to say that the catalyst was Abigail Plummer, however pungent the argument she spread. And it was not Sam Greeley, whose remark that pigs in the swill thought of other living critters in the world as nothing but jackasses and boobies was repeated widely from one end of the town to the other. There were many factors, among them the Depression, which had gnawed away for years like an underground fire at confidence and self-respect until minds were worried and nerves strained. As the speeches of the political gentlemen themselves indicated, the time was ripe for the winds of change to blow, and blow they did. They blew a hurricane that shook down sere and yellow leaves from stout oaks undisturbed since the administration of William McKinley. It was an unusual election.

In Granite Hills almost every registered voter in town went to the polls. Old ladies in wheelchairs appeared who had not stirred out of their houses in years; practically the entire population of River Street; cynical citizens whose opinion was that the more it changed, the more it was the same thing and who, normally, couldn't care less if the town had elected a horse. Asa Francisco was there, with his wife and six sons: eight votes. Asa's family had never before even registered to vote. They lived on a farm down a back and muddy road and seldom came into town, except, once in a while, the boys showed up to buy staples—coffee and sugar, cigarettes and whiskey—and to raise hell. No one ever remembered seeing Asa's wife. Yet on election day there they all were, in an old farm wagon. Sam Greeley voted, and Nettie Hill and her boyfriend, Zeke Peterson, and Ory Carter and her husband, Doug. Ory and Doug stood in line in front of Judge Clawson and Jerome Green; behind them were the four Cartwrights and Waldo Larsen.

Jerome was feeling feeble; he wouldn't have come at all if the Judge hadn't insisted—not because, he said, they needed his vote, but because it wouldn't look right if Jerome wasn't there. He'd promised to come for Jerome in his car; and it had been about what Jerome had expected from the Judge—he'd arrived just on the dot of when that good radio program started, after dinner.

Come between me ever since I've known him, Jerome was thinking; he glanced around with a bleared and disillusioned eye at the crowd. The hell Harley don't need my vote, he told himself, and caught sight of Waldo Larsen who wasn't hard to see, since he towered head and shoulders over almost everybody else. "I'll be damned!" Jerome said aloud. He bellowed at the top of his lungs, "How'd you get out, you son-of-a-bitch?"

"Door unlock, didn't you?" Waldo said. He grinned mildly and waved a hand. "How go you cribbage game? You vant ten cents I owe you?"

Jerome grunted. Well, maybe he had unlocked the door;

he was getting so forgetful these days he couldn't remember half the things he ought to.

The Judge nudged him. "Shut up, Jerome. You've lost us Ma Crittenden's vote already."

Heads had turned, and the lady in question was staring at Jerome with a baleful and reproving eye, which indicated all that was necessary about somebody being foul-mouthed in public.

Jerome snorted. "Let her vote any goddamned way she wants to," he began. "Who gives a continental, pie-eyed—"

"—pink-whiskered apple pie," the Judge said, to distract him. "You know, Jerome, what this crowd reminds me of? Poetry."

"Poetry, hell!" Jerome said bitterly. "I ain't interested in— it does? Are you nuts?"

The Judge quoted, speaking softly:

> "Up the road to the movie show,
>   Came Sal and Solly and One-toe Joe,
>   Half-assed Harry and Foolish McCloy,
>   And Mother Pareek and her idiot boy—"

In front of him Ory Carter spun around. She said, "Ain't it too bad there's so many of us?"

Self-respect rose, as one defeated town officer put it, speaking before the election and not about the same thing, "like the Phoenix, from the ashes of the Depression." The winds of change blew; and they blew Willy Meader into the sheriff's office, much to his own surprise, for, knowing that the organization was not behind him, he would have said he was defeated before the voting took place.

On the morning after the election he went around to the dairy office to see Abigail Plummer and found there sitting at her desk Arthur Bickford, who congratulated him in a mild way and said that Mama was at home resting. Responsibility stuck out all over Arthur. He said, "What can I do for you? You know, I'm running the business here now."

"Just wanted to see Mrs. Plummer a minute," Willy said. "At home, you say?"

"You better talk over your business with me. I'm, uh, by way of being the man in that household now."

"No business. Wanted to thank her for campaigning for me is all, Art."

"She's worn out. I don't think she ought to see anyone."

"Sorry to hear it. Well, she's lucky to have such competent help, Art."

Something in his tone set Arthur to prickling.

"I may as well say right now," he began, "that I was dead set against her stumping the town for you or anybody else. Talking politics, house to house, so soon after a death in the family, it wasn't suitable, and I don't know what the town could have thought."

It being evident what the town had thought, Willy said nothing.

"She ought to been home, in mourning, helping Mo-reen and Nettie look after that baby. I, uh, told her so."

"I can imagine," Willy said. "See you, Art."

He found Abigail working in her kitchen with Julie's baby sleeping quietly in a cradle near the stove and Nettie deep in some kind of concoction she was mixing at the bread-board. The kitchen smelled of spice and roasting meat, and Willy, entering, felt his mouth water.

"Smells good in here," he said. "I ought to know better than to bother ladies cooking, but I wanted to say thanks, Abby."

"Why, I'm glad you did. We had a nice landslide, didn't we?"

"Thanks to you, we did."

"Oh, mercy, no. It's a sensible town, really."

"It was, too, thanks to you," Nettie said. The clap-clap of her spoon in the mixing bowl increased in sound and velocity. "Let me tell you, I went down and voted myself, and I ain't ever. I always figured that whosumever run, one side or t'other, didn't make no difference who beat, they was all crooks, but Abby says to trust you, Mr. Meader, so I did. It's Miles's birthday today and I'm cooking and I ain't got time to talk, but they's coffee on the stove and I've just took a batch of my spice cookies out the oven. Abby, get Mr. Meader a cup and some cream and sugar, and I don't care how many of them cookies you put on the plate for him."

"Why, thanks," Willy said. "I was hoping."

Abigail smiled at him as she put the coffee and cookies on the table and then sat down in the chair opposite. He couldn't see that she looked different from usual—a little tired, perhaps, a little strained around the eyes.

"This is all for Miles's birthday party," she said. "We're having all the Cartwrights and Mr. Larsen. That's quite a batch, and Nettie's been up to her elbows in flour. The kitchen's been untenable. She wouldn't let me in here, if somebody didn't have to baste the roast and tend to the baby."

Willy couldn't see anything of the baby but part of a red and puckered face. It was hard to think of anything to say, under the circumstances, and he took a drink of coffee, hoping the cup might hide anything that showed in his face.

"She's very much better," Abigail said. "We were worried for a while, but now I think she'll do. Thanks to Nettie."

"Thanks to nothing!" Nettie said. "You set up nights with her as much as I did. Let me tell you, Mr. Meader, she's brought that baby through the dark valley, no matter how much she blames me for it. And that baby ain't the only one in this town owes life and living to Abby Plummer. There's folks that would be starved to death today, and me, I'm one of them. Let her talk! About herself is the only thing in God's world you can't trust her word for. Abby, Mr. Meader could use another cup of coffee."

"No, thanks," Willy said. He got up hastily. Receiving the approval that an elected officer gets from one of his constituents was pleasant, but he was a modest man and he was getting uncomfortable. "I'd like to say thanks again," he said to Abigail. "I did plenty of sweating yesterday. I didn't think I had a prayer. Looked to me as though the opposition was too strong."

Nettie snorted. "Them weasels! Even with half the jails and all the cemeteries on the voting list, they couldn't of beat you, Mr. Meader. The first thing you better do is git the names of them jailbirds and dead people off of there—"

"Nettie," Abigail said, "that's pure gossip, and you don't know it's so. I don't want to listen to it."

"Ory Carter," Nettie began dangerously, "she said—" She glanced around and met Abigail's silence. "That roast smells awful hot. I better look at it myself."

"And you've waked up the baby," Abigail said. She moved over to stand by the cradle. The baby was beginning to stir and whimper, and she put a gentle finger down on its cheek. "We've named her Sarah," she said. "I've always thought Sarah was a nice name."

*　　*　　*

In January, Larry Cartwright finished his law course and passed his bar examinations. He was in the top quarter of his class and, as he told Nan, had shed part of his pin-feathers. The rest would probably get singed off.

"And now you have to grow flight feathers, darling," Nan said. She spoke with a certain sadness, and he knew why. He was going back to Granite Hills. She was not.

He had been afraid, after her desperate outburst following Julie's funeral, that he had lost her for good and he had gone back to the city with a heavy heart. To his infinite relief, she had phoned him almost at once.

"Larry, I need to see you. Come to dinner?"

"Nan, thank God, yes! To all your dinners, always."

Her voice was quiet, the hysteria gone. When he arrived,

she walked into his arms and laid her head wearily against his shoulder, where, he told her, it belonged.

"Yes. It does seem to."

"Nan, what other people do can't separate us . . ."

"No, it can't. I have to say that we can't begin by pushing each other around. We can't say somebody has to give and it won't be me."

They had not talked much that night. They had been too glad to be back together, too shaken at what had almost happened. But they had talked since, soberly working out a compromise, confronting the wall that had started to raise itself between them and finding it, after all, not insurmountable.

She would be in Boston until classes ended in June. Then she had a chance to go back to Berkshire; she would do that until September, if he still felt, by then, he wanted to stay in Granite Hills. She didn't blame him for not wanting to stay in the city; she didn't, either, not for good. If he wanted to start somewhere on his own, that was what he should do.

"I can't see you working for a corporation lawyer, running errands, Larry."

"Well, there is that, Nan. On your own, if you get a sock on the nose, it might not take too long to stop the nosebleed. But it takes years to get the corporation lawyer's errands run."

"I'm trying to make sense to myself, Larry. I need time."

"There are other country places besides Granite Hills. I'm not going to dig my heels in about going there, if there's a chance it'll break us in two."

"It won't. Right now I can't go back. I don't know whether I ever can, but I'm not digging in my heels either. I think, the way you feel, you should go. I'm not going to have it hanging over us that I kept you from doing it, if you feel you should . . . just because I can't seem to put myself back together." Her voice wobbled a little and she steadied it. "I'm working hard, and work's helping. It's a long time until June. Or maybe October."

"It's going to be rough, just seeing you weekends, whenever I can make it."

"Don't tell me how rough it's going to be. I'll be living for those weekends."

"I'll see we get them, if I have to walk."

They left it that he would go, find out what practicing law in Granite Hills was like. He admitted that, with what the setup seemed to be in the town, he might not be able to earn a penny. If, at the end of the summer, things didn't work out, and she still felt the same, they would take it from there.

She said, kissing him good-by at the train, "I'll try, Larry."

She was trying, he knew. And she did need time. The wound was still too open, too raw. She still could not talk about it, and had not, since her first frantic outburst, and he did not want to press her to talk. He did not know all of Julie's story, or what had gone on between Nan and her mother. It was like trying to sort out pieces of an incomplete jigsaw puzzle. He could not reconcile the Abigail Plummer whom he liked and for ample reason admired with the woman who, seen through Nan's eyes, had not lifted a finger to help Julie when Julie could have been helped. Abigail Plummer, on the night he had put her aboard the train, had been half out of her mind with worry. There had been no doubt that she was trying to do what she could and that Julie wouldn't listen. As a last desperate resort, Abigail had tried to reach Nan.

Nan knew that. He had barely got home that night after leaving Abigail's message, the urgent plea for help, in Nan's mailbox, when she had phoned him.

"Larry, where's my mother? I called the hotel. She's checked out."

She had been out and around the town all day, moving from place to place, sitting in parks, walking, had taken a long bus ride. Trying to make up her mind; and when she finally had, it had been too late. In the morning, when word had come—a telegram—Nan had been packing, getting ready to take the day train home.

So close, so near a thing it had been, the timing off by a half hour or so; and the subsequent terrible event then had driven home the final spike of misunderstanding, of blaming —of guilt?

No one should be blamed for this punishment out of proportion to the crime. For anger, perhaps, for stubbornness, for differences, between two people who loved each other, which in time could have resolved themselves as infinitely nothing compared to the return to love of the dearly lost.

She had to have time. Larry wanted to go to Granite Hills because the needed job there might be one he could do, but not alone for that. Nan might someday be able to put blame —if she had to blame—where blame must truly lie, on the reasonless bad luck which seemed at times and with intent to choose its victim. As if, out of nowhere, out of a cloud or an ill wind blowing, some bleak-faced evil leaned, pointed a ghastly finger, saying, "That one." And then piled it on.

He hoped; and hoping, would wait.

He was surprised, a little bewildered, by the welcome given him in Granite Hills. Having been prepared for the toe of somebody's boot, he told his father, he was handed out a reception. The brethren of the bar were cordial; one or two of them went out of their way to see he got a few cases. Judge Clawson shook hands, remarked that he was glad to see some new blood around. It was about time, he said, that some of the younger generation came back to the town. He wished Larry the good luck he deserved and went on to say that there might be more of that around for everyone, now the Depression was beginning to let up.

It was quite a fulsome speech.

"What gives?" Larry asked Willy Meader after a while. "I'm having a pretty good time here. At least, so far nobody's tried to singe me down."

Willy grinned and was noncommittal. He said the elections last fall had shaken things up some. "Heard a piece on the radio awhile ago," he said. "Nice young feller talking about water bugs. Said they was about the oldest family of insecks in the world today. Living fossils, he called 'em. Ain't changed in ten million years. Ain't likely to." Behind his desk, once Jerome Green's, Willy stretched his legs and went rambling on. "We had one down to our house, other day, in the kitchen, come out of a paper bag of stuff from Charles Plummer's grocery store. My housekeeper—her name's Mrs. Roach, so she called it a water bug—she's been gunning for it, setting up nights with the fly swatter. Caught sight of it once or twice, but turn on the light and flick, it goes back into the woodwork."

"Can't breed there all by itself," Larry said. He could be deadpan too.

"Couldn't say. Ain't familiar with the critter's personal life. It's February. Could be like the cats and dogs, out looking."

Could be, Larry thought.

The Judge's office, being appointive, could not have been affected by the election, though gaps were still apparent in the closely woven order of his friends, whom perhaps he missed. The decisions emanating now from his bench were impeccably sensible and just, so far as an observer could tell; some of them showed a wealth of knowledge about and comprehension of the law. He seemed not to remember ever seeing Larry before and apparently held no grudge against having been asked questions concerning Waldo Larsen's trial.

The devil, perhaps, was sick; but, in the meantime, Larry fared better than he had hoped to, and while far from affluent, he made enough over and above his living expenses to finance an occasional weekend with Nan.

*   *   *

The Depression, by April, did seem to be slowly wearing itself out. In Granite Hills the wheels of the economy creaked and stopped, creaked and moved and stopped, creaked and moved. There were jobs again, few at first, then a few more. Doug Carter, Ory's husband, found steady work again and began to whittle down his mountain of bills. Ory, with no regret, resigned her job of scrubbing the courthouse floors. She left them, she said, clean. Dr. Graham and Forrest Eastman, the town druggist, bought house lots on Cranberry Mountain; Cartwright Bros. got the contracts for both houses. Abigail Plummer's new grocery store was finished, though not yet stocked. Its bright new paint and fresh shingles, at the north end of Main Street, stood out against the grays and browns of older buildings eroded by the Depression; the sight of it might or might not have sparked the lethargy and discouragement of the lean years; at any rate, repair work and new paint jobs began to show up here and there along the street.

Charles Plummer had seen, as yet, no reason to discontinue his grocery store. He did not intend to until his mother's establishment was finished and running. Through the winter he had done a good deal of thinking and had thought himself out a plan. Let her have the boob trade, she'd get that anyhow. He himself would restock his general line; for groceries, he would get in fancy and expensive specialties for the summer trade. He was already doing that for some regular customers who could afford luxuries and for friends like the Judge. He guessed his friends would stick by him, and the summer trade, with hard times letting go, would surely pick up. He would do this for a while, until just the right occasion and set of circumstances showed up, and then who knew what might take place? He checked his insurance policy and moved out Clarice, along with his household goods and records, to a rented house on Maple Street.

All winter, and through into spring, Waldo Larsen hauled the Cartwright kids to school and Chris and George to work in the dump truck along the Starball road, kept open by city snowplows. Waldo, in his earlier days, it turned out, had had a job as third assistant keeper at an offshore lighthouse. He recalled that a schoolteacher had been provided, by state law, to teach the head keeper's five children. Not that he vanted strange vooman kicking around, he told the glum chairman of the Town Council, whom he went to see, but five Cartwright kids got to get to school. Cheaper to send down snowplow? More than four kids, hard to get to place, the law said schoolmarm or else, vasn't it?

The year turned hopefully to summer, and on a weekend in early June, Larry Cartwright, a little sadly, went down to help Nan move her things to Berkshire.

And on the fifteenth of August, Sam Greeley came up before Judge Clawson and got thirty days in the county jail for creating and maintaining a public nuisance and for resisting arrest.

Sam Greeley, as he had promised to do if the November election went to suit him, had got rid of his pigs. Since by then they were big enough to market, he would have done this anyway, but to make his usual winter's expenses and keep his word as a progressive citizen at the same time gave him a deep sense of satisfaction. He *was* progressive; he had voted, hadn't he? He had stood just inside the dingy window of his shack, watching while Willy Meader and another man unknown to him inspected his empty pen, and grinned to himself as he watched them walk away.

Just about two jumps ahead of them devils, he'd been. That stranger must be the new Board of Health, now that he and the rest of the town voters had thrun the most of them scalawags out. Well, the old one hadn't bothered him, not after he'd chased that other young feller away with the shotgun.

The winter had been long and solitary. Sam came through it all right, walked on his own two feet right up over the top of March hill. He was a little more tottery than he had been in the fall; his hands were a mite more shaky, didn't see quite so well as he'd used to, but that was the cold weather for you—took it out of a man. He'd had to drink quite a lot more than was his custom to keep from getting blue on the long nights; had the jimjams a couple of times, not that it signified. One night, about three in the morning 'twas, he'd seen the *Mary T. Randall* under full sail go off down the river in the moonlight, a pretty sight and about time. He'd been quite surprised at daylight to find her hulk lying in its usual place out there in the mudflats. Well, that was a quick trip.

In the spring he bought another batch of young pigs and put them in the same pen. They didn't seem to thrive. Didn't fill out the way they ought to. Sickly. Got bogged down in the muck, couldn't seem to handle themselves in it. Too bad he hadn't bothered to shovel some of that out before he put the new batch in. Still, seemed he could recall that that muck had been frozen at the time. Yes, it had been. Hard's a rock. No man could've shoveled it. He watched over the pigs with anxiety and affection, but one by one they died. Bitterly he buried them where they lay, in the pen. If that muck hadn't been soft and deep, easy to shovel, he told himself he never could have done it.

The last two came to grief in August. They would come to no man's swill, sooey-pig them however he tried, but stood unmoving, immobilized, their sad snouts resting on the mud, the tears running from their eyes. They had sunk too deep at last.

Look at that! Sam told himself. Them pigs is cryin'.

Well, a pig was too fine and intelligent a critter to be let to suffer.

He got his gun and shot them both, and left them. He was through with pigs. He wasn't even going to bother to bury them.

In the August heat the pigs went the way of all flesh. Sam's neighbors, not one but one and all, complained to the sheriff's department. Tried beyond endurance, they could do no less.

In jail Sam brooded. It was a meager life, shut away from the light of the sun. No peanuts and no liquor, and their cook didn't know how to make a clam chowder a man could eat. Had the nerve to send in raw sliced tomatoes, when anyone would know that the cussed love apples was poison except cooked, and out of a can. Try to poison him, would they?

He began brooding about poison. Funny, the way them pigs went, just stood still and died, nothing to hold them up but what they stood in. Never had a batch of pigs go like that before in his life. No reason to. Only thing, what if somebody'd poisoned them?

Who'd do a thing like that? Who had it in for him? Never had but one enemy, and that was Joe Crow and Joe was dead. Died two—three—no, seventeen years ago, down in Sailor's Snug Harbor. Left me his book and his extry pants. Wasn't too bad a pair of pants, except too small, and that book was interesting reading, too, his blankbook where he'd writ down the story of his life. So marked the place, good and black, where him'n I had that fight down to Cuba, made out I was to blame when I wasn't, he was. Knocked me slap over a table and then I knocked him over one. Same table. Madder'n the devil because I didn't pick out a different one. Could've at least done that, s' he.

Thought when I see them pants, he'd let bygones be bygones. "Joe's left me his pants," s' I, and I shed tears. But when I come to read his book, I see he was still cuddling his bile. Now, I wonder if he could've poisoned them pigs? Come to think of it, though, Joe's dead. 'Twasn't Joe.

In Sam, the human syndrome, all the symptoms converging, addling the head, festering. Almost ninety-one years of memories, a heavy weight on a man. Been here, been there. Stood on his own two feet, never bothered anybody. And this was all the whole works come to, ended up in jail. Who done it? Who was aginst me?

Abby Plummer begun it. She was the first sicked Willy Meader on to me. She complained. Who was it to? Was she the one poisoned them pigs? No. She ain't the woman to poison a pig. I heard, round 'lection time, that she was crazy, but she ain't the woman to poison a pig. It was them ones she complained to, then. Who?

Somebody with pull. Somebody who could push the law at a free man, send round, say, "You don't live your way, you live my way," somebody thinks he holds the whole world in his hands.

"He's got the whole world in his hands."

God. Abby Plummer had complained to God. She would. "God," s' she. "Strike down Sam Greeley's pigs."

Put the blame on a disagreeable cold sliced tomato, or on the man who grew the tomato and sold it to the jail kitchen. Blame the creatures which produced the manure to fertilize it, the sun which ripened it in time to be red on Sam Greeley's plate, the day he was let out of jail. Blame the bottle he bought and finished on that day by three in the afternoon; his mother, Minerva Creasey Greeley, who brought him into the world inherited from her mother, Jennie Creasey, she whose distinguished line went back six thousand years to Adam, the first man, and to Eve, his wife. Place blame according to the magnetic pole toward which your own spirit draws. No matter. It was the tomato, sign and symbol of negation and disregard, that tumbled Sam over the edge, sent him wandering up Main Street with a full kerosene can in his hand.

Charles Plummer was at his office desk in the rear of his store totaling the day's sales to enter them on his books; the cash from receipts was in the canvas bag beside his hand. He was nearly ready to leave for the bank to make his deposit, when he saw the man come into the store. Hell, some boob wanted kerosene. Let him want it. Come back tomorrow. It was only a few minutes before the bank would be closing doors for the day.

Then Charles leaned forward, looking, galvanized. The fellow didn't want kerosene, he had plenty. Enough to give away. He was going around from shelf to shelf, pouring it out of the nozzle of the can. Charles gathered himself to jump, opened his mouth to yell. Then he stopped, watching.

Fellow was that drunk, Greeley, from River Street. From the looks of him, he was wambling around, he was more than half-seas-over right now. And kerosene, poured around over stuff, could mean only one thing.

I be goddarned! Charles thought. Hey, this is all right.

This was opportunity knocking at the door, slap in the middle of a sunny afternoon, so there wouldn't be any doubt as to how it had happened. This was a chunk right off the slab of Old Man Good Luck himself. If the shebang blazed up too fast for him to make the front door, he could snake it out the back door. And leave it open. He sat still and waited.

If Charles had been behind the counter and the store full of customers, it would have made no difference to Sam, so deep-drowned was he in single-minded purpose. This was Abigail Plummer's store, which she owned and where he had traded for years. She had got God to kill his pigs; he was going to burn her store down. He shook the empty can, tossed it on the floor with a clatter, felt in his pocket for matches.

Sure, he had matches. Lit his pipe on the way up here, hadn't he? No, the pipe was cold in his pocket. Frantically Sam felt his clothes, patted his pockets, one by one, all over. No matches. Not a match.

Well, this was a grocery. Must sell matches. Must be some somewhere.

He began going from shelf to shelf, hunting. Feeling of stuff. Cans, cans, cans. Hard. Tinny. Matches would be paper packages, soft, papery. Here was something. Couldn't read the label without his glasses. Where were his glasses? He didn't have them either.

He ripped open the package. Hell and damnation. Soda crackers!

Smelled good. Smelled darn good. Little mite keroseney, but he'd had worse.

He ate one. Ate another. Darn if he wasn't hungry! Eat something, might help that dizzy, flyaway feeling in his head. Had that for a while now, as if he might spin right around and fall down.

Sam sat on the floor eating crackers, one after another, the motion of his hand to his mouth growing more and more slow until it stopped. Presently he sagged over sideways and went to sleep.

Charles picked up his canvas bag and came out of the office, his heels cracking down on the floor, making it fast in case anybody should by chance come in. He hauled down a package of matches, ripped it open, set the entire box aflame and scooted it along one of the kerosene-soaked stalls.

"On the shelf, right over your head, you clunk!" he said.

He went back through the office, opened the back door wide and left it open, strolled leisurely around into the street and down toward the bank to make his day's deposit. Time enough when he got back to call the fire department.

There were not many people on South Main Street that afternoon, points of interest being at the north end—the drugstore, which was having a one-cent sale, and Abigail Plummer's new grocery, where Norman Hardwick with two helpers was unpacking goods to stock the shelves. Norman had not planned to open until tomorrow, but everybody was curious about the new store's modern equipment. He was a vicarious man—it certainly would be something he himself would want to see—so he decided to unlock the doors and let people in. The aisles were quite crowded when the fire whistle blew, to everyone's complete surprise.

Where is it? people asked each other, staring anxiously into faces. Had anyone counted the blasts?

Abigail, in the dairy office, counted two blasts. That meant somewhere nearby, in the Main Street area. She stepped to the door, looked. People were just beginning to come out on the sidewalk, glancing up, down. Along the street she could see Charles standing in front of his store—not, as other people were, as anyone normally would be, scanning the sky for smoke rising over the tops of buildings, watching to see which way the crowd was running. He was peering, with absorbed attention, into his own plate-glass window.

Charles's? Abigail thought. The store? Or why is he doing that?

The whistle blew again and he did not stir. At the sound of the fire truck starting up, blocks away, he did not turn around. There could only be one reason for that. Of all the people around, he knew where the fire was.

She caught up her jacket from the hook behind the door and slipped into it as she hurried along the street.

"Charles?" she said, coming up behind him, she saw through the window what he was seeing—thick smoke shot with sullen orange gleams. From somewhere—from Charles? —came a rank smell of kerosene.

Charles glanced around. "I called the fire department," he said. "Not much use. Looks like the old shebang's going up for fair."

He had his hands in his pockets; the quill toothpick he

used was in one side of his mouth. With his tongue he flipped it to the other side. "I went to the bank," he said. "Gone about ten minutes. When I got back, she was full of smoke, starting to blaze some. Back door was open. Wasn't when I left. I tried to get in, see where it was coming from, did get in. Partway. Place stank of kerosene enough to knock you down. I saw the kerosene can. Fell over it, got covered with the stuff. I just barely made it out and shut the door. That," he said, flipping his toothpick, "is why you don't see any smoke outside yet."

"Charles, what are you saying? That someone . . . ?"

"How else, Ma? Use your head."

"Oh, no!" Abigail said.

Was he lying? That clipped way of speaking, the casualness that wasn't really casual . . . How many times before? "See you, Ma. Going fishing with Jack, back suppertime." And not fishing, and not Jack, and back hours after suppertime.

"Charles—"

She stopped, leaned suddenly forward, fixed on the window. Something in there had moved. Through the smoke, in horror, she made out a shuffling, staggering figure, a pair of hands, groping, briefly there, as quickly gone.

"Charles, there's somebody in there!"

"Couldn't be, Ma. I looked."

"Charles, there is! Charles, help him!"

"Open that door? *Now?* You must be crazy!"

The fire truck in the next street uttered a wail that rose, fell, and died, and was supplemented from inside the store by a muffled, choking scream.

She pushed past him, thrusting him out of the way, tore open the door. Black, oily smoke rolled past her and she vanished into it.

Charles made no move to stop her. Under his breath he said softly, "So you go."

Waldo Larsen, driving past to fetch the Cartwright kids from school, saw her go. He had heard the fire truck, had been keeping an eye out for it and for where the fire might be. The gush of smoke from the open door half blinded him, but there was fire, all right, and that lady . . . that lady . . .

He stopped the dump truck where it was in the middle of the street, raced across the sidewalk. He did not so much shove Charles out of the way as run over him, sending him sprawling, and lunged into the smoke which was now shooting murky tongues of flame.

The fire truck, lumbering around the corner and up the street, found itself nose to nose with the dump truck; the jolted firemen took a minute or so to untangle themselves. It had been a sudden stop. By that time Waldo was back on the sidewalk. He had Abigail, who was unconscious, and, before he fainted, he showed, clenched in one hand, the charred collar of a man's coat.

Now to a raw, sliced tomato, to Adam and Eve, to the slovenly ragtag-and-bobtail of Sam Greeley's times, things, events, the final item compounded the issue, hurried it to its certain end. Abigail Plummer once gave her son a store, and that was the last piece of the jigsaw cut, the hidden, terminal twig of the monkey-puzzle tree. The firemen, after the ashes of the store had cooled, found what was left of Sam.

The poor devil, crazy as a loon, they said. Set the store afire, God knows why, and then couldn't get himself out in time.

In the hospital Abigail slid in and out of dreams.

"Burning," someone kept saying. "Burning, burning, burning."

"Fred, let Grace alone, you're driving the poor child crazy. Trust her, and show her you do. She'll be all right."

Grace. Lost so long ago. She had not been all right. Trust . . . you must have somebody you can trust.

Felix saying, "Like a lion's back. A big old lion, sleeping in the sun," meaning the field of grass, tawny-colored. Charles, running in the grass, shouting, his young, flawless face turned up, crying because he wanted to look into the sun and it hurt his eyes.

The brook ran, *rabble-dabble, rabble-dabble;* the water made a hushing sound along the beach, and three small girls came out from around the corner of a ruined house. One of them helped another across the brook.

The green snake was dead; Jos killed it, poor thing. How strange that I should just now have felt it moving in my hand.

Someone took her hand and held it, and the dreams fled away.

"Nan," she said. "My dearest Nan. Is it all right now?"

"Yes, darling, it's all right now."

So, then, it was.

She said, "Will you look after Sarah? I think she should belong to you."

On the afternoon of Abigail Plummer's death Willy Meader was in his office sitting at his desk. Court was in session upstairs, the last case of the day just ending. Willy had left the courtroom early. He was tired. He had testified as arresting officer in four cases, none of them very unusual, and mostly sad. They had come out as long years of experience had told Willy they would. Kids—some kids—had got probation; drunk drivers, depending on who they were, were let off or fined. Willy would be picking most of them up again before long anyway.

Well, he'd seen it coming. No good thing, he supposed, could last too long. Quite a number of Clawson's friends were beginning to raise heads again around the courthouse.

Busy, too. The Judge was fluttering his wings, getting ready to take off.

Looked like you couldn't keep a bad man down. Not if he had backing.

What the hell ailed these people? Inherited tendencies from the pioneers? Willy didn't doubt for a moment that the pioneers had all been heroes. They'd sailed into a new, unexplored country with nothing more or less than what they'd stood up in. Picked up what they needed where they found it, because they had to or starve. A man could do that then, but no one was starving now. If he did it now, some other people would be out of luck. The case just finishing upstairs was one in point.

Joe Eastman, the druggist's son, a nice young fellow, seventeen years old. Coming home one night late, he heard a radio playing in Frank Wilson's corn patch. Sneaked in there, stole the radio, drove off with it in his car, and Frank had seen him do it.

Frank had been losing a lot of corn, some to kids going on picnics, some to plain ordinary folks who liked corn, but mostly to coons. He'd read in the newspaper—one of the fillers it had been—that if you stuck a battery radio in the corn patch and left it on, it would scare the coons away.

His testimony had been that a radio was the last thing in the world he wanted to listen to but he guessed he could put up with one in the cornfield. Lying in bed at night, he could hear it carrying on to itself over there; and he was awake on the night when it had suddenly stopped playing. He had got out of bed and seen Joe Eastman come from the field carrying the radio, climb into his car, and drive away.

"I awready had writ down the number of that car," he said. "Parked her there round dusk, he did, and I see him go off down the field with his gun. Coon hunting, I surmised. But anybody parks out by my corn patch nowadays, by God, I write his number down."

Joe told the court that the radio was his own. His uncle from Milwaukee had brought it to him for a birthday present, when he'd visted East last summer. This was the only point on which Larry Cartwright had been able to catch him. Larry had looked up vital statistics; Joe's birthday was on the tenth of December.

Neat and combed, in his good dark suit, matching socks and necktie, Joe was a nice-looking, respectable young kid. Attentive to questions, respectful.

"Yes, sir," he said. "My uncle doesn't get East in the wintertime, so he brought me my birthday present when he came."

At about that time Willy had got up, prepared to leave the courtroom. He'd heard about all he wanted to. As he went out, he heard Joe repeating that he'd been with his girl that night to a dance and saying what orchestra it was and what they played. His girl would back him up, he said.

Oh, well.

People were stirring around upstairs, preparing to come down. Another session over, thank God.

Larry Cartwright came in, prowled over by the window, not saying anything. He looked played out.

"So Frank's old and half-blind," Willy said. "Illiterate. Can't be depended on to get the numbers on a license plate straight."

"Uh-huh," Larry said.

"Hell," Willy went on. "Reads his newspaper and the Bible. Not two weeks ago, I saw him shoot a hen hawk flew off with one of his pullets. Prettiest shot I ever saw. With a twenty-two. Never even hurt the pullet, he's still got her. She's somewise bald on the rump, but she's still coursing around. What's the trouble with you? Joe got off—didn't you expect it?"

"The bench was impressed," Larry said. "Ha ha." He came over and sprawled, rather than sat, in the chair by Willy's desk. "I'm pooped, Willy."

"Real neat-looking young lad," Willy said.

"Uh-huh. Considerate, too. On the way downstairs I heard him say that it was a darn shame and he'd be glad to give his own old radio to Frank, if it would help any."

"Well," Willy said, "they come and they go. Into the woodwork when the light comes on. Out of the woodwork when it goes off again. Ten million years. Ain't changed. Ain't likely to."

"Seems so," Larry said.

He was worn out, Willy could see. He was, as Willy himself was, as most of the townspeople were, heartsick over Abby Plummer, and with more reason than most, since Nan Plummer was his girl. Nobody knew yet whether Abby was going to make it. So far, Willy had heard, it was nip and tuck with her, bad burns and smoke poisoning. He couldn't think of anything to say to Larry about it. What was there? He rummaged thoughtfully in a drawer of his desk, brought out a bottle of bourbon and a couple of paper cups.

"Here," he said, pushing a filled cup across the desk.

"Thanks." Larry picked up the cup, sniffed it, set it down untasted. "I'd fall flat on my face, Willy."

"Good for some things, though," Willy said. "And most things is relative. Damned if you don't look as if you needed it. You heard from Abby since noon?"

"Yes, I called. Not good. They don't know."

"Oh, hell," Willy said. "Hell and damnation." That, he thought, was a helpless kind of a thing to say.

"Hospital let Waldo go this morning."

"I heard. Saved his hand, didn't they?"

"They think so. They wanted to keep him a few days longer, but Waldo put up a fuss. Said thanks and walked out. He drove home with me." Larry managed a wan grin. "Told me he knew of some stuff out in the woods that laid all over what those fellows were putting on his burns."

"That guy must be made out of iron."

"Guess so. I hope he stays away from Charles Plummer

till his hand heals. He told me Charles didn't even try to stop
Abby going in there."

"You swallow Charles's story?" Willy asked.

"I don't swallow any story that takes off from Abigail
Plummer's being crazy."

"Nope. And I ain't swallowed it either. For the reason of
why she did go into that fire. You and I know she ain't crazy.
She ain't a fool, either. Thing is, I think she saw Sam. If she
did, then Charles must've too. Says he didn't." Willy took a
small sip of his drink. "I don't know what that adds up to.
Where's any proof of anything? Abby ain't able to talk."

"She may be. She's said a few words to Nan."

"I hope so. I don't know; but there's a rat gnawing away
at me, says loud and clear that Charles Plummer stands to
inherit quite a wad if anything happens to his mother."

"I'm not entitled to tell you," Larry said. "But you don't
run off at the mouth, Willy. The thing is, Charles doesn't
know it, but he doesn't."

"That so?"

"I didn't draw up her will—I couldn't, seeing that Nan and
I will marry. But recently she's been transferring the rest of
her legal business to me. Her regular man in Bristol did her
will. It's signed and attested by two reputable Bristol physi-
cians that she was of sound mind when the will was drawn.
I don't know what's in it, except for that and two items
which she mentioned, I suppose for her own reasons—well,
yes, I know what they are. She wants, she said, to be buried
on Randall's Hill, and that Charles, when he found out that
he wasn't getting anything but the store he already has—
had—would use any pry, any excuse, to prove that she wasn't
of sound mind. I guess she thought I knew enough law to
help some, in case he made things hot. After what happened
upstairs today, I doubt if I do."

"Oh, hell," Willy said. "Today was a triumphant occasion.
Means the boys probably won't ask you to run for county

attorney, you're too damn smart. Know too much law, I heard. Things get around. My guess is you'll run anyway. That right?"

"I like you, Willy," Larry said. "Once in a while you have a word for something that restores my faith in—well, whatever there is."

"You going to waste that bourbon?" Willy asked. "If you are, I'll pour it back in the—"

The doorknob clicked and Judge Clawson stuck in his head. He said, "I thought so," and entered, closing the door behind him. "Willy, as usual, disgracing the elective offices."

"That's right," Willy said. "Have some?"

"Don't care if I do." He came across the room, dapper and neat in his street clothes, his handsome head of silver-streaked hair apparently just combed, with water to accentuate the wave. "I hear," he said, taking the cup Willy handed him, "that the town's conscience is dead."

"What's that?" Willy said. He stared at the Judge, not quite understanding, afraid that he had understood only too well.

"Abigail Plummer," Clawson said. "About half an hour ago."

Willy did not look at Larry. For some reason, not knowing exactly why, he pushed back his chair and stood up. Then, embarrassed at showing whatever it was he had shown, he sat down again.

"Well," the Judge said, "I hope she likes heaven." He swallowed the last of his drink, tossed the cup at the waste-basket. "If she don't, I'd hate to say who inside the pearly gates is going to have to shove over."

"Not you, here, now, though," Larry said.

He, too, had got up. White-faced, he towered over the Judge who took a step backward.

"Oh, no disrespect. No disrespect intended. A poor joke— the passing of such a lady is of course a terrible shock to everyone." He waved a hand. "Must be on my way, see you all tomorrow . . ." The door closed behind him with a muffled click.

"Not yet," Larry said, between his teeth. "Not yet, Willy. But, by God—" His voice choked in his throat.

"That's right, son," Willy said. "You go be with your girl. She's going to want to see you."

Alone, Willy sat for a moment unmoving, before he reached for the paper cup which Larry had left on the desk untouched. He held it for a moment level with his eyes.

"To bigger pockets, God damn them," he said, and emptied the cup distastefully into his wastebasket.

Standing on top of Randall's Hill, the Plummers, Abigail's family, were watching her go down. Charles, stocky, round-headed, stood flatly in his good shoes and Sunday suit of a hairy, dark-brown material which yielded nowhere and made him look still blockier than he was. The picture of dignified mourning, he stared at the undertaker's imitation-grass mats placed over the raw earth around the grave. Here on the un-sheltered hilltop the wind was blowing hard, a fall north-wester; the green carpets had had to be anchored down with stones.

She had had her blasted way for the last time. She was being buried where she'd wanted to be, so who gave a damn? He supposed, now that he was head of the family, he'd have to pay out of his own pocket the charges for perpeutal care of the eight-grave lot in the town cemetery where Uncle Jos and Pa were. Never mind. He wouldn't miss what it cost. His head was full of dreams, visions of sugarplums to come. The man of substance, the man with money and real estate, the chauffeur-driven man, sought after for committees, lodge offices, boards, clubs, councils; the trustee of schools, the director of banks—damn them, they couldn't keep him out now. There'd be nothing he couldn't have, no place he couldn't go and be welcomed. He could kiss his foot at them all. Anyone who thought different could be rocked right back into the place he belonged, and would be. She had plagued him, frustrated him all his life. So she was gone, and let the grass grow.

Beside him, Elsie stood, an anonymous pillar of black. No one could tell how Elsie felt; she was obliterated by her mourning garb. Her veil was long, further lengthened by a fringe of round black tassels, stylish, too, ordered from the most expensive shop in Bristol. During the church service it had hung in scalloped folds as it was supposed to, with all the somber dignity of decent grief; but here on the hill the wind unsettled everything. The cemetery was alive with blowing leaves, as the big hardwoods let go. All colors, red, orange, yellow, brown, poured past, plastering themselves to the sides of old gravestones and to the backs of hats and suits. They not only stuck to the thin web of Elsie's veil, but the veil billowed. She could not hold it down. The tassels only added to her difficulty. In any especially wild gust the veil would stream out and the tassels pop like pistol shots.

Whenever this happened, people's heads would turn. Charles twice gave her the full blast of his glare. What did he think, she asked herself indignantly, her black-gloved hand groping to no avail among the slithering folds, that she was flapping her veil on purpose? Just let him mind his own business. Show people that he was grieving for Ma, the way Maureen was. Poor Maureen, wasn't it too bad that that homemade veil was so plain? It wasn't becoming at all tucked back over her hat that way, made her look old; or maybe it was her eyes, red like that, and her face just beglammed with tears. Her handkerchief was wet as a sop, you could see it and all wobbed up into a ball. Wouldn't you think she'd have had the foresight to brought two?

I wonder what of Ma's things she'll want. Ma's 'lectrict mixer, Elsie thought with longing. Well, I could tell Maureen, "Maureen," I could say, "you know Ma once give me that 'lectrict mixer."

Who is there now to trust? Maureen was thinking. She did not look at Arthur who stood, his hat off and held against his chest, his taffy-colored head bowed—sorrow in person listening to the minister. Maureen stared at the raw grave and wept, and did not care who saw.

What is a good man? Larry Cartwright asked the tall slate stone. You could read A GOOD MAN IS and that was all. Heaped-up, fallen leaves hid all but the first four words of the final inscription. What was a good man in the days when John Constant Randall's stone was cut?

There was his father over there, and Willy; and Waldo Larsen with his bandaged head and his ruined hand in a sling.

Checks and balances, he thought. The scales of justice, one side up, the other down? How many decent men to balance the spoilers, the sharks, the thieves and murderers? How many pin-feather lawyers?

The minister was beginning the final words of the service. Nan, beside Larry, slipped her hand into his. For comfort, he thought, and his heart turned over. For me, as well as Nan.

Big white clouds tore across the sky and the wind yelled down out of Canada, with somewhere from far back of it and a long way off, a remembered smell of snow. The minister said, "Dust to dust," and a yellow moosewood leaf as big as a dinner plate spun out of the air and plastered itself across his mouth. There had to be silence while he plucked it away.

NO RENEWALS!

PLEASE RETURN BOOK AND REQUEST
AGAIN.